Advance Praise for *The Complete Social Media Community Manager's Guide*

Marty and Lauren have emerged as undisputed thought leaders in the rapidly evolving social media arena. We all benefit from their years of knowledge succinctly poured in this "how to do it" book. This book defines the roles and guides us through the process of establishing and operating as a social media community manager—an essential role for every business even dreaming of online sales if not today, then soon. This is essential reading for every person involved in growing their business.

> —BRUCE CLAY, President, Bruce Clay, Inc.

Effective social media marketing goes way beyond posting to Facebook and Twitter. A good social media community manager knows how to engage the community, deal with crises, and get the most marketing mileage out of time spent on social media. No one knows more about squeezing every inch of value out of social media than Marty and Lauren. Their posts on the aimClear blog are my go-to resource for social media knowledge. In The Complete Social Media Community Manager's Guide, you'll find tips for getting started, behaving well, creating valuable social media content, and measuring success. This book provides a roadmap for new and experienced community managers alike, and should be on the bookshelf of anyone responsible for corporate social media.

> —MELISSA MACKEY, Search Supervisor, Gyro, Contributor, Search Engine Watch and Web Marketing Today

This is the playbook every business needs in its back pocket for success! The Complete Social Media Community Manager's Guide *is a roadmap to public relations success.*

> —LISA BUYER, Social PR Publicist, Journalist, Specialist

Marty and his team at aimClear are the smartest social media marketers on the planet, period. I've had the pleasure to present advanced Facebook marketing with Lauren and know her to be a smart, insightful community manager with first-hand knowledge of what it takes in the trenches. After the first book from the aimClear team, I know they can bring the knowledge. I'm so excited to get my hands on this book. I expect to learn from these masters, myself.

> —WILL SCOTT, Owner, Search Influence

Marty Weintraub and Lauren Litwinka go beyond the psychobabble to cl...
the importance of social signals and content on marketing, providi...
able tips to better understand metrics, best practices and human be...

> —LAURIE SULLIVAN, Senior Writer, MediaPost; Chairperson, Insider Summit

Marty Weintraub and Lauren Litwinka are social dynamos. They have the uncanny ability to explain complex social media strategies so that anyone can understand them and put them into action. Marty and Lauren have hit a home run with this book.
 —BILL HARTZER, Standing Dog Interactive

Since the role of community manager started to proliferate across the marketing world, community managers have been largely making it up as they go along. This timely guide fills a huge void in the field and will lend a sense of structure, purpose, and measurement to the social media community manager's role.
 —ANDREW GOODMAN, Cofounder, HomeStars

Weintraub and Litwinka have hit the social nail on the head. This book has all the information you need to be successful in Social Media Marketing, all in one information-packed place. It covers everything from the value of "Like" to how to manage your campaigns.
 —ALAN K'NECHT, K'nechtology Inc.

Here's the social media big picture delivered by two of the brightest minds in the industry. An actionable, big-picture guide for every community manager out there. Finally, a way to cut through the "social media noise" with laser focus.
 —MARK KNOWLES, President and CEO, Pixelsilk

Marty Weintraub is the reference the interactive marketing industry turns to when it comes to social media strategies. This book lays out a detailed road map all companies should follow on their quest for building and engaging communities online. The Complete Social Media Community Manager's Guide *is now mandatory reading for our entire marketing team, and the everyday reference for our social community manager.*
 —MARC POIRIER, Cofounder and CMO, Acquisio

A busy community manager's salvation! Like having Marty whisper over your shoulder.
 —DENNIS YU, Chief Executive Officer, BlitzLocal

While there are clearly many reasons to read this book, you really only need one and that's Marty Weintraub. His knowledge and passion for this subject makes this a must read. Social media is here to stay and so is Marty! So pick this book up and you will learn something to drive your life and your business.
 —BARRY M. ZELICKSON, Senior Vice President, Border Foods Companies

Marty has the extraordinary ability to not only deconstruct the complexities of the various social media channels and explain them to the uninitiated, he also elucidates a series of complex, non-obvious inter-channel relationships that will advance the proficiency of experts in the field.
 —TODD MINTZ, Senior Account Manager, PPC Associates

Complete with job expectations framework, sample templates, PR safety harnesses, and community thrill tips, this book is a must-have resource to ensure your social media roller coaster ride is an intentional joy (versus an unexpected nightmare) for both you and your community.

—ANGIE SCHOTTMULLER, Chief of Conversion Marketing, Unbounce.com

This is the master course you wish the universities could offer, and as professors, Weintraub and Litwinka are the best in the business. No matter how tools and social platforms may continue to change, the essence of strategy and execution outlined in this book will serve as the solid foundation for community managers for years to come.

—MICHELLE STINSON ROSS, Columnist, SearchEngineJournal

The world's best CMs attend every @aimclear event around the globe. The rest follow the steps in this book.

—JIM DAHLINE, Internet Marketing Consultant

Not many people "grok" social media and the benefits of smart community management. Not many people are Marty Weintraub and Lauren Litwinka. The Complete Social Media Community Manager's Guide *will be required reading for most forward thinking companies. Read it and benefit from it before your competitors do.*

—BRYAN "@THEGROK" EISENBERG, New York Times Bestselling Author of *Waiting for Your Cat to Bark?*

Marty is the mad scientist of social media campaigning. He is not only an author and a very entertaining conference speaker but also a hands-on marketing professional working with real clients on real projects producing real results. This book will give you an insight view into the strategic thinking of Marty and his aimClear team and is an amazing source for current or upcoming social media professionals.

—STEFAN HEEKE, Siemens Corporation

For years, marketers have been wondering how to get the most of their social media campaigns. Finally, Marty and Lauren have created the first authoritative tactic-based, results-focused handbook for social media management. From content marketing to crisis management, from reputation monitoring to paid organic amplification, readers of this book will develop a sound foundation for social media success. This book is stuffed with hardcore strategies that will revolutionize how you measure, manage, and optimize not only your social media presence, but your entire online marketing program.

—JOSEPH KERSCHBAUM, Coauthor, Pay-Per-Click Search Engine Marketing: An Hour a Day

Being a Social Media Community Manager is all about promoting and protecting "The Brand" while navigating the hurricane forces of social media in motion. Marty and Lauren are the "been there/done that" experts. If you are engaged in the social media universe without this book by your side, your insurance coverage had better be current.
—James L. Young, Westman, Champlin & Kelly, P.A.

This is a comprehensive guide that helps social marketers of all experience levels understand what it takes to be successful in such a fast-paced field. Whether you're a small business owner seeking to learn or an experienced social community manager, this guide will not only help you learn about social media best practices but also how to quantify and analyze your success.
—Gary Henderson, CEO, Interactivity Marketing

Stop wasting time tinkering on every social network you can get on to just because it's cool and because your competitors are on there. When it comes to thinking about and executing a successful, holistic, and structured social media program that delivers real results for your company, this book covers everything you should know, and more.
—Imelda Khoo, Global e-Marketing Manager, Tektroniks

The Complete Social Media Community Manager's Guide *is by far the most comprehensive tome encompassing every key piece critical to being a successful social media manager. Marty and Lauren have collectively been living this community management world for in excess of a decade, and it shows, from providing excellent advice on the ROI bugaboo of social media, to listening effectively and creating the kind of content customers care about. Whether you have a seasoned veteran running your social media efforts or you've just begun the hiring process, get this book for them immediately.*
—Christopher Swanson, CEO of PureDriven

Marty and Lauren steer you clear of those hollow dime-a-dozen "social gurus" and deliver the goods. Get insights and tips ripped from the front lines of social media management.
—AJ Kohn, Owner of Blind Five Year Old

This guide is essential to any social media manager who needs to stay on the bleeding edge of community management and at the same time keep a foundation in time-honored practices and good judgment. Marty and Lauren created a comprehensive guide that I would have killed to have even a year ago. As a business leader, you need to have trusted sources in an ever-changing environment and this book hits that mark way beyond my wildest expectations!
—Heather Lutze, CEO, Findability Consulting & Speaking

The Complete Social Media Community Manager's Guide

Essential Tools and Tactics for Business Success

Marty Weintraub

Lauren Litwinka

WILEY

John Wiley & Sons, Inc.

Senior Acquisitions Editor: WILLEM KNIBBE
Development Editor: KIM BEAUDET
Technical Editor: LISA GRIMM
Production Editor: DASSI ZEIDEL
Copy Editor: LIZ WELCH
Internal Copy Editor: LINDSAY SCHLEISMAN
Editorial Manager: PETE GAUGHAN
Production Manager: TIM TATE
Vice President and Executive Group Publisher: RICHARD SWADLEY
Vice President and Publisher: NEIL EDDE
Book Designer: FRANZ BAUMHACKL
Compositor: KATE KAMINSKI, HAPPENSTANCE TYPE-O-RAMA
Proofreader: REBECCA RIDER
Indexer: TED LAUX
Project Coordinator, Cover: KATHERINE CROCKER
Cover Designer: RYAN SNEED
Cover Image: © VASILIY KOSYREV / iStockPHOTO

Dear Reader,

Thank you for choosing *The Complete Social Media Community Manager's Guide: Essential Tools and Tactics for Business Success*. This book is part of a family of premium-quality Sybex books, all of which are written by outstanding authors who combine practical experience with a gift for teaching.

Sybex was founded in 1976. More than 30 years later, we're still committed to producing consistently exceptional books. With each of our titles, we're working hard to set a new standard for the industry. From the paper we print on, to the authors we work with, our goal is to bring you the best books available.

I hope you see all that reflected in these pages. I'd be very interested to hear your comments and get your feedback on how we're doing. Feel free to let me know what you think about this or any other Sybex book by sending me an email at nedde@wiley.com. If you think you've found a technical error in this book, please visit http://sybex .custhelp.com. Customer feedback is critical to our efforts at Sybex.

Best regards,

Neil Edde
Vice President and Publisher
Sybex, an Imprint of Wiley

This book is dedicated our aimClear team. You are the very best.

Thanks for all of your hard work, friendship, and support while we

wrote this book, and for being such incredibly empowering allies.

Acknowledgments

First, we could not have written this book without incredible support and encouragement from our families, Wiley/Sybex, the aimClear® team, and our dear industry friends.

Thank you so much to aimClear's leadership team, our families, and our closest relations for holding the business and our lives together. We owe particular thanks to our Wiley/Sybex Acquisitions Editor, Willem Knibbe, for envisioning this book, choosing us to write it, helping us grow as authors, and for being completely unconditional in his trust and support. Know this: Willem is one of the very best in the marketing book industry and deserves credit for the results as an artist, mentor, and reliable friend.

We also want to express our highest gratitude to Technical Editor Lisa Grimm. Lisa's dedicated feedback was impeccably empowering and made a huge difference! That's exactly what this book needed. Thanks additionally to Kim, Dassi, Pete, and the whole Wiley/Sybex crew. You guys totally rock.

Lindsay Schleisman, in our Saint Paul office, added fabulous professionalism to the editing and formatting processes. She's quite a writer in her own right and spent many late nights doing really hard work that mattered so much: proofing, formatting, and handling countless important things. Thank you, Lindsay, for being so unconditional at crunch time. Alyssa Friesen contributed the personal dashboard case study, which is immaculate, as usual. Thank you to Laura W., Matt, Manny, Merry, Kathy, Molly, Joe, Erica, Megan R., Dan, Mike, Quentin, Ryan, Laura P., Reed, Gretchen, Anna, and Megan D. for their remarkable contributions to our company.

Thanks to Danny Sullivan and Barry Schwartz for truly being Marty's muses and for writing so eloquently as quintessential ambassadors of the industry. We'd like to extend additional thanks to Chris Sherman (Third Door genius futurist), Chris Elwell (Third Door), Bret Tabke (PubCon), Laura Roth (Incisive), Mike Grehan (Incisive), Todd Mintz (SEMpdx), Bryan Eisenberg, Sarah Power (ThirdDoor), and Laurie Sullivan (MediaPost).

About the Authors

Marty Weintraub is CEO of aimClear®, an Inc. 500–honored search and social marketing agency. His first book, *Killer Facebook Ads: Master Cutting-Edge Facebook Advertising Techniques* (Sybex, 2011) is critically acclaimed as a harbinger of the social PPC revolution.

Client credits include Intel, Siemens, Tektronix, United Health Group, Ning, SecondLife, MarthaStewart.com, *The Washington Post*, and other iconic global brands. aimClear has managed social advertising campaigns generating more than a trillion impressions, and was named a top workplace in Minnesota by *Minnesota Business* magazine. The agency has become internationally recognized for its work in psychographic and demographic targeting, especially as pertains to Google, Facebook, YouTube, LinkedIn, and retargeting.

A fixture on the international conference circuit, Marty's recent and upcoming keynotes include SES London, MediaPost Search Insider Summit, Charlotte Search Exchange, SEMpdx, and OMS, as well as many appearances over the last five years at SMX, SES, mozCon, PubCon, eMetrics, and others all over the world.

Marty has written extensively for respected Internet marketing publications, including SearchEngineWatch, Search Engine Land, and Search Engine Round Table, and has been quoted in others, from AdAge to MediaPost. aimClear Blog was cited among Technorati's Top 10 Small Business Blogs, Cison's Top Ten Social Media Blogs, and PRWeb's 25 Essential Public Relations Blogs You Should Be Reading. Marty was named the third most influential PPC professional in 2012 by PPC Hero.

He has been described as "not your typical agency type," a "social media maverick," and "more innovator than follower." Marty enjoys camping, canoeing, fishing, patronizing James-Beard-award-winning restaurants, and fine wine.

Lauren Litwinka is an Online Marketing Account Manager and Publications Manager at aimClear. Her areas of expertise include cradle-to-grave community management, killer search and social ad writing, online journalism, and holistic social befriending, as well as content aggregation, creation, and strategic syndication.

After purchasing sacks full of winter-weather gear, Lauren waved goodbye to her wonderfully supportive family and moved from her hometown in New Jersey to Duluth, Minnesota, joining aimClear in 2009. Intensive work with multinational clients in search, social, paid, and organic has inspired her to compile and publish case studies and in-depth tutorials on aimClear Blog and other trade publications such as Search Engine Watch. She loves to explore the beautiful side of business-to-business marketing in her monthly column pieces featured in Search Engine Land.

Lauren has ample hands-on experience training companies across a variety of verticals, from beauty product retailers to industrial manufacturers. Leveraging insightful data based on traditional demographic research and cutting-edge conversation mining, she helps brands build and thoughtfully engage community members in a meaningful and effective manner. Leveraging honed paid marketing chops, she enjoys tossing an assortment of paid social ad units into the mix to amplify organic activity and prominence, yielding real results that rock.

Throughout the year, Lauren covers multiple mainstream industry conferences as a well-regarded member of the press. You'll find her churning out coverage at finger-breaking speed via @beebow on Twitter. When she's not live-tweeting, Lauren speaks at aimClear's Facebook Marketing Intensive Workshops, sharing top-shelf community management tactics and best practices.

In her spare time, she enjoys taking photographs, writing stories, drawing drawings, cooking tasty food, and sampling hoppy beers. Lauren's art, featured throughout sections of this book, can be found online at facebook.com/DeepCereal. She currently lives on the shores of Lake Superior with her sweetheart and charmingly enormous Maine Coon.

Contents

Chapter 3

Hit the Ground Running! 77

Chapter 4

Content, Reputation, and Hardcore Listening Hacks 141

Chapter 5   **Finding Themed Conversations: The Superior CM's Edge**   **175**

Chapter 6   **Dominate with Paid Organic Amplification**   **207**

CONTENTS ■

Introduction

The Internet has exploded in a massive confluence of social media and corporate reaction. A blazing hot new profession, social media community manager, has emerged from a cottage industry of geeks. The profession of community manager is the full-on standard in nearly every big business.

Social media matters as much to small and medium-sized businesses as it does to huge brands. Common citizens tweeting and an individual's YouTube video posted on Facebook literally caused a revolution. Social media accidents have destroyed products and people.

If you're excited, concerned, or outright curious about how to market your business in social media, this book is the right choice. We explain why understanding social media is imperative and provide in-depth tips for managing your personal or corporate presence.

This book pays a lot of attention to how social works: as a distribution system for direct response and to promote content. Also we're focusing on identifying audience (psychographics), content strategies, how to pay social communities for organic boost, and public relations.

When you finish this book, you'll understand the real value of a like, how to represent yourself across all social channels, from Pinterest to Twitter, and you'll have ideas of how to engage customers and sell things. Because this text is packed with tools, tips, toys, and classic social marketing hacks, you're in for a seriously deep dive into what it means to be a social media community manager marketer!

Who Should Buy This Book

This book is for anyone who tweets, posts to Facebook, makes YouTube videos, or monitors anyone's reputation, from multinational corporate types to small businesses, educators, and everyone in between. This includes

- Marketers who already work as a community manager for a company or agency
- New social media marketers looking for an overview
- Entrepreneurs seeking to promote their products and/or services in social space
- In-house pros and agency types
- Professors wishing to augment curriculum with cutting-edge social media psychographics, channels, strategies, and tactics for marketing and real-world anthropological analysis globally
- Advanced social marketers seeking a serious edge

- Online marketing managers wanting to grow the capabilities of their team
- Advertising agency and public relations professionals seeking an edge in social media marketing
- Small business owners wanting more site traffic, friends, business, and prominence for their brand
- Anyone wanting to thoroughly understand how organic and paid social work together

There's something in *The Complete Social Media Community Manager's Guide* for everyone. Whether you are a newbie or an advanced power social monster, you'll find nuggets of information, many of which are potentially transformational to your thinking about social as a marketing channel.

What's Inside

Here is a glance at what's in each chapter:

Chapter 1, "The Social Media Community Manager's Role," lays the groundwork for the gems this book has in store for you. First things first: It's important to embrace the fact that being a community manager these days is a fascinating fusion of various roles, previously assigned to multiple areas of most marketing agencies and in-house departments. This chapter defines the role and objectives, tackling everything from determining brand voice to understanding social return on investment (ROI).

Chapter 2, "Timeless Tenets of Non-Gratuitous Social Behavior," focuses on best practices that modern-day community managers should embrace to succeed. As a community manager, it's your job to engage the community surrounding your brand in the various social media channels in which you operate. But how do you encourage those conversations? Is it ever OK to promote yourself? What actions should you avoid to avoid angering your friends, fans, and followers, not to mention the natives? In other words, how should you act in social media? This chapter offers basic behavioral advice for the smart CM.

Chapter 3, "Hit the Ground Running!" explores the business nature of social media and how to create a scope of work (SOW)/budget request from the basics you gathered in Chapter 1. We'll explore the terminology used to create such documents, which can be used to sell social media to the boss. Then we'll take a deep dive into the variety of social media channels in which to implement the tactics laid out in the SOW.

Chapter 4, "Content, Reputation, and Hardcore Listening Hacks," looks at one of the pillars of community management: content. Everything that publishers publish and users generate is content. In this chapter, you'll learn how to listen to content for the purpose of reputation monitoring, sharing, and creating your own content.

Chapter 5, "Find Themed Conversations: The Superior CM's Edge," digs deep into the importance of sharing and how to go about finding content to share with your community. It also delves into finding appropriate users to befriend and conversations to participate in. From Best-Content-on-the-Block Sharing to tips on leveraging Google search and Chrome, this chapter has it all.

Chapter 6, "Dominate with Paid Organic Amplification," dissects the paid side of organic social channels and uncovers the benefits. The only social that is truly free is within communities of those who already like your Facebook page, follow your LinkedIn profile, and otherwise subscribe by any model. In this chapter, you'll learn how social communities limit what others, outside your community of friends, can see. You'll also consume a systematic study of ways to pay communities to reenable the missing organic features and dominate the distribution system.

Chapter 7, "Community Crisis Management," is your go-to guide for successfully navigating the rough seas of social media. Sometimes, the same community CMs cultivate, care for, and connect with on behalf of their brands can turn against that brand or each other. In this chapter, we'll dissect social media crisis management from the top down. That includes establishing a crisis protocol, implementing house rules for branded social spaces, employing best practices for kicking people out of your community, and even tips for maintaining a cool head and a steady blood pressure. We hope you'll walk away armed with the right tools and knowledge to face any social media conflict, quarrel, or red-level disaster.

Chapter 8, "Measuring Success! State-of-the-Art Social Metrics," explores the plethora of social analytic tools available on the Web. There are so many solutions out there that attempt to lend ordered metrics to the social media chaos. This chapter highlights analytics tools that we usually reach for.

Appendix A, "Social Media Community Manager Job Description," features a granular look at crucial skills and essential duties for the CM role, along with verbiage you can use for job descriptions, blog posts, tweets, and other outreach.

Appendix B, "The Big List of Community Management Tools and Analytics," houses a list of awesome tools for today's data-driven community manager—everything from content aggregation to holistic automation to hardcore analytics.

Appendix C, "72 Must-Follow Online Marketing Geniuses," boasts a selected round-up of folks who know what's up when it comes to social media, complete with each of their Twitter handles for easy contact!

When you see this icon in the margin, it means there's an asset you can download from www.sybex.com/go/communitymanager or aimclear.com/cm/.

Things change quickly in social media land. Visit aimclear.com/cm/ or www.sybex.com/go/communitymanager for valuable free resources updating information in this book.

How to Contact the Authors

We welcome feedback from you about this book or about articles and books you'd like to see from us in the future. You can reach us by writing to lauren@aimclear.com and marty@aimclear.com. For more information about aimClear consulting services, upcoming speaking engagements, and other fun stuff, please visit our website at www.aimclear.com.

The Social Media Community Manager's Role

1

Being a community manager these days is a fascinating fusion of various roles, previously assigned to multiple areas of most marketing agencies and in-house departments. This chapter defines the role of the community manager.

Chapter Contents

Be There or Beware!

The New Marketing Mash-up Player

Data-Driven Community Outreach: The Holy Grail

Determining Brand Voice: Who Are We? Why Are We Here?

Understanding Social ROI

Social Media and Attribution

Be There or Beware!

The act of communication is nothing short of a total marvel, paramount in the preservation and perpetuation of cultural beliefs and functional civilization. From leisurely storytelling to sharing vital information, it is a way for one person to say to another, in so many words, "This is what I think! This is how I feel! Can you dig it?"...and it's been like that forever. The biggest variable is the constant evolution of communication mechanisms.

Today, tons of conversations—consumer-centric chatter, complaining, praising, smack talking, and evangelizing—take place online. But as few as two generations ago such exchanges were neatly confined to the family dinner table, under hair dryers at the salon, around the knitting circle, on the bus, in the park, on the phone, etc.—much to the chagrin of companies hungry to sell products or services and understand how consumers feel about them.

The emergent adoption of personal computers, household dial-up modems, the Internet, and thus, the gradual shift of these conversations from offline to online in the mid-1990s was huge. Throngs of people—consumers—were connecting and communicating faster, easier, and more frequently than ever before. AOL email, Instant Messenger, chat rooms, forums, and eventually social networks like Facebook were total game-changers for human interaction and the dissemination of information. But shiny new communities didn't solve anything for companies. They were walled gardens accessible only by account holders with a username and a password. Unfortunately, search engine spiders, corporate spies, and uninvited flies on the wall were strictly excluded. Inside those walls, oh, the sweet, juicy gossip to behold!

Even as users flocked to popular new communities, marketers were still out of earshot of customers, potential or existing, and therefore, as out of the loop as they had been 50 years back. Any walled garden or digital platform with direct message (DM) functionality meant Target Customer A was communicating with friend, a.k.a. Target Customer B, and Brand X not only couldn't do anything about it, but had no clue who was talking to whom about what, or, of arguably equal importance, the sentiment of their exchange. No spiders meant no content indexed. Search engines weren't effective for that kind of reputation monitoring.

Brands were at risk of catastrophic damage—because who was there to stop it? Companies didn't have community managers in the digital trenches, on the hunt for brand mentions, ready to field angry rants or dispel inaccurate claims from dissatisfied customers. Such omnipresence was more or less impossible, and far from common practice. Likewise, companies couldn't offer incentives or recognition to shoppers who endorsed their brand to friends. Countless opportunities to turn average consumers into brand evangelists and turn disgruntled buyers into believers, thereby creating a beloved, prosperous company, flew the proverbial coop by the flockload.

Until now.

Social Media: The "Always On" Channel

It happened. The wall came down. Well, sort of, in some places. Facebook, for example, gradually morphed from a no-exceptions closed-circuit cyber-campus into an environment welcoming of high school students and, eventually, anyone with a valid email address. The garden underwent perpetual (if not infuriating) renovations until Facebook decided to let companies in too. That's right! Search engines still weren't on the VIP guest list, but brands could *finally* enter the social playground to set up shop, giving customers a place to air grievances and heap praise. It wasn't the equivalent to copping a squat at the dinner table when family members bemoaned or lauded recent shopping experiences. But Facebook took significant steps in exciting directions and the community manager role went mainstream.

Community managers had a new beast on their hands when microblogging channels hit the scene. Twitter was revolutionary, giving everyone and his dog a mouthpiece that was, by default, public to the world and crawlable by search engines. Video-hosting and -sharing sites gained popularity, and suddenly everyone was uploading their own video clips, everything from OMG-adorable kitties to epic skateboard wipeouts—even product and service reviews. An assortment of similar social communities cropped up and gained mass. People began to delight in sharing their two cents as consumers and as citizens of a digital world. Social sharing has quickly become second nature.

The majority of contemporary consumers are, in one way or another, operating online—around the clock—surfing, shopping, commenting, rating, raving, ranting, perusing, recommending, and weighing a healthy mix of all this user-generated content (UGC) as they move closer to or away from a purchase decision. When it's 5:30 p.m. in Minnesota, and we aimClearians are punching our cards after a long day in the shop, community manager clients of ours in Sydney are just getting into the office with an 8:30 a.m. cup of coffee, and their customers are logging onto Facebook, ready to engage. We come to work at 8:30 a.m. Central, but that's just after lunch in London, and even back at home, people have been awake and angrily tweeting @ClientBrand for three hours already.

These conversations don't stop. They are real. They're rampant. And they're happening whether companies are listening or not. The most titillating development over the past century is that now companies *can* listen.

The Art of Vigilant Monitoring and Engaging

Yes! Part of the wall's come down, and billions of consumers are active online at any given part of the day, any given day of the week, from all corners of the globe. For the first time in history, marketers have unprecedented access to social chatter, from the crucial to the casual. If brands are not listening, if marketers are not keenly devoted to monitoring all relevant conversations, if community managers aren't at the helm ready to engage when customers reach out or whisper smack to their friends, nasty brand damage is imminent. Be there. Or beware.

Bear in mind, there is no blanket coverage across the Web when it comes to reputation and community monitoring, no simple solution for companies to catalog every atom of conversation surrounding brand terms, products, or services. Google Alerts are an awesome start, but they aren't enough, simply because not all content is crawlable or indexed. Which sites are crawled and what content triggers Google Alerts is up to Google. Also, the Internet is just too big. No search engine can keep track of all of it. Companies and community managers need a more comprehensive monitoring strategy. Social listening software and social customer relationship management (SCRM) tools are available to organize the conversation happening about your brand online, often at a high cost and sometimes contingent on social network APIs—but it is paramount that a human still sift through this for qualitative analysis.

Brands need a green-beret rep in every channel, at every portal, under every digital bush and rock, armed with the most sophisticated listening tools and monitoring 24/7, because social never sleeps. Marketers need a cohesive and strategic action plan for proactive engagement, crisis management, and everything in between. This isn't new.

 Note: Even mainstream customer relationship management (CRM) software or tools, like SalesForce, have built-in modules to monitor multichannel chatter.

Social media community management isn't what's next. It's already every online marketer's job description. You need to be the definition of a diligent, vigilant, hard-core social media community manager. We're confident this book will show you how.

The New Marketing Mash-up Player

In order to be effective, community managers (CMs) must possess a solid understanding and practical fluency in public relations (PR), search engine optimization (SEO), pay per click (PPC) advertising, analytics, and content marketing. It's a tall order to be functionally literate in *all* these classic roles, because such skills can be highly specialized. Also, most companies do not cross-train PR team members in PPC, SEO jocks in PR, and other combinations.

Therefore, to understand the next-gen community manager's role, we'll spend a few minutes reviewing marketing fundamentals, timeless tenets that have served our industry well for generations. The confusion that still exists surrounding online marketing, even after 20 years, still surprises us. The good news is that things have not changed much for decades (or longer), certainly since well before the Internet's rise. Let's dive in and remember to review the basics of what it means to be a marketer!

There are essentially two major types of marketing in the world: search and contextual. Search means that marketers respond to users' questions with answers. When a user types a keyword into Google or Bing and clicks Submit seeking answers on a search engine results page (SERP), that's called search.

Contextual is also commonly referred to as display or walk-by. Users don't search and they're not necessarily seeking solutions at the time of exposure to marketers' content. A great example of contextual marketing would be those "Ads by Google" you see in major online publications such as the *New York Times*. Readers are exposed to ads relevant to what they're reading, not what they search for. Usually when one refers to banner ads, they're talking about contextual.

Both search and contextual marketing come in two delicious flavors: paid and unpaid. Paid search marketing is known as PPC. Major search channels Google, YouTube (owned by Google), Bing, Yahoo!, Yandex, Baidu, and other mainstream engines dominate the paid search market. Unpaid search is commonly known as SEO.

Eyes, Ears, and Brand Representation

In social media, the minimum any community manager must do is partner with PR to understand what the goals are for online reputation management and to passively listen for opportunities to capture online brand sentiment potential for crisis. Reacting to positive, neutral, and negative feedback from the customer-mob is optional, but often called for and something to plan for.

The next level of social media commitment is to undertake assertive outreach, researching and joining communities that align with your brand values in some way. Once your brand is established by building relationships in these communities, it often makes sense to sweeten the mix with social advertising.

Being worried about one's reputation is not new. Fervent desire to successfully exist in the pack is undoubtedly as old as human instincts. Certainly during Madison Avenue's Mad Men glory days, skinny-tied PR gray-hairs took the pulse of customer and prospective customer bases to stay in touch with users' affinities, complaints, and opinions. The 1962 community listened and reacted and undertook triage on behalf of the brands. Companies crowed about victories and worked to mitigate public #fails.

The role of social media community manager is the modern representation of a classic listen-and-react role as described earlier. Facebook now has nearly one billion members; a large percentage are fanatically engaged, every day. YouTube, LinkedIn, Twitter, Pinterest, Foursquare, and niche players such as StumbleUpon scream at scale and are continually sprouting up and growing deeper.

Note: Social media channels have such massive penetration that interactions mirror users' physical lives!

Attaining Social Prominence

The first goal of any marketing channel is to define its value proposition and obtain a prominent presence. Look to simply be present by providing contextually relevant content. The more targeted those users are, the better. In other words, we want to be in the right place, among users who matter, and in ways that fit in and stand out according to the channel's voice and tone. This applies to search, social, billboards, newspapers, and sponsored golf outings. The community manager's primary goal is to attain social visibility in ways that blend in and stand out, according to the voice and tone of the channel.

In the real world, you would never run naked through the airport (or at least we hope you wouldn't). In social media, there are plenty of behaviors just as glaring and, as in life, companies need to behave in ways that are acceptable. It's OK to be disruptive, but customers have limits in every channel, physical or virtual.

Organic Prominence

An organic social media impression means a brand did not pay the community to be seen. There are many methods and tactics to attain organic social prominence, most of them simple. As an example, if the brand has 50,000 Twitter followers, a percentage of those followers are logged into Twitter when the brand tweets. A measurable percentage of those followers might interact with the brand's tweet, by retweeting, replying, and sending direct messages. Brand visibility and user engagement are great examples of organic impressions and represent a key component of social media prominence.

The simplicity is similar in most social channels. Posting to a brand's Facebook wall is most highly visible to those who have liked the brand's page. The same holds true in YouTube, StumbleUpon, and nearly all social communities. Think of likes and follows as users subscribing to receive the brand's posts organically. That's a really simple way to think about prominence, right?

Paid Prominence

Brands can also attain prominence by placing ads. Figure 1.1 shows one type of Facebook Ad. The area to its left (Iridium Jazz Club) is organic. Paid and organic units—that is, blocks of content standalone or in a feed—live in a variety of locations on Facebook and in other communities. Where social sites place paid units is all about how that community is monetizing the site. Paid and organic units often appear in the same proximity on a page. When paid ad units appear in a place where traditionally organic units also appear, that is called paid inclusion. Since users usually seem to trust organic content over paid, any ambiguity about what's what is great for marketers.

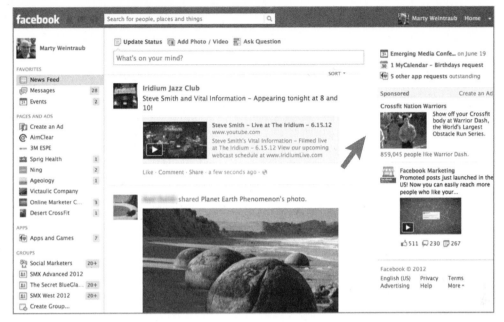

Figure 1.1 Facebook Ad, a paid unit on the right sidebar an advertiser purchased

We'll discuss the blurred lines between paid and organic prominence in Chapter 6, "Dominate with Paid Organic Amplification," in the paid-organic section. Figure 1.2 shows how paid prominence is mingled in traditional Twitter space, a promoted post sandwiched between otherwise organic feed items.

Figure 1.2 Comingled paid and organic Twitter feed items

Impact on Search Engine Optimization

A huge part of the modern community manager's role is about search engine optimization (SEO). Sure, prominence on any social media site *within* that site is easy to understand. You participate in Facebook and want to be visible in Facebook. For the investment in social, you want activities in channels to be visible to others in the channel.

In addition, there are other central nodes of visibility, the most notable being in Google, Bing, and other search results. When someone searches for keywords, it's a cool thing for your social media meanderings to show up in the results. Yep, public-facing pages from social media sites are indexed (listed) in mainstream search engines, including international ones like Yandex, Baidu, and Yahoo! Australia.

The lines between social media and SEO have been blurred for years, as marketers have grown more and more concerned about how social activity is indexed and reflected by mainstream search engines. In fact, one of the first lines of reputation defense is to push an unflattering result down in the SERPs by creating social profiles from channels that engines favor. These days, LinkedIn, Facebook, and Twitter profiles tend to show up prominently in Google and Bing. Powerful niche blogs and forums, where users' account profiles are public facing, can be super powerful in the SERPs, especially when marketers build true links on relevant anchor text to the profile.

Social Signals and Google+

Traditionally, search engines evaluated links, trust, keywords, metadata, and other on- and off-page attributes when ranking websites. Though metadata formats have changed with the evolution of new tag sets like Schema (www.schema.org), many traditional ranking factors still apply.

Over the years, search engines also began to look at social signals from mainstream communities. When users in Facebook and Twitter take content hot by retweeting, sharing, and otherwise trafficking content in public, search engines "see" the activity and surface content in transient waves. Bing, because of its business relationship with Facebook, is hyper-sensitive to Facebook social signals.

Google is another story. One of the biggest changes to SEO over the last 20 years occurred in spring 2012, when Google took social signal ranking factors to a new level with its fledgling social community Google+ (Figure 1.3). Following someone in Google+, known as subscribing to a circle, means that the follower's SERPs are much more likely to receive suggested content as a result of the followed user's sharing.

Google+ totally blurs the line between social and SEO, and it's now essential for brands to crank out an optimized Google+ feed and strive to get other users to subscribe in circles. No longer do we just target keywords. Marketers must now also target users to qualify them to receive socially prioritized SEO.

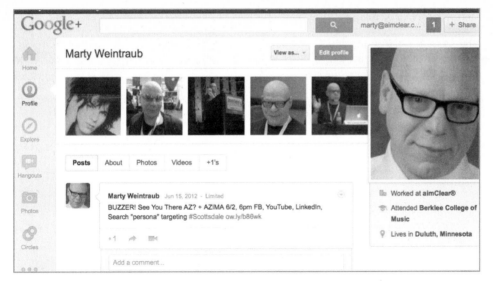

Figure 1.3 Google+ is now essential fare for SEO.

Social Advertising Partner

SEO is not the only thin line community managers traverse. The new hybrid CM also needs to be informed and fluent in social advertising formats that affect how content is visible in mainstream social channels.

Social media communities need to make money from the massive influx of users to widespread adoption of their sites. That means selling advertising so marketers can gain visibility, otherwise unavailable by organic activity alone.

As you'll learn in Chapter 6, Facebook intentionally limits virility unless you reenable key organic features by opening your wallet. Also, there is not always clear delimitation in Facebook as to what's organic and what's paid, so some ad units deliver astonishing results as Facebook users act on what they believe to be trusted organic listings when, in fact, they are paid. Ah, we love paid inclusion!

Twitter, LinkedIn, YouTube, StumbleUpon, and other communities sell advertising as well. Although each somehow blurs the lines between paid and organic units on the page, the message is clear: For the greatest chance to attain optimal prominence in social media, brands need to advertise. Because community management has the ability to inform on consumer behavior, sentiment, and trends in real time, CMs need to attain fluency in social advertising methods for maximum effectiveness.

Figure 1.4 is a screen capture of YouTube Ads, which are powerfully effective to drive views of your own videos and even send users back to your website to study, hang, and convert.

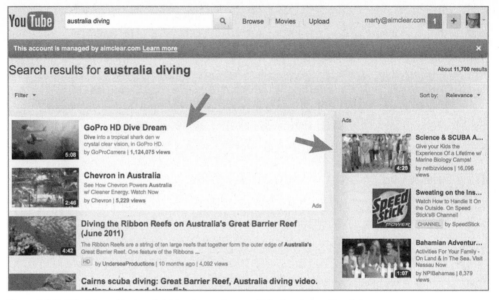

Figure 1.4 YouTube Ads can drive branded video views and even traffic back to the brand's website

Interestingly, while buying ads in social channels is all about attaining prominence in that specific channel, in-channel visibility from social ads often results in additional sharing of the promoted material. This content propagation can cause viral activity. In turn, the viral sharing can influence search engines, especially if users radiate the sharing out to Google+. Wow, it's a brave new world!

Public Relations Team Member

We know that community managers affect SEO, which means that a certain baseline of non-spammy output in social sites is required. Think of it as an "Identity feed." The question begs to be asked, "Where is this daily or weekly content going to come from?"

Well, let's think about that content. Though much will be generated on the fly, sharing ideas and inspirations from others and our own brand, baseline (minimum) social feeds need to reflect the true personality and goings-on of the brand. Since channels like Facebook, Twitter, and Google+ are inherently social, then our brand's output needs to also engage users consuming the feed for maximum success. We'll explore this deeper in Chapter 4, "Content, Reputation, and Hardcore Listening Hacks."

Community managers also stand ready to make the feed an exchange, truly bi- and multi-directional. In other words, since conversations will break out, the CM needs to be ready to participate. That sounds a lot like traditional PR to us and public relations pros are excellent folks to source for modern CM training and duties. No traditional role in the marketing mix is better equipped to crank out appropriate baseline content along lines of relations including media, investor, community, customer, internal, human interest, and crisis management. These relationships are timeless staples of PR.

As social signals have become critical mash-up feedstuff for social and SEO prominence, so has the understanding of classic public relations thinking become crucial. It's official now. PR is an absolutely essential skill set for community managers.

Data-Driven Community Outreach: The Holy Grail

Many community managers, as they manage profiles, are content to sit on the brand's wall, greet social users who stop by, and "mind the store." That's only part of the picture.

The modern community manager is also charged with identifying related communities where users may have an affinity for the brand's offerings. The art of ascertaining which communities may hold interested users can facilitate healthily assertive acts of engagement and friendship as CMs leave the comfortable environs of their own walls and head out to meet people and engage them on behalf of the mother brand.

The Demographic Research Ethic

We would never undertake SEO or search PPC without doing keyword research. Reciprocally, it's foolish to commence community management without doing social demographic research to reveal the inventory available to target users within a social site. Just as SEO artists use Google's keyword tool, a utility designed to serve search advertiser targeting, social organic targeting is best researched using paid social advertising tools. Good examples are

- Facebook Ads creation tool
- YouTube placement and keyword research tools
- LinkedIn Ads tools

Social media sites are loath to give up exact proportions of community makeup but are forced to pony up the data where the sites sell advertising. Another awesome place to look for social inventory is where sites allow users to search for content. Say we're targeting travelers. Using paid and organic tools to do demographic research for campaigns is fundamental to online marketing because the engines and communities have to give up the information in order to sell ads and service users.

Figure 1.5 shows examples of inventory in YouTube, Facebook, and LinkedIn.

Using the YouTube search box to identify users' interests

Using the Facebook Ad creation tool to research user concentrations

Using LinkedIn Ad creation tool to research themed groups for participation

Figure 1.5 Inventory in various social channels

Making More of the Right Friends

There are myriad approaches to holistic befriending via social media channels. We'll discuss this in great detail in Chapter 2, "Timeless Tenets of Non-Gratuitous Social Behavior," from targeting the right friends to conveying a sense of familiarity and interest, expanding conversations with thoughtful questions to reaching out without selling and enhancing rebroadcasts with insightful editorials.

As previously mentioned, the first step is demographic research to identify social media influencers and potential friends from a number of channels ranging from Facebook and YouTube to forums. We then challenge CMs to take these "friend leads" and convert them to organic friends over a period of time, at a "cost per friend lead" calculated from how much time the friend conversion takes.

Quality is much more important than quantity. Let's use the LinkedIn group in Figure 1.5 earlier, where we've uncovered focused clusters of LinkedIn users. We know from our demographic research using the LinkedIn Ads creation tool that there are 14,301 such users. It stands to reason that as we bring ourselves to participate in those groups on behalf of our brands and ourselves, we will make friends with others of similar mind.

The premise here is that once we've identified users who demonstrate affinities related to our brand, we can go meet them where they hang out. It's better to make fewer of the right friends than oodles of unfocused peeps who are much less likely to be interested in the same topics we are.

Modern Community Building Key Performance Indicators

So, what do we look for as indicators of successful community building as the front end for marketing efforts? As mentioned, such metrics are not necessarily about quantity of friends, rather about their congruency with the marketing mission. Of course it's good to have both. We love the intersection of quality and quantity.

There are two main considerations when evaluating strength-of-community. First, we want to know the percentage of the demographic segments targeted that like, follow, and otherwise subscribe. If there are 13,301 users in LinkedIn's hospitality-related groups, then we ask what percentage of those users follow our brand in LinkedIn and/or become personal contacts.

The next consideration is usefulness-of-community. What is having this collection of like-minded users good for anyway? Are we successfully converting them to customers and/or serving existing customers? Are community-building efforts truly entrances to the purchase funnel? Do we regularly drive traffic back to sites we own to accomplish key performance indicators (KPIs)? Does building the community result in SEO prominence in Google and Bing SERPs?

Later in this chapter, in the "Understanding Social ROI" section, we'll take a detailed look at what KPIs can be monitored and measured. The stronger and more focused the community building effort is, the more likely it is we'll see KPI conversions. Start with community-building goals that are about connecting with the right users, after identifying them with demographic research.

Determining Brand Voice: Who Are We? Why Are We Here?

Close your eyes. Imagine your company's dream community manager. What does he/she look like? (For the sake of pronoun simplification, let's assume it's a she.) Better yet, pretend your team sent this model CM to a business event—a networking cocktail hour. The marketing team collaborated prior to the gig to establish her intent: The social media community manager is there to mingle, meet prospective clients, catch up with familiar ones, chat with likeminded professionals, and, above all, represent your company with grace and enthusiasm.

Determining Your "Person"

What's your hostess with the mostess wearing? A corporate uniform? A branded hoodie? Perhaps a polo with the company name stitched on the breast pocket? Maybe the spokesperson representing your brand is in ripped jeans, a cozy rock-band t-shirt, and scuffed-up Chuck Taylors—just what the target audience might wear on the weekends. Or is the CM walking around in a theme-park mascot outfit, complete with full mask and bodysuit, just like the cartoon character on your corporate website?

How does the community manager talk? Is dialogue fixed in the third person plural, the *royal we*, resolutely conscious of the company for which she's speaking? "Our approach is this," "We weren't aware of that," "We're sorry to hear that," "Tell us more," and so on, even though this community manager is clearly the lone representative in the room?

Or are voice, tone, and content unabashedly direct? Does the CM discuss personal interests, extraneous as they may be to the company, to encourage and sustain a friendly conversation? Would she be overheard saying, "Get out of town, I *love* that restaurant!" to another attendee, even if your business has nothing to do with fine dining?

Is your dream community manager some hybrid placed gracefully on the spectrum between polar opposites: the corporate talking head and the groovy girl people want to be friends with, who cares about her job? Does the CM have a neutered voice and impersonal tone that could put up a wall between your company and potential customers? Will there be little return on investment (ROI) because the CM is too busy socializing?

These are essential questions every business on the quest for a seriously amazing social media community manager must ask and establish upfront. In short, how do you envision your brand being represented in cyberspace? What, *who*, is your company avatar?

Choosing an Appropriate Avatar

An avatar is a term used to describe how people (that includes companies) represent themselves online, essentially a social media persona. The combinations and possibilities are as endless and as complex as the actual guy or girl behind the computer monitor advocating for the brand. Regardless of the freedom given to an actively engaging community manager, in the end it's a commercial avatar, that is to say, an avatar participating in social media for corporate gain.

As happy-go-lucky as social media interactions can feel, if participation in a social sphere is on behalf of a company, the goal is to *gain* something for the company: links, organic prominence, awareness, promotional opportunities, PR value, traffic, and so on. Community managers are community marketers. Mission: market. That's not to say being absolutely fabulous and appreciated isn't part of the package.

Note: One takeaway from this book we hope you'll embrace is that the true secret of social media is to give more than you take.

To this day, there is a remarkable lack of consensus regarding the right avatar for a brand. Appropriate social media usage for a company and level of transparency are open to interpretation. Marketing commercial goods and services in an environment where people are just hanging out could have ugly ramifications. Social media is still very much the Wild West for online marketers. That said, there are tiers of transparency to take into account when crafting a commercial avatar:

- Is corporate affiliation revealed?
- Is the CM's ultimate mission apparent to the community? (Remember: The ultimate mission is marketing!)
- Are personal elements (authentic or altered to mirror target audience) such as age, gender, ethnicity, orientation, social status, or location disclosed?
- Does the company CM bare *personality* traits—shades of who's behind the computer screen? Is tone obviously sarcastic, patient, compassionate, excitable, or knowledgeable?
- Is the community manager's goal to become a beloved presence in the social community, or is the purpose to lurk and listen to brand chatter?
- Does the company want a staunch defender of the brand in times of crisis, or a passive participant or mediator?
- Who owns the avatar? The brand? The individual community manager? An agency or client? (This is already becoming an important dialogue among attorneys.)

These concepts of identity, transparency, and ownership beg a discussion of the continuum of black hat vs. white hat tactics—in other words, the range of what's acceptable, shady, legitimate, manipulative, fair game, illegal, and so on.

If a fully corporate avatar is selected, does that conflict with the terms of service (TOS) of the marketing platform? If the CM is to parade around as a fabricated character meant to embody the brand spirit or target consumer, is there a breach of trust, rules, even laws in a certain jurisdiction? Do a gut-check prior to dipping your toes into any social media channel. Be totally honest with yourself and the community.

Let's cruise through some common avatar models and corresponding attributes to demonstrate the range of possibilities and combinations a commercial avatar may embody.

The Data-Driven Community Manager

- Honest and transparent in role
- Extremely well-developed persona
- Forensic psychologist/profiler
- Targets lists of authority users by topic; only manipulates to serve
- Makes the right real friends
- Makes them think they thought of it
- Persona derivative of blogger team, or mostly fictional
- Feels emotional and shares
- Strategically defends brand and leverages opportunities for the win
- Sells by sophisticated, nurturing, and subtle maneuvering
- Builds links by sharing remarkable content
- Ownership is negotiable

The Press Secretary

- Uses real name; puts personal reputation on the line
- Fully transparent; represents company interests
- Not focused on link building or SEO (directly)
- Communicates directly on behalf of the brand
- Persona owned by blogger (of course)

The Admin Press Secretary

- All features of press secretary model, but uses pseudonym
- The key difference is ownership (not a real persona; ownership open to interpretation)

The Lovely Celebrity Spokesperson, Endorsement Included

- All features of press secretary model
- History, reputation, and authority
- Often much more expensive
- Built-in readership and buzz
- No question of ownership or transparency

The Walled Garden Forum Lurker

- Not transparent; doesn't reveal association with clients
- Lurk and report; fly below the radar
- Participate selectively to gain street cred
- Loner, limited engagement
- Never sells anything
- Does not attempt to influence, except in extraordinary circumstances
- Makes few friends in forums that do not require friendship to search and view chatter streams
- Makes some/many friends if required to search and view chatter streams
- Limited or no influence on behalf of clients, selectively engages to counter threats only by gathering information

These are but a taste of the multitude of avatar models we've noticed in the wild. Any combination of model attributes can be employed. The role and identity of a community manager can be as customized as a swank new car, specific to a company's objectives, industry, morals, whatever. Community managers *are*, as it were, some of the most powerful vehicles for brands eager to get into the minds and hearts (wallets, too?) of consumers and the vast empire of social media.

Hungry for some real-life examples to put this all into context? Grab your forks for a three-course meal of social media community manager case studies. Most echo elements of the classic and beloved Data-Driven Community Manager and Press Secretary models, with noteworthy variations. For now, we'll focus exclusively on each brand's Twitter presence, and the CM avatar they've designated for that specific conversation-based channel. The goal here is to hone in on how each brand verbally and visually represents itself in an untamed stream of tweets, rather than how the community manager manages its own branded corner of the World Wide Web, such as a company Facebook page. This is all about voice, face, and overall identity.

First up, a few demonstrations of unified brand presence, then on to examples of multiple brand representatives.

Unified Brand Presence

Check out GNC's main Twitter presence, @GNCLiveWell. Popular brand, respected company, pretty household name. How has this legacy brand chosen to represent itself on Twitter? Figure 1.6 gives us some hints.

Figure 1.6 @GNCLiveWell Twitter bio

Branded avatar (here, avatar will mean the 128×128-pixel image associated with a Twitter account). Branded name. Branded handle (username). An almost impersonally succinct bio. Not even a city in the location. GNC is operating omnipresent in the USA!

There isn't one shred of personality in this key introduction. We haven't the faintest impression of who's on the other end of the monitor typing out tweets for @GNCLiveWell. Male? Female? Buff? Trim? Mommy blogger of four? Twenty-something college grad frat dude? Sports nuts? Yoga pro? Carnivore? Vegan? We don't know. There's pretty much zilch to glean from the bio, avatar, name, and handle. If GNC's community manager were at that cocktail party with your dream CM, "it" would be a giant asexual foam red square with white blocky text, kicking it by the punch bowl.

GNC assumed a unified brand presence for its social media model. All tweets are in the third-person plural state, further removing any sense of the individual. The CM is participating on behalf of GNC, always and forever. Everything is in terms of "we," "us," and "our." Topics of conversation with fans and customers fall somewhere under the GNC umbrella: general health and fitness, branded products, and daily deals. Extraneous chatter simply for the sake of socializing coming out of this feed is unlikely; everything is in some way related to GNC's business and target market.

That said, the tweets are informative, helpful, and enthusiastic. @GNCLiveWell uses exclamation points to mark passion, and easy-going shorthand Internet jargon, such as "Thnx!" for "Thanks!" and even the slightly tacky AOL-4.0-tastic "u" for "you," as shown in Figure 1.7. An overall welcoming and amiable tone, definitely not a corporate bullhorn with the sole mission of blowing branded content out the feed with no concept of two-way engagement.

Figure 1.7 @GNCLiveWell customer service tweet

Let's move on to a similar case: @VasqueFootwear. Take a peek at this company's Twitter bio in Figure 1.8.

Figure 1.8 @VasqueFootwear Twitter bio

Nearly identical to @GNCLiveWell in terms of branded representation. Company logo as the avatar, branded name, branded handle, and even a similar bio: "The official twitter account of Vasque…" followed by a brief description of the company, "…a leader in outdoor performance footwear," which is helpful, because we had never heard of Vasque before. Location: "Red Wing, MN." Nice. We know where Red Wing is—one of our aimClearians grew up there. This bit of contextualization helps humanize the entity.

A quick skim of tweets unearths the unified brand presence, that *royal we*, showcased in Figure 1.9.

Figure 1.9 @VasqueFootwear sample tweet

Similar to @GNCLiveWell, there's personality marked by exclamations and genuine eagerness to assist and share, but the community manager's identity is irrelevant, hidden behind a branded mask. It seems to be working for this company. Though a majority of the tweets are Vasque product–centric, they're not noisily hocking links to e-commerce pages for hiking sneakers. Figure 1.10 shows Vasque Footwear's CM diligently monitoring tweets from both jazzed and frustrated customers. After listening, the brand's CM engages thoughtfully.

Figure 1.10 @VasqueFootwear monitors @Mentions and engages.

@VasqueFootwear must have some additional brand reputation monitoring strategy in place. Check out the tweet chat in Figure 1.10: The user didn't directly @mention Vasque, but its community manager's hawk eye picked up the generic brand mention and pounced on the opportunity to engage. We'll take a deep dive into tight brand monitoring tools in Chapter 4, so to all you deadeye super-ninja CMs in training, stick around.

A commendable portion of all tweets from this company is @mention based, that is to say, conversation based. Too often we see companies, typically those that fall under the unified brand presence umbrella, miss the boat with Twitter. Rather than utilizing its supreme conversation functionality as a tool for powerful customer service and proactive engagement, they treat it as a one-sided RSS feed to blast out links to the mothership (branded content, that is).

In this case, Vasque's CM chats with customers and followers about its products and topics related to outdoor activities, and the material is rich. The more you study this company's Twitter stream and approach to community management, the easier it is to see why they're a beloved regional brand.

Onto another example: @MayoClinic. Let's review the tweet-stream from one of the most prestigious treatment centers in the world.

Combing back through a month of tweets, you can count the @mentions on one hand (*cough* two fingers). Clearly not a very digitally interactive brand. The bulk of tweets are one-way broadcasts aimed at no one in particular, just a mass of 360,000+ followers (Figure 1.11). Almost all point back to branded content. Little to no personality. As-removed-as-it-gets Press Secretary. Unified brand presence all the way.

Figure 1.11 @MayoClinic tweet-stream

Check out Figure 1.12—time to dissect the bio.

Figure 1.12 @MayoClinic Twitter bio

All right, pretty much what you'd expect. Branded avatar, handle, name, and a bio that reads like a pamphlet: "An integrated clinical practice, education and research institution…" Hang on now, what's this? "Account maintained by @MayoClinic/ MCCSM," and a hotlink to another page. Let's follow it (Figure 1.13)!

Figure 1.13 @MayoClinic community manager Twitter list

Interesting! @MayoClinic has leveraged Twitter Lists (we'll talk more about those in Chapter 4) to introduce the individuals contributing to the branded Twitter-stream. We can assume that the "team of people that make up the Mayo Clinic Center for Social Media" all have their hands in @MayoClinic in one way or another. Nice to put a few faces with the big blue square, even if they aren't represented whatsoever in the stream.

So we have our first taste of multiple brand representatives. Let's move on to some more examples that employ this model in a more transparent way.

Multiple Brand Representatives

aimClearians fly all over the world to speak at online marketing conferences and visit with clients. None of us are immune to the occasional flight delay or double-booked seat or similar travel frustrations. We may even have sent an angry tweet or two to @AirlineX after such experiences.

Unlike @VasqueFootwear, whose customers are stoked about their awesome new kicks and can't wait to tell the world about them, we know from experience, and from a perusal of our next case's tweet-stream, that generally when passengers engage an airline, it's to complain. Kudos to @DeltaAssist for being on the ball with warp-speed customer service and replies to weary travelers armed with a smartphone and Twitter application.

Figure 1.14 provides a top-down review of this Twitter presence devoted exclusively to customer service.

Figure 1.14 @DeltaAssist Twitter bio

At first blush, this appears to be another case of unified brand presence. Branded handle, branded name, branded avatar, "we"-laced bio: "We're listening around the clock, 7 days a week. We try to answer all tweets..." Delta's certainly got the always-on channel part well understood. But come on, no *one* person can handle a task like that. They'd have to be a cyborg CM. That or they'd have to have multiple community managers operating in shifts so each hour of the day in each time zone around the world is covered fully.

Bingo.

@DeltaAssist introduces us to its team of 14 community managers with a branded background wallpaper, shown in Figure 1.15.

Figure 1.15 @DeltaAssist community manager roster

Characteristic of Twitter feeds with multiple brand reps, each CM initials his or her tweet to display ownership. Amber K. signs her tweets "^AK" so you can tell it's her, and although you don't know her last name or her hair color or whether she prefers dogs or cats, it helps humanize the customer service exchange. Those three characters begin to break down the wall between anonymized brand and customer, making it more person to person. Instead of "We're sorry to hear your flight was canceled," you get more empathy: "I get it, I'm human, too, I know flying sucks sometimes—I want to help make things better." Powerful stuff!

@Starbucks is another example of a branded account that taps into the personalities and prowess of multiple community managers. CMs are introduced playfully in the bio: Brad, Lee, and Paige (Figure 1.16). You don't know anything about them beyond their first names, and unlike @DeltaAssist, they don't append initials to their tweets. Brad's tweets are indistinguishable from Paige's, likewise with Lee's. Branded handle, name, and avatar neuter individuality, but personality shines through in the trio's tweets, populated with smiley faces and exclamation points. You can't see who's tweeting what, but that doesn't seem to discourage their 2+ million followers.

Figure 1.16 @Starbucks Twitter bio

@MallOfAmerica shakes things up by including hotlinks to the personal Twitter bios of its three community managers, Bridget, Sarah, and Erin (Figure 1.17).

Figure 1.17 @MallOfAmerica Twitter bio

You have to click each link to visit the PR gals' own Twitter profiles and learn more about them, but at least now you have the chance to do so (Figure 1.18). It's a real game-changer to know that even though you're tweeting with a branded avatar, the woman answering your question about where to get awesome yogurt in the largest mall in the country is a yoga-loving shopaholic with funky taste in jewelry.

Figure 1.18 Mall of America community manager Bridget Jewell

Whenever links to branded content are shared, no one CM is attributed. They save initialed tweets for @mentions, from chitchat to customer service.

Last but not least for this section, @foiledcupcakes. Figure 1.19 shows us a new breed of multiple brand rep accounts. Branded handle, straightforward bio similar to what we've studied thus far: "Chicago's exclusive gift cupcake delivery company! Order a box of cupcake love & we'll handle the rest!"

Figure 1.19 @foiledcupcakes Twitter bio

Then, a twist: personal interests. "Loves Hugh Laurie, shoes, karaoke." And what's this? A photo of real-life human beings! No square brand logo here, not even an overlay of the company name on the ladies. Official Twitter name for this account is "Mari-Kelly-Kristina." Are they some of the folks in the photo? Likely, yes.

We met Mari at an online marketing conference in the Windy City back in 2010. From personal experience, we can say this is one of the more laidback companies we've encountered, both on and offline. You're never quite sure who's firing the tweets on the other end of the monitor, Mari, Kelly, or Kristina, but whoever *she* is, she has a bright, adorable, sassy personality and isn't afraid to make friends by chatting about things that are in no way related to inventory (though really, it wouldn't be the worst thing to gab about cupcakes all day).

The community manager(s) for @foiledcupcakes keep it light and fun on Twitter. They don't sell themselves. Foiled Cupcake's CM seems to, above all, use the channel as a tool for socialization, with the secondary mission of generating brand awareness. The CM is tweeting like a human being without a sales agenda under a branded name, admirably dissolving the wall between company and customer (Figure 1.20). It seems like customers are friends with the company by way of Mari and the ladies, and eventually they morph into cupcake purchasers.

Figure 1.20 @foiledcupcakes Tweets

Understanding Social ROI

Social media ROI is a daunting concept. This is especially true because classic web analytics were tooled to evaluate traffic to websites, not social media communities owned by third parties. Still, there is much that can be measured and the role of community manager is integral in this process. Let's dive in.

K.I.S.S. Social Media KPI Chart

As social media has become inexorably intertwined with search engine optimization, so too has the spectrum of goals. In the spirit of K.I.S.S. (Keep It Simple, Stupid), we set out to reduce classic and potential KPIs to a streamlined chart, expressing a matrix of analytic possibilities.

Use the chart shown in Figure 1.21 to spawn creative thinking as you construct social media metrics that reflect evolving realities. From the most basic traffic KPIs to multilevel social/SEO mash-ups, brainstorming on this grid of analytic options may be of benefit to your team.

Figure 1.21 SEO KPI K.I.S.S. chart

Chart Usage Fundamentals, Top Down   Start with five variables above the gray line: category keywords (nonbrand), brand keywords, links, shares, and social visibility. These are the building blocks. Examples are

- Social media that drives traffic to our website and converts
- Social shares resulting in chatter
- Social visibility that results in organic prominence in search engine results pages

Path One: Straight Down to the Left or to the Right   Add another layer of segmentation. Follow the arrows to either the left or right from the building blocks to "On Page," "Off Page," or "Segmentation" to form KPIs. Examples include

- Links earned by social resulting in chatter that generate likes and other subscriptions
- Shares by traffic by loyalty (returning visitors)

Path Two: Left, Then Right Follow the arrows down to the left and then to the right. This yields SEO KPIs that are more complex, including

- Shares resulting in conversion segmented by geographic area
- Social visibility that cross-pollinates to other channels that result in likes
- Links to off-site properties (like YouTube) that boost organic prominence in Universal SERPs for geographic-specific keywords

There are 640 possibilities on this chart, many of which are already widely adopted. Some apply to SEO and are great to have on a social KPI chart. Others range from innovative and immediately useful to more theoretical expressions. Use the chart as a starting point to discover new KPIs.

Creating analytics mechanisms to report on some of these KPIs is an interesting matter. Some combinations are super easy to conceptualize and execute in Google Analytics using Advanced Segments and other analytic packages. Others require more sophisticated systems and are difficult to isolate or even impossible to measure except for feeling lift. The idea is to get those creative KPI juices flowing. We hope you enjoy this chart as a starting place for creative social media KPI thinking.

Lead Gen vs. Sales

Some sales are either too expensive or complex for us to expect a user to click "Buy now" and pony up their credit cards. From mining leads for universities to selling multimillion-dollar business-to-business (B2B) equipment, very often the first step toward a completed sale is generating a lead. Direct response means eliciting an action from a user now. That can be either a completed sale or a lead.

The important consideration is whether the actions we seek from users happen now or later. You might hear the phrase "first-touch conversion." That means that a marketer got a user to complete an action the first time the user was engaged by a paid or organic result. While first-touch conversions are absolutely possible in social, they most often come from ads. Another common term is "last-touch conversion." This speaks to the last channel a user was in, leading to the conversion action.

Keep in mind the following basic division of actions:

- We are generating either a lead or a sale. This is dependent on the length of sales cycle for any particular product or service.
- A sale can be many things, from cash purchases and event signups to likes, subscriptions, and follows. The final action is the sale conversion.

Social Media and Attribution

Attribution, as pertains to the marketing process, means the order of channels a user touches on their way to a conversion. A user may see a television commercial, search for the brand, find the brand's Facebook page, like it (thereby subscribing), see the brand's wall post three weeks later, click on a mobile Facebook Ad targeted at them, send him/herself an email so as to remember later, and head over to the brand's website on a different laptop to convert. Whew! That's pretty deep and the complexity of the sequence of interactions is representative of the inherent challenges of measuring social media.

The problem is made more acute because our ability to gauge user behavior in social communities is limited to what each individual community tells us with built-in analytics. LinkedIn tells us almost nothing. Facebook Insights offers fantastic data about users in general but hardly anything about individual users. YouTube Insight analytics are cool but also limited, providing only general data.

Social communities can yield sales, leads, direct response, and first- and/or last-touch conversions. Often, communities built by brands result in sales that are less direct and barely measurable by this generation of web analytics. Here are a few key concepts for community managers to keep in mind:

- Analytics to measure attribution chains don't totally work because there are sometimes hops that are not completely measurable.
- Emergent platforms to measure attribution range from free (Google Analytics multichannel funnels) to more costly (Adobe SocialAnalytics, Convertro, Acquisio, and others).
- Last-touch conversion is usually possible.
- Tag all social ads with source, demographic segment, and creative elements.
- Whenever possible, place the conversion mechanism (form, buy button, etc.) on a site you own. Ask your friendly web developer to set a cookie on all new traffic to your site and build a visits history by concatenating each new visit to the site, matriculated to the source and any other tagging variables.
- Remember that zooming out always works. Total Cost Of Marketing All Channels / Total Conversion = Total Cost Per Conversion. As social media programs come online, study the effect on the total program, including search—paid and organic—in all channels.

It's important to understand that not all social media conversions are easily attributable, end to end. Such is the fickle nature of today's web analytics paradigm. If you're not working in a true attribution analytics environment, start by learning Google's multichannel funnels and explore paid tools.

Social as a Subscription Channel

At its core, someone liking, following, adding to circles, and so forth is equivalent to subscriptions or relationships—it's the same as someone subscribing to an email list or newsletter. Treating social channels like subscription lists or like email lists of old can be a highly effective approach for brands to monetize social.

For instance, when someone likes your brand Facebook page, they are signing up to see things you post in their newsfeed, on a prioritized basis over other brands they have not subscribed to. The same holds true in Twitter. After the user follows, your updates show up in their main feed.

Say a brand has earned 25,000 Facebook likes. Each time the brand posts, a measurable percentage of users will see the post. Facebook gives us that metric. Some users will click through to either the Facebook brand page or directly to the content that was highlighted on the wall. That is analogous to the "email open" metric in an e-marketing campaign and subsequent traffic to the internal or external asset being promoted. Out of the number of visitors driven to an asset, a certain amount of them will take an action. Over time, this can result in sales. Treating social media follows, likes, and so on as subscription marketing is the new wave, as classic becomes new again.

Setting Realistic Social Media Marketing Goals

Your job as community manager is to lead the team and set realistic expectations rooted in business objectives. What's key here is not allowing any stakeholder to set unrealistic goals. Educating multiple audiences about social media best practices and setting attainable goals is fundamental to the CM's role. We strongly encourage you to challenge the realism of plans others make. Your boss's wanting a certain social media result in a certain timeframe at a desirable cost does not mean it can be attained. Reciprocally, it's important to reach for the stars.

Because most nonagency marketers don't have the opportunity to touch dozens or even hundreds of case studies each year, we've learned that it's essential that marketers making the plan insist that objectives, strategies, and tactics be rooted in the company's overarching business goals and objectives so that there's a strong foundation for a holistic marketing communications presence. Chances are your boss does not know jack about social. Keep in mind that *you* may not know squat about something important the boss knows. Be open-minded.

Here's our list of planning questions. Some of them may not apply to every project, but most of them do, at least in some way.

Building a Kick-Ass Social Media Marketing Plan

The secret of building a kick-ass marketing plan is to ask and answer the right questions. In fact, the best way to do it is to use all the question words. Yep, you know, those five big "W" words and the one "H" word: who, what, when, where, why, and how. We apply the "W" words and "H" first to groundwork and then execution.

Marketing plan means constructing a written outline of what will come and setting expectations as to how we're going to get there. It seems simple, but there are often many moving parts. It's best to lay out the important variables, ask crucial questions, and write down the answers.

 At this point we'd like to introduce the first downloadable resource in the book, which is denoted by that spiffy icon in the margin. Right now, before we go any further, head over to www.aimclear.com/cm/chapter1 or www.sybex.com/go/communitymanager and grab the marketing plan preparation template for your own use. Download the zipped file.

You'll want the files handy. Have a close look at the docs and then read this chapter again. Apply the process to a real-life or role-played case study of your own. We want you to test this system to create a marketing plan right away.

There are three versions of the file in the zipped directory. The first is blank (marketing-plan-blank.docx) and the other is completely filled out with sample answers (marketing-plan-sample-answers.docx). The third zipped doc is a finished ready-to-deliver marketing plan made up of statements derived from the example answers (marketing-plan-complete.docx).

Note: It's easy to turn questions answered into marketing plan statements simply by reformatting answers from the completed questionnaire. For instance, if the question is "Who do you want to sell to?" and the answer is "53-year-old female Latinos in East LA," then the marketing statement is, "The demographic segment is 53-year-old female Latinos in East LA."

Great! Let's get started. A marketing plan is just that: planning. So, you also better allocate time and invite key stakeholders and anyone else you find valuable to help. One tip: Think about the first session in advance, in the shower, while listening to music, or on a flight. The best marketing plans come from passionate marketers who don't candy-coat obstacles, who challenge conventions, and who show up at the planning party ready to rock!

Preproduction: What Are You Marketing?

It is paramount that the brand's purpose be defined and that the CMO, marketing director, or owner is clear on what the brand's promises and purposes are. It's tragically funny how often a brand fails to do this, and it ultimately creates a shaky foundation. What are the planning basics you need to know? Are you building a program to last indefinitely or are you planning a seasonal campaign? Usually companies need both base programs and campaigns. Create the base program and then additional planning for fixed-length campaigns to run on top of the foundation.

Most social media plans differentiate between what is programmatic (ongoing) and campaigns (fixed length):

- What countries will you be marketing in?
- Will you only be marketing in English?
- What channels will you use?
- Is this ongoing or fixed length? If fixed, how long will it last?
- Will you have organic and/or paid campaigns?
- If you're using multiple languages, do you have translation teams in place or will there need to be a third-party team? If yes, who?
- Will this be a fully in-social effort or involve the promotion of external assets like website landing pages, other social communities, and so on?
- What pages, apps, and profiles need to be (re)built, and who is going to build these assets? Will the team be in-house or are external vendors required? If external, then who?
- Make a list of existing in-community social pages and/or external landing pages and content that is the closest you have to facilitating whatever a KPI conversion is. For instance, if Facebook likes are the KPI, then tell us what tab in Facebook you're going to send users to.

Demographic Research

What are the interests and affinities of your customers and prospective customers?

- What channels do your customers and potential customers frequent?
- List the top 20 characteristics of personas susceptible to your KPIs (here, you can leverage the broad and precise interests in the Facebook Ads creation tool).
- Are there occupations that suggest the presence of meta buyers or internal employees who make purchasing decisions for larger groups of people?
- Specify common usages of the products and what goals they should accomplish.

Strategy and KPIs

Now that you have the data, it's time to ask the right questions. For starters, what is the expectation of monthly KPI conversion volume at what cost-per-action (CPA)?

What are the goals? Be explicit regarding expectations of monthly KPI conversion volume at what CPA. (See the K.I.S.S. KPI chart). For example, some goals might include:

- Friendship, subscription, and subsequent content marketing
- Direct response via organic social and/or paid prominence
- Branding impressions leading to increased brand searches over time

- Media and other influencer outreach: passive or aggressive
- Links and citations
- SEO and organic prominence in mainstream search engine results
- Other

ROI Modeling

What will social media cost and what ROI can you expect?

- For any paid channels, what results can you expect in terms of media spend, traffic, conversion quantity, overall cost, and cost per conversion (see Figure 1.22)?

- For organic social, what results can you expect and at what cost?

- Adding paid and organic together, including any agency or third-party fees, what are the costs and conversion expectations?

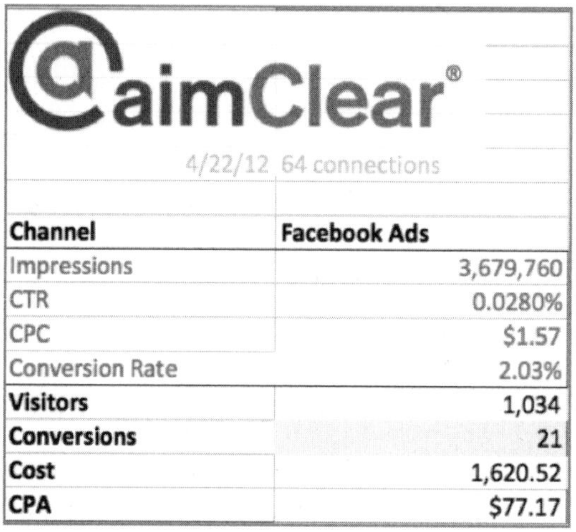

@aimClear®

4/22/12 64 connections

Channel	Facebook Ads
Impressions	3,679,760
CTR	0.0280%
CPC	$1.57
Conversion Rate	2.03%
Visitors	1,034
Conversions	21
Cost	1,620.52
CPA	$77.17

Figure 1.22 Predictive modeling for Facebook ads

Channel Tactics, Creative, and Testing

What paid and organic social channels are you testing?

- Social media mirrors and amplifies physical life. How is/are the product(s) currently sold, with how many conversions per month, and at what CPA? Include offline and other online channels. Is there any information here that might contribute to your understanding of how this product can convert in social media?

- What channels should you market in? Paid? Organic?

- What are the messages that will motivate a community member to convert to your KPI?

- Provide any written collateral materials (such as PowerPoint slides, sell sheets, value proposition statements, case studies, and any other materials you can leverage to call creative).
  - State the differentiation points from whatever any competitor says.
  - How is your messaging the same as everyone else?
  - Why will your efforts succeed over others?
  - What are the significant challenges and classic objections?
  - Is your messaging disruptive? How? Why? Why not?
- Have there been any brick, broadcast, search, print, or other collateral ads surrounding this product? Are they working? If yes, who were they targeted to and what were the messages?
- Are you attending any real-world events (consumer expos, trade shows, etc.) to promote your brand? Which ones? Which messages have worked? Is there a theory as to why?
- Who will be listening, responding, and monitoring the wall?
- Will your team partake in healthily assertive outreach in communities other than your own profiles?
- Include a list of approved product claims, or is this information easily available on the landing pages or brand identity center?
- What are the brand standards? Can they be superseded? Who approves the exceptions?
- Are images on the website and/or in brochures (PDFs) fair game for ads?
- Is any/all text on the website approved as derivative text for ads?
- Who will sign off on all ads, creative, targeting, and so forth?

Reporting and Optimization

What reports will be generated and when?

- Will they be derived from standard output from mainstream platforms using standard reports (for example, Google Analytics, Facebook Insights, Adobe SocialAnalytics)?
- Are custom reports required, and if so, what information needs to be included and who will construct the report?

Team and Responsibilities

Who will work on this account and what access credentials do you need?

- Supply the name and contact information for the technical liaison with whom you can discuss mechanical specifics of providing assets.

- How will you track conversion?
- What analytics will you use to track traffic? Is conversion tracking set up? If not, can you be of assistance?
- Where in the attribution chain can you not track your efforts? What are the workarounds?
- What do you anticipate the media spend will be moving forward, assuming you reach a palatable CPA?
- Please provide credentials where possible:
  - Analytics
  - AdWords
  - CMS
  - FTP
  - Any subdomains that would be good sell URLs (for example, buy.domain.com)
  - Bing
  - LinkedIn company page
  - Facebook page
  - Twitter
- Is there a geographic area you want to focus on first?
- What is your three-month media spend limit?
- Anything else you want us to know?
- Provide the name and contact information for your team member contact:
  - Primary contact
  - Contact for logistics (meetings, etc.), if different
  - Targeting and ad-signoff contact
  - Analytics contact
  - Accounts payable contact
  - Technical/development contact
  - Design contact

The role of social media community manager is a quickly evolving and fascinating mash-up of traditional and online marketing roles. Be ready to become the next-gen hybrid marketer. The voice and how the avatar represents a brand's interests should be carefully determined and dictated by a brand's purpose. Think of such decisions as part of a social stylebook. Build a kick-ass marketing plan by asking lots of questions, which subsequently get turned into statements. When the plan takes shape, it'll provide clear direction, strategy, and goals for the entire team. Onward!

Timeless Tenets of Non-Gratuitous Social Behavior

2

As a community manager, it's your job to engage the community surrounding your brand in the various social media channels in which you operate. But how do you encourage those conversations? Is it ever OK to promote yourself? What actions should you avoid to prevent angering your friends/fans/followers, not to mention the natives? In other words, how should you act in social media? This chapter offers basic behavioral advice for the smart CM.

Chapter Contents

The "Know Me, Love Me" Standard

Conversation-Seeding Engagement Tactics

Self-Promotion without Spamming

13 Utterly Annoying Behaviors to Avoid

The "Know Me, Love Me" Standard

The greatest irony of social media is that marketers believe that marketing is somehow different than ever before. That's not true, not much at all. Long before the Internet existed, let alone social media channels, brands worked hard to connect, earn friends, and build community. Embrace this timeless axiom next time you're freaked out about understanding social media. In every generation of community management, the best way to make friends is to be friendly.

The finest way to earn likes is to model likable behavior and not be a jerk. The best way to socialize customers surrounding brands is to be, well, appropriately social. The best way to motivate folks to engage is to be engaging yourself. The best way to be a thought leader is to lead thinking.

Yep, community manager types need to be friendly, likable, social, and deeply passionate. Otherwise one might argue that person should not have a CM job. Community managers need to be the life of the party, measured, and know when to be tasteful, when to shut up, and when to listen. The CM needs to be a natural, the kind of presence that tastefully works social settings to the max. When aimClear hires employees for this line of work, we look for candidates who are total people magnets—forces who know what to say and have all the right moves in real-world physical situations.

You know the type, right? She glides into the room, moves easily between small groups of people, and tête-à-têtes. She seems effortless, traversing the line between thoughtfully lurking and leading conversations by way of healthily assertive tactics. She answers questions with questions to keep the conversation going and means it, she really wants to know the answers.

Our prototype CM is informed about vital topics that permeate dialogue in the conference room and community, so much so that the engagement stimulates dialogue as appropriate. You know the type! To know them is to like them and be inspired. Great community managers know what to do. They are socially informed and handle themselves appropriately in social situations. Somehow this person takes your breath away.

I (Marty) was very lucky to learn about being social from the vantage point of being on stage. In the 20 years or so of my professional music career, which included everything from recording Pizza Hut jingles to playing in stadiums in support of records I helped record—not to mention the hundreds of second-rate VFWs and bars in which I played—I enjoyed the outrageous pleasure of being *artificially* prominent because of my role. I'm sure that I was not that big a deal and maybe even bordered on creepdom. However, my look, appearance, and shtick worked extremely well with the crowd. I had artificially enhanced street cred because I was the cute dude in the band. Check out the hair (Figure 2.1).

Figure 2.1 Coauthor Marty Weintraub, circa 1988

I also knew how to act, strike a pose, and say the right things. Heck, I even learned to *mean* the right things. I'd meet young ladies who thought I was super groovy/cool even before I opened my mouth, because, again, I was the guy who played keyboards, had hot '80s hair, and danced really well, among other appealing characteristics. Then, when it came time for me to become deeper friends, the opportunity was mine to screw up. In other words, I had the benefit of authority and representation. The lights were shining. I had the advantage.

I looked the part. When it came time to actually interact, the exchanges were so easy. I'm a people person. Dude, it felt like I could make friends with anyone I wanted because of the combination of bully pulpit and my personality. If I had not been in the band, I certainly would not have received the same level of attention. It takes both attributes to be a socio-professional leader, a community manager if you will. Usually one must be in a position of authority and representation, as well as be a total people person. I pretty much got whatever I wanted, whenever I wanted it.

Those experiences back in the day proved pivotal to my career over the last 20 years, during which I've been inserted into many socio-professional situations. The cocktail parties in Hollywood during my years working at PolyGram required the same skill. When networking at speakers' receptions at conferences, I relied on the same acumen and verve. Anyone confident enough to be in public networking on behalf of any entity, including themselves, needs to have an intangible charm, that thing that sets them apart. You know the type. To know that person is to love them. We call those star qualities the "Know Me, Love Me" Standard.

Those experiences of youth embodied amazing lessons that have lasted my whole career. It was priceless to learn the confidence that comes while holding the advantage of authority and representation. We've trained hundreds of community managers to share themselves from that position. The premise of the "Know Me, Love Me" Standard is that you're so friendly, likable, informed, and engaging that others are drawn into friendship. It nearly always works.

Importance of Unrestricted Outreach

In all social media, the ability to reach out to users you're not friends with is one of the most powerful social tools on Earth. Coupled with Know Me, Love Me, the ability to say things to users you don't know is often a clear path to friendship.

Most channels allow some level of person-to-person contact with folks you don't know, because selective accessibility is the universal requirement to making new friends. In other words, you can't make new friends if you can't reach out to people in friendship. Reaching out in friendship is the data-driven community manager's secret path to new relationships with qualified users targeted by interests that matter to him.

Participating in Facebook on Behalf of a Brand

Most of us understand the notion of a Facebook user liking a brand. Also, the concept of users making friends (following each other) is an easy model to grasp. But what about if it's the other way around: a brand reaching out to a user? Brands are not allowed to friend a person in Facebook. Facebook solved that issue by allowing users to interact with Facebook as either themselves or as any brand they are administrator for. At the top of every brand page for which you're an administrator, you'll see a way to toggle back and forth between surfing Facebook as the brand or as yourself.

This technique opens lots of doors. A Facebook user who is an administrator for a brand page can move in and out of surfing Facebook as themselves and as a brand they are representing. Facebook offers the option under the Edit Page tab, as shown in Figure 2.2. The most common question we receive is from CMs who want to know, "Should I be myself?" Remember this mechanism for later.

Figure 2.2 Great community managers are confident participating in social situations on behalf of a brand, online and in real life.

Know Me, Love Me Examples

The good news is that it's super easy to get folks to respond on Twitter, gain a Facebook friend, and reach other goals. Often, simply following another user results in a follow back. However, with some thoughtful legwork and an informed and magnanimous approach, the process of mutual following can result in a much stronger friendship, rooted in a more intimate connection. The examples provided are personal to aimClear (the business), but the tactics work for any brand. Such techniques also work in any social channel with similar dynamics to Twitter: for instance, the ability to reach out in friendship to users you don't know as well as recommend content.

Recommending other users' content is a powerful method for making friends. The secret is to avoid being self-promotional, gushy, or gross, and to add some value to the citation. aimClear is a thought leader in the area of psychographic targeting. We want to gain Twitter followers who are interested in the subject, because that's one of the main things our community is about. I start with a Google search for "psychographic targeting."

There are two articles of interest, as shown in Figure 2.3, indicated by the arrows. One of them is on Mashable by a blogger named Jamie Beckland (Figure 2.4), and the other is on eConsultancy by a blogger named Doug Kessler. We don't know either of them, but they've been writing about our emergent topic, psychographic targeting, for more than a year. It's easy to find the authors' Twitter profiles from their name and the topic. Sure, sometimes your friend-targets don't have Twitter profiles, but authoritative bloggers almost always have Twitter handles. Let's take the first friendship steps with Jamie and Doug now. They'll make fantastic additions to our community.

Figure 2.3 Google results showing articles written in the last year about an important topic that defines our business

Figure 2.4 Mashable post on our topic, found by Google search, written by Jamie Beckland

After researching Jamie's Twitter handle (using Google) and that of the blog that published the article, I tweeted a recommendation for the post and author. It was quickly retweeted by one of aimClear's followers, a nice little extra because Jamie will see it (Figure 2.5). We also followed him on Twitter. Following your friend-target early in the process is not always needed. Usually waiting to follow does not affect the ultimate goal: mutual friendship.

Figure 2.5 My tweet shouting out to @Beckland and @Mashable, highlighting the post written by my friend-target

Within a couple of hours, Jamie tweeted to thank us for the shout-out (Figure 2.6). Because of the way Twitter rolls, all his friends saw it. Just that in itself is a lovely result. Now Jamie is aware of aimClear and the seeds of friendship are sown. We don't need the follow yet. It will come in time as we interact.

Figure 2.6 The seeds of friendship are sown. Jamie Beckland thanks us in front of his friends.

The next thing to do is set up a Twitter search (Figure 2.7) to keep our eyes on what Jamie, our new friend-lead, is discussing and with whom, so we can interact with him as appropriate. Count this one in the win column, even if mutual friendship takes a few days. We'll make friends with Jamie. Our interests are similar and he seems to be an influential writer.

Figure 2.7 Twitter search for @Beckland in TweetDeck to keep our eye on Jamie

Figures 2.8, 2.9. 2.10, 2.11, 2.12, 2.13, and 2.14 chronicle an interaction we had with a Facebook user that resulted in friendship. We saw Laura on the Zappos brand page, noting in public that she was pleased with her sandals order and enjoys the Zappos CM's humorous work. Let's assume our marketing assignment is to make friendships that ultimately result in sales of an accessory congruent with shoes, say insole cushions.

Figure 2.8 Laura on the Zappos wall

Remember the unrestricted direct message (DM) capabilities in Facebook? I did not mess around, and sent her a charming DM right away. This is a bit aggressive and the essence of Know Me, Love Me. Another option is to engage on the brand page first before taking this private. I guess we were feeling frisky that day. A key thing to note here is that my mom actually needs arch support and I was telling the truth. The best social media outreach is, in fact, when you tell the truth and don't game people.

Figure 2.9 First DM to Laura

She DM'd back right away. How cool is that! We already have a private conversation going.

Figure 2.10 Laura gets back to me.

Then she must have checked out our blog from my Facebook profile, taking a minute to find out who I am. This demonstrates great potential as a friend.

Figure 2.11 Laura's getting personal.

More often than not, we wait for users to friend us first, which is very often the result of Know Me, Love Me. In this case, I reach out in friendship first because she's exactly the right kind of friend.

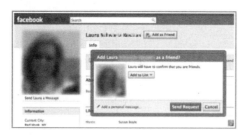

Figure 2.12 Friendship request to Laura

She accepts the friendship inquiry.

Figure 2.13 Laura accepts the friendship request.

We check out her Facebook page and, wow, Laura is promoting our blog post. Win, win, win! Know Me, Love Me rides again!

Figure 2.14 Laura promoting aimClear Blog right away

There are many ways to engage in social media to earn friends, likes, and follows. Be yourself and don't game users. Sometimes that means *being* the brand. Chat about things you know and care about, from a place rooted in a deep understanding of what you're talking about. In Chapter 4, "Content, Reputation, and Hardcore Listening Hacks," we'll dig into building an up-to-the-minute expert content RSS dashboard so you've always got great sharing material at your fingertips.

Conversation-Seeding Engagement Tactics

Any community manager worth her salt knows the importance of healthy two-way conversation. Actively and consistently engaging community members in topical discussion is essential to any company's successful social media campaign. Woe to the brand that uses a twitter-stream or Facebook page as a corporate megaphone! The instantaneous, far-reaching functionality of today's social channels is unparalleled. Marketers who misuse these tools not only miss precious opportunities to connect with target customers, community players, and potential influencers, they also expose themselves as arrogant, incompetent, and foolishly archaic to the world of social-savvy consumers. Bottom line: The best way to get social media engagement is to be engaging.

In this section, we'll explore 11 superb conversation-seeding engagement tactics social media community managers should feel proficient with and implement daily as they charge forth into the digital trenches. The platform of execution isn't crucial. Some tactics revolve around content that might be best suited for a company blog (we'll identify those), but the conversations they generate can unfurl pretty much anywhere—comment thread, niche forum, Twitter, Facebook, and so on—that's really up to the brand and community manager hosting the dialogue. Ample best practices come included with each of the big 11. Let's get started.

"Thank You" and Other Magnanimous Gestures

"Thank you" is a basic coupling of words taught to us as children to convey gratitude for something someone has done. This remarkably simple yet powerful phrase can change the course of someone's day and perhaps, by extension, the world. It is the butterfly effect mapped to humanity. Instead of unleashing a hurricane in another country, a tide of positivity is generated from its utterance. The results of thanking someone are often as spiritually genuine and gratifying as the gesture itself.

In the realm of social media, it's no different. One of the most sincere ways a marketer or community manager can begin a conversation with another human is to personify humanity. Brands who recognize something someone has accomplished and then express gratitude in response don't go unnoticed. (We hope you'll glean from this section that, in fact, there are various forms of rewards for brands that exemplify such thoughtful behavior!)

Of course, this tenet is and has been a part of traditional customer service for decades: Man buys product from shopkeeper, shopkeeper thanks him and wishes him a nice day. We like to encourage brands and CMs to up the ante by employing the element of surprise: thanking social community members or expressing similar magnanimous gestures of human interest for an achievement that has little or no direct effect on the thanking brand.

Consider a local business that thrives thanks to regular customers in the community. Imagine the delight that a campus CM and staff and students of her college might feel when @LocalBusiness tweets: "@CommunityCollege Thank you for being amazing! You & the class of 2012 make [town] proud!"

The relationship between that local business and the college isn't overt, and the gesture isn't self-serving. The business isn't asking students or the school to spend money or endorse products. @LocalBusiness is simply reaching out a hand for a high-five: "You do good work, and your community appreciates it. Booyah!"

Beyond expressing thanks, it's about acknowledging life's passages in non-gratuitous ways—recognizing periodic signposts across professional and personal life. Sharing tidings of congratulations, good health, and good luck has a twofold objective: to make someone's day, and to start an organic, compassionate conversation. No ulterior corporate agendas here.

Log in to Facebook. What greets you in the upper-right corner of the screen? Notifications of upcoming events such as friends' birthdays (Figure 2.15). The reason the Facebook team does this is because they understand that a lot of human interaction is celebration on various passages: a new job or office, a company award, a marriage, a baby, anniversaries, and yes, birthdays. The data-driven social media community manager should be an omniscient master of magnanimous gestures. When a personal or professional milestone occurs in the community, the CM should be there, a living, breathing fluorescent "way to go!" banner.

Figure 2.15 Facebook alerts users to friends' birthdays.

Keeping track of life passages and milestones across possibly dozens or hundreds of community contacts can be dizzying without a bit of structure and organization. Some events will be brought to the community manager's attention on the fly: noticing one user tweet another, "Happy birthday, @friend!" and then jumping in the thread with similar well wishes, as shown in Figure 2.16, for example.

Figure 2.16 A birthday tweet takes 6 seconds and makes someone smile. That's not soon forgotten!

To supplement the spontaneous, we advise clients to create some kind of database, an Excel spreadsheet or a basic Notepad document, that features prominent people and complementary businesses in their community or vertical. Make a commitment to skimming local news and press releases. Is something happening to someone that the CM should engage? *Use* what's happening as a springboard for candid engagement. Reach out and touch the participants accordingly, with a shout-out on Facebook, a dedicated tweet, or some other social gesture. Don't gush and don't be a creep. Be cool. Be natural!

For brands with a strong regional presence, creating an editorial calendar featuring upcoming local events is an excellent route. Follow along with examples like that shown in Figure 2.17. Casually plug the event with excitement and support the activities that matter to the community: high school car wash fundraisers, town festivals, county fairs, chili cook-offs, city marathons—the works.

Figure 2.17 Luther Auto promotes the Twin Cities Jazz Festival.

The goal here is to show that you care about the community and its citizens— that you see them as more than dollar signs and numbers on an invoice. A company wouldn't exist without customers, and customers wouldn't be the same without their culture and community.

This concept most definitely extends to the other end of the human emotions spectrum. Wherever there's joy, there are inevitable hardships. Expressing sympathy or concern can mean just as much, if not more, than sharing in successes. It shows the brand is there for support in low times, too. Don't underestimate the impact a simple "sorry to hear..." or "you're in our thoughts" tweet may have on a community member's worried mind.

Bear in mind, thanking the community or making some other magnanimous gesture is the *start*, the *seed* of the conversation. When the target of such thanks responds with "you're welcome," don't let the situation go stale. Jump back in with another thoughtful response or inquiry to stoke the fire. Which leads to our next tactic...

Asking Questions

Close on the heels of thanking members of the community comes another brilliant and effective conversation-seeding tactic: asking the community questions. This is another fundamental element of human interaction. Imagine meeting someone for the first time or catching up with an old friend over dinner and drinks. What is the shape of the conversation? Simple, uncomplicated, thoughtfully posed questions, such as these:

- What do you do for a living?
- What do you do for fun?
- How have you been?
- Who did you see at the party last week?
- What are you having for dinner?
- Got any fun weekend plans?

When the responses come back, some new questions that build off them come to mind and are posed. More responses, more questions. Aha! A conversation.

Let's apply that to the world of business. Picture an artisan vendor in Seattle's Pike Place Market. A tourist stops to linger at the merchandise, even politely notes, "I like your work." If the vendor responds, "Thank you," and nothing else, he's missed the boat, and likely, the sale.

Think of his booth as a company blog. The shopper is a reader who commented on a recent post: "Thanks for this great info! It will be useful for my business." He took the time to type out that he digs what the company has published. If all the blog CM does is swing in and say, "Thanks! Glad you enjoyed the post," the conversation has ended before it began.

Comments in a blog are a conversation, not a "Hi, thanks, goodbye." Each comment is an invitation for a greater dialogue. Hone in on any element of the commenter's note to let that person know you actually read it. Thoughtfully probe. Answer with questions. Milk a discussion out of a standalone post.

Community managers interested in building a natural rapport with consumers need only be in the right place at the right time with the right attitude, ready to ask the right questions of the right people. One of the reasons this tactic works so well is that, well, people absolutely love talking about themselves. Ask what their favorite X is and they claw at the keyboard to reply (hmm, hopefully not *literally*, unless your friend-target is a feline, in which case, yay kittens!).

Beyond retorting to users who stop by a comment thread, empower the company CM to start her own conversation by posing questions to the community that vary in form and content. Everything from a "Hi, how are ya?" first tweet of the day to a strategic Facebook Poll to encourage chatter and even gain a bit of consumer feedback. We just love it when we scope out a brand's Facebook page and it's rich with chatter-sparking prompts peppered between links to branded and nonbranded content. Some questions are apparent, as in Figure 2.18.

Figure 2.18 Tweets to wish good morning and ask about fans' weekends are effective and easy.

Some are "disguised" as a game. Gap is one brand that knows what's up. Check out Figure 2.19.

Figure 2.19 Gap asks a simple question via its Facebook Page.

Here, Gap has used a quality photo of a stylish product they market as the catalyst for a community discussion for their Facebook community. They're keeping it somewhat brand-centric, but they're opening the door up for anyone in the community to contribute personal opinions and feedback. Some responses have nothing to do with Gap or clothing at all. That's not the point. The point is Gap's community manager has successfully posed an incredibly basic question and started an intra-community conversation as a result.

Another way to work beautiful photos into this tactic is to turn it into a trivia question, demonstrated by Rosetta Stone's Facebook community manager in Figure 2.20. There's no big-ticket prize for the winner, but sometimes people are just satisfied to revel in the fact that they got it right.

Figure 2.20 Rosetta Stone leverages gorgeous travel photography to launch trivia questions and similar prompts.

Here are some other awesome types of questions marketers can pose to their community.

Multiple-Choice Questions   Basic trivia or opinions. No prize, just for fun. For example, "What year did Hawaii become an official state?" or "The best kind of pizza topping is A) mushrooms B) pepperoni C) anchovies D) 12 million extra pounds of cheese!"

True or False Questions   Same as multiple-choice questions. For example, "Dogs are color-blind: True or False?" or "Bacon is a food group unto itself: True or False?"

Fill-in-the-Blank Statements and Questions   We've noticed these tend to resonate best with various communities due to the increased open-ended nature. For example: "The best place to vacation is _____" or "My all-time favorite band is _____." If the CM asks people what they like (or don't like), or what their #1 this or that may be, they're likely to respond.

Offshoots of Current Events or Trending Topics   At a loss for questions to ask the community? Turn to the news. Was there a recent event relevant to the company's region or industry that community members may be chattering about or feeling particularly opinionated about? For example, a company with strong local pride might ask: "Could you believe the [hometown sports team] game last night?!" or a fashion company could post: "Couldn't believe some of the getups at the Academy Awards on Sunday! Who wore your favorite gown?"

Facebook Questions and Polls add great visual variety to the content CMs post on Facebook. Check out Figure 2.21 and Figure 2.22 for a taste. The break from typical status updates, even those that house questions, might be the extra incentive that gets users to participate. If your company isn't already leveraging them, start (testing) now.

| 📝 Update Status 📷 Add Photo / Video ▦ Ask Question |
| What's the most super ultimate zombie movie of all time? |
| Add Poll Options   🌐 Public ▾   Post |

Figure 2.21 Facebook Questions are a great way to seed engagement from a community.

Deep Cereal asked: What's the most super ultimate movie of all time?

☐ Night of the Living Dead
☐ Day of the Dead
☐ All the Pretty Horses

Figure 2.22 Facebook Polls offer a variety of optional answers to a question.

Check out www.facebook.com/help/facebook-questions to learn more about Facebook Questions and Polls.

Sharing Third-Party Content with Value-Added Rebroadcast

We'll dig much deeper into tools, techniques, and best practices surrounding sharing content in Chapter 5, "Find Themed Conversations: The Superior CM's Edge," but for now let's highlight the basics of this effectual conversation-seeding tactic. Sharing third-party content with value-added rebroadcast can fall under the "Asking Questions" umbrella, but it features one otherwise omitted element: third-party content! Go figure. All of the examples showcased in the previous section were straight-up forms of the CM asking the community a variety of questions in a variety of formats with no supplementary content at which to point users.

Rebroadcasting killer third-party, noncompetitive, complementary content and contributing your company's two cents on the matter is an absolutely fantastic way to inspire dialogue among community members. In fact, we recommend to clients that this sort of content represent about 80 percent of the content they share across social media, with 20 percent being branded, owned content. CMs don't have to reinvent the wheel. There are a gazillion pieces of wonderful content floating around in cyberspace that someone else already wrote! It's not feasible to spend hours writing a fabulously stimulating blog post every time the community needs to be fed. All the data-driven community manager has to do is identify quality content (again, a topic we'll dissect fully in Chapter 5), thoughtfully editorialize with a viewpoint or ask users theirs, and then share the link with added value as a tweet, Facebook post, Google+ update, and so on.

Figure 2.23 shows Ben and Jerry's employing this tactic with considerable latitude and humor.

Ben & Jerry's @benandjerrys   27 Jun
Is this the turning point? bit.ly/NOUUBd Let's Get the #DoughOut of Politics! #CitizensUnited #democracy4sale
Expand

Figure 2.23 Ben and Jerry's sharing content with rebroadcast

Figure 2.24 features a screen-capture of the article to which B&J's linked.

Figure 2.24 The Ben and Jerry's CM stokes conversation on Twitter by sharing an article about politics.

Politics don't have a heck of a lot to do with ice cream, and discussing them *can* be a bit risky (you never know who you're going to freak out with heavier topics of discussion). Nevertheless, the ice cream behemoth's CM takes the opportunity to rebroadcast a topical article and add his/her personal two cents.

Check out Figure 2.25 for an example of the community manager for @DogFishHead tweeting a link to a third-party news article. The content is topical (hooray for beer!), the added value is concise, clever, and all things considered, kind of moving.

Figure 2.25 Dogfish Head tweets a beer-related article with a poignant, rhetorical question.

Remember: Your goal as a marketer is to leverage relevant, quality content created by others and

- Share it with the brand's community
- Add an opinion
- Pose a question
- Offer a discussion point
- Seek community feedback in a brief editorial snippet

Cool alternative alert! Rather than hunting down content from around the Web to share with the social community, take advantage of Twitter lists. Create lists dedicated to tweet-streams manned by folks who habitually share amazing content. Retweet what they share (or map to any social community). If you do your homework upfront, much of the content coming from that stream should be pre-vetted for authority, authenticity, and relevance. *Et voilà!* Time shaved off already pretty much effortless content streaming.

But wait, another special bonus: If the CM rebroadcasts these power Twitter users in Twitter, her company can get on *their* radars, as long as their Twitter handles make it into the retweet. For example: "Whoa, that's pretty intense. What do you think? RT @PowerUser: Government bans all kittens everywhere from everything [link]." The @mention ends up in @PowerUser's stream. Curiosity piqued, he or she may reach out to thank you and continue the conversation about the content shared.

This leads to a very brief look at the various ethics of retweeting.

Some people believe that when a Twitter user decides to retweet another, nothing at all about the original tweet should be altered, because any changes should be attributed to the retweeter, although they appear to be attributed to the original tweeter without that tweeter's consent. Perhaps in support of this concept, Twitter itself implemented a "new Retweet" feature near the end of 2009. The feature, among other things, removed the ability to modify a tweet upon retweet in any way whatsoever. The original tweet was preserved in its entirety, and the retweeter could add no editorial whatsoever. Some felt that was rather control-freakish of Twitter. We're inclined to agree. At the very least, upon retweeting someone else's tweet, we strongly recommend taking the opportunity to editorialize with added value—that is, adding some sort of thoughtful comment or question to precede the RT@Handle. That said, it's the "maintaining the original tweet" that we're talking about here. Moving on....

Some will argue that when a Twitter user decides to retweet another, minor adjustments may be made to ensure the tweet length is less than the maximum 140 characters. Common and generally accepted hacks include Internet slang abbreviations (tomorrow = tmrw, people = ppl, and so on).

Some maintain since *you're* the one retweeting you can modify the retweet however you want. Of course, you really *can* do *whatever* you want. Just be sensitive to attribution. Consider leveraging a "h/t @PowerUser" (h/t is short for *hat-tip*, a thank-you or a shout-out) rather than the standard "RT," short for retweet, which implies that what follows the RT was originally tweeted by @PowerUser.

Vanity Baiting Synergistic Publishers

This tactic is similar to the previous one, but with a stronger emphasis on the *creator* of the content shared, rather than the power user re-broadcaster, or even the content itself.

Businesses serious about success should already have a finger on the pulse of the mainstream publications and top writers in their industries. In doing so, brands can stay abreast of emergent trends and technologies, and show their social communities they're knowledgeable and on the cutting edge. Being familiar with the published top players in the biz can also help companies and CMs feel like they're part of the in-crowd. With the right approach and some strategic vanity baiting, they really can be.

If your company hasn't done so already, sit down and make a comprehensive list of the publishers and writers in your industry, complete with contact information (email or, ideally, Twitter handle) and corresponding publication(s), such as links to the blog(s) or news site(s) where they regularly publish articles or other forms of content. Ask coworkers, ask the C-suite, ask Google, heck, ask your own community (yay, crowd-sourcing for easy answers!) any or all of the following:

- Who's breaking the latest news in our field?
- Where is the news showcased? What are the popular online journals and news aggregators?
- Who are the editors, the columnists, the forum moderators?
- Who in our industry does the social community listen to and look to for insight and information?
- Who are the published mini-celebs in our niche?
- Who are the authority powerhouses?

Once the list is assembled, get to work. Encourage the community manager to scope out highlighted publications on a regular basis. Tweet links to the top-shelf content. Some truly choice online publications cull roundups of daily awesome articles from around the Web. Jackpot! Stay up to speed and never run out of content to share.

Now, here's the vanity bait bit: Don't *just* tweet the title of the article and a link to the post. And don't *just* @mention the publication. Go the extra mile: @mention both the pub and the author of the article. You'll get on the radar of the CM behind the publication, who should be dutifully monitoring brand pings across the Social Web, as well as the radar of the author, who should be monitoring his/her personal brand (yes, people in a professional context are *personal* brands).

If either party cares about human interactions the way a deep social media community manager *should* (right? nod), they'll reach out in some way and thank you for sharing their content. Some will move it to a DM environment so as not to appear overly gratuitous. Others may keep the thread out in the open, because, what the hell?

Fine friend of aimClear, SEOmoz's @jennita is a community manager who knows how to play the game, and she plays it well. Take a look at Figure 2.26, in which she tweets a link to a Search Engine Land article, written by @beebow.

Figure 2.26 @Jennita cleverly vanity baits and thoughtfully attributes both publisher and author with two @mentions.

Now, if all the writer (or publication) does is thank you, you know what to do. Skim back over the Asking Questions section. Stoke the fire. Answer with an inquiry. Thoughtfully touch on an element of the post, or ask about a case study they referenced. Ask their opinion on the matter, if not overly stated in the piece. Use your brain—be creative. Don't be a creep, don't be a gushing geek, and don't surrender without trying! The goal with this tactic is to, yep, you guessed it: Start a conversation!

Awards

Nothing brings power users and ordinary digital citizens together like an awards ceremony! Picture the Oscars. Throngs of celebrities from a common industry (in this case, film) gathering in one place to be honored, commended, and admired on live TV. And for every beautiful celebrity clad in couture, there's an average citizen sitting at home, watching the event, tweeting, "OMG I can't believe what she's wearing!" or some similar sentiment with folks across the country.

Luckily, companies don't have to wait around for such a star-studded event to leverage this same principle and reap its benefits. They can create their own awards, nominating the brand community manager as the glowing host and inviting anyone they want to the party.

Friendly shout-outs à la #FollowFriday, when one Twitter user endorses another to his or her community—"Follow @PowerUser, he is the go-to source on Local SEO and, mmm, West Coast seafood!"—are like the second cousin to the life passages. They're joyous hat-tips with multifaceted results:

- Share ultimate resources with your own community.
- Compliment a power user; get on his/her good side.
- Start a conversation!

The same concept applies to awards, it is just a bit more structured and scalable. For example, aimClear pal Matt McGee created the SEMMYs (http://semmys.org) back in 2008 as a way to honor all the great content produced by peers across the search engine marketing industry. Nomination categories range from Small Business to Local Search, Blogs & Blogging to Link Building, Social Media to Analytics, even Rants. It's a delightful annual awards event that brings together industry celebrities and community members for a humbling, positive cause.

Here are some more ideas to get your marketing and CM team's gears turning:

- Create a weekly, quarterly, or yearly roundup of anything relevant to your industry. "This Week's Best Blog Posts about X!" or "The Definitive 2012 Guide to X, as Told by 54 Industry Pros!"
- Shine the spotlight on someone in your industry, maybe a new person each quarter, or provide a rundown of the top contributing folks that year, broken out by category and area of expertise—"This Month's Must-Follow PPC Pro!" for example.
- Aggregate the aggregators! Scope out the top content aggregating sites in your industry, ones that are filled with content pre-vetted for authority, virility, and category. Pick your favorite posts from the week, month, year, whatever, and slap a trendy award name on it: "The Hottest, Most Super Awesome Amazing Stuff on [Aggregator] This Week."
- Create your own version of the SEMMYs mapped to your industry, ask members of the social community to nominate their favorites, and then organize a voting party or judge panel to pick the winners.

Tempered Shout-Outs and Righteous-Indignation Callouts

So, we've learned that brands can always start a conversation with a compliment. Of course, another way to seed spirited discussion is to take the opposite route and be a little feisty.

Tempered shout-outs and righteous-indignation callouts are a fascinating tactic to employ in social communities, but it's best to turn to this tactic when there's a well-established social community in place, one the company CM has spent ample time with, gained the trust and loyalty of, and genuinely befriended.

Is there a hate-spewing troll kicking around on the company Facebook page or blog comment thread, or polluting the brand @mention column with nonsensical spam? Maybe it's an extremely angry ex-customer slinging insults and harassing comments at the CM and other community members, or maybe it's a competitor's CM just being a snot on your brand's home turf. Don't be afraid to call him out! And don't be shy about using that callout as an opportunity to turn negativity into a positive brand-centric dialogue.

Straight up, defending against criticism that feels unwarranted is one chief duty of the social media community manager. It's not juvenile bickering, it's defensible righteous indignation: the CM is answering the criticism (level of sass employed open to interpretation), standing her ground, and playing the game, knowing full well the best defense is a good offense.

In this case, the reason CMs and marketers want a well-established social community on their side is just that: to have a well-established social community on their side. When the going gets tough, we like to remind clients to not discount the loyal band of fans their CM has helped cultivate over time. More often than not, when an unfriendly critic or bully enters branded space, that community will rise up on behalf of the brand and of the CM, defending both with words of support and encouragement, and consequently, "putting the stomp on" said bully. There's something glorious about knowing a heated mob of digital citizens have got your back. It makes the CM feel all warm and fuzzy inside.

Be advised! There may come a time when that heated mob turns against your brand for whatever reason. Chapter 7, "Community Crisis Management," deals exclusively with intracommunity bloodshed and crisis management. There, we'll outline unbreakable tactics for avoiding sticky situations, preparing for the inevitable, and implementing best practices for when the cyber-shtuff hits the fan. For now, let's move. We've got more tactics to explore!

Reviews

Creating and sharing reviews of complementary, noncompetitive products, services, whatever, is a great way to start a conversation between the CM and the social community, and even the party being reviewed. Brands know (or should know) how much of an impact online chatter can have on reputation, and they are (or should be) monitoring that chatter like a social media community manager hawk.

For the first time in history, anyone with Internet access and a social media account can affect the reputation of a person or a company online, which is something that is polarizing by nature. Social media is often one live-streaming review pool in multicolor. Smartphones changed everything. Before people are finished eating dinner in one of New York City's latest swank establishments, they're on Facebook Mobile, posting pics of their plates and an overall opinion of the dining experience. Today's moviegoers don't even wait for the credits to roll before they tweet feedback on the latest summer blockbuster. Brands' reputations are, more than ever before, in the hands of consumers, and at the mercy of trigger-happy fingers clutching iPhones and Droids.

Consumers *and* community managers looking to get a company's attention for a friendly or feisty chat need only tweet a mention about the brand or affiliated product and how they feel about it (Figure 2.27).

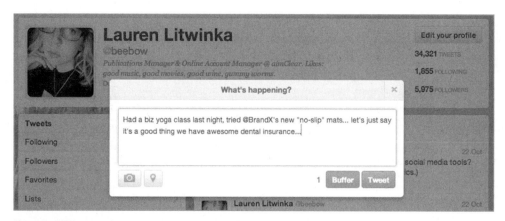

Figure 2.27 CMs can spark a conversation in as little as 140 characters, often less.

If the company is serious, its CM will respond. Thus begins your conversation, the tone of which will likely be shaped by the initial review. Positive reviews beget sunshine, pussycats, maybe even a little future discount for the friendly evangelization. Hooray! Negative reviews beget conversations tinged with awkwardness, fumbling apologies, stubborn and ineffectual silence, or even a little righteous-indignation call-out in reverse. If the conversation is public, say, on Twitter, that may very well draw in haters, lovers, supporters, and so on of the company under the microscope, not to mention your own social community who's listening to what the CM puts out there. Social media community managers with nasty-worded reviews must understand they're at the helm of a potentially volatile thread. You can be brazen, but prepare for the tide to turn either way. The brand you pick on (however legit the complaint) may have a fiercely loyal community that will rise up and squash you. Or your complaint might resonate with a group of potential friends/customers who had similar experiences. You never know!

CMs interested in leveraging reviews as a way to drum up conversations among users (less of a focus on the party being reviewed) need only insert a thoughtful open-ended question in the post, sometimes in lieu of their own opinion (see Figure 2.28).

Figure 2.28 CMs can also seed conversation with the community by asking questions.

Want to up the ante? Write a little blog post or shoot and post a quick video review of a recent consumer experience *you* had as a marketer. Remove your actual opinion from the tweet, Facebook post, LinkedIn update, and so on, and replace it with a tiny URL pointing at your content. Finish with a dreaded ellipsis. "So... Had my first experience with @Brand yesterday... [link]," for example. What brand mentioned therein could resist clicking? KPI = traffic to your mothership company site and a healthy surge of eager adrenaline for the CM being pinged.

Boots-on-the-Ground Personal Journalism

An offshoot of reviews, this conversation-seeding tactic emphasizes the individual community manager's role as an active participant in the real world. Thanks to smartphones, social media, and the Internet in general, *everyone* is a field reporter for their own TV station; everyone's a publisher for their own daily newspaper. Multichannel broadcasts rich with photos, video clips, and other supplementary goodies make for some truly conversation-worthy content.

This goes well beyond basic product reviews and into the exciting and totally attainable realm of boots-on-the-ground personal journalism. When social media community managers break news to their communities, they're feeding valuable content to a place where people can consume, discuss, and rebroadcast. It's a powerful tactic with substantial benefits. All CMs eyeing this tactic need to succeed is a smartphone, a green light from the boss, and an adventurous spirit.

Check out the stunning photo in Figure 2.29. It was tweeted by an ordinary girl on the street after Duluth, Minnesota, was rocked by heavy and unexpected flooding. She cleverly directed the public tweet at the *Duluth News Tribune*, getting her bit of personal reporting on the radar of professional journalists.

Figure 2.29 Twitter user directs picture of Duluth flooding to Duluth News Tribune

Figure 2.30 shows another flood-related tweet pic, this from a Minnesota senator. Tweeting updates and photos from his iPhone, this fellow, who is in a way a community manager on behalf of District 7 (Figure 2.31), is bringing ongoing news to the folks listening at home.

Figure 2.30 Duluth Senator tweets photos and ongoing news about recent local flood

Roger Reinert
@RogerForDuluth

This is the official Twitter page of Roger Reinert, current State Senator for District 7 – Duluth, Minnesota.
Duluth, MN   http://facebook.com/rogerforduluth

Figure 2.31 @RogerForDuluth Twitter Bio. He's no reporter, but he plays one on Twitter!

Tacking the appropriate topical hashtag to this tweet helps ensure it will be seen by all eyes chatting about the great #DuluthFlood. Smart move! It opens up the audience to all those interested in the topic, not just @RogerForDuluth's own social following.

Naturally, the concept of personal journalism sparks a discussion on avatars, the representation of a brand in social media. How much individual personality do you want the company CM to have? For this particular conversation-seeding engagement tactic, the more personality the CM has, the more authentic the coverage becomes, the more communities will tune in, and the more genuinely engaging conversations will become.

Live Coverage

We tell clients they don't have to be the luminary or thought leader or undisputed master of their field; they just need a member of the team present when said thought leaders get together and dish two cents on breaking news, developments, emerging technologies, trends, or other special techniques, tactics, and takeaways that apply to their specific industry.

Providing coverage of industry conferences, expos, trade shows, conventions, seminars, and networking events is an extremely powerful way to contribute topical, valuable, authoritative content to your community without being obnoxiously and perpetually self-promotional and still remaining the author of the material you're sharing.

Live coverage of industry events represents a valuable trifecta:

- The boss-man is happy the content being showcased in the company blog and across company social media assets was actually, you know, created by the company. Third-party sharing is *essential*, but it's important to contribute owned content as well.

- The social community is appreciative of the wealth of information gleaned from the coverage.

- The community manager gets to learn new things while establishing the brand as a participating and knowledgeable force in the biz.

Now, on to specific tactics and best practices.

If your company's community manager has the bandwidth and cheetah-fast fingers, it's ideal to have her live-tweet industry events, much like an on-the-scene journalist, delivering immediate reporting and feedback to the readers at home (your social community). Support this on-the-fly coverage with comprehensive write-ups to be posted on a company blog and then syndicated across branded social channels.

The live-tweets are what help garner instant attention and popularity, whereas the blog posts provide long-lasting value as proprietary resources for the community that can have legs well beyond the event itself (not to mention draw traffic to the mothership site and associated social assets).

Want to beef up the coverage? Arm the CM with a flip cam or other portable recording device to capture rich multimedia content she can feed the community. This doesn't have to be a Hollywood production. Snag a few minutes of footage in the expo hall (if permitted!) or casual interviews with speakers and attendees. Embed in blog posts, post to YouTube, share on Facebook, the works.

Keep on reading for some of our favorite tips to make the most of live coverage.

Create an events calendar.   Create a Microsoft Excel database or Google calendar that keeps track of industry events (and any corresponding event hashtags) in the area (or around the world, if your business has the budget!). From mainstream conventions to casual meet-ups (even online tweet-ups), be aware of what's going on and attend when the CM can. Don't know where to start? Scope out online directories that calendar trade shows and conferences across various industries. Check out prominent industry publications, forums, and other online social circles to see where the cool kids hang out. Seriously lost? Go ahead and Google "[industry] conference" (add [city] for regional results). Do your homework. Get involved.

Monitor conversations.   Create keyword columns in TweetDeck or a Twitter client of choice that track hashtags specific to events of interest. Follow conversations before, during, and after events. Participating in conversations *before* the event can help pave the way for smoother social interactions in real life. Monitoring *during* certainly gives you a deep look at what's going on in real time. Take note of other companies that are tweeting up a storm. Are they competitors, or non-foes worth befriending? Are they doing anything differently? Better? Are they getting retweeted more? Learn from them. (Then, either befriend them or destroy them!) Keep tabs on conversations *after* to learn what's happening next for a given event and its following.

Get to know the speakers.   Create an Excel database of speakers for events the CM plans to follow. Include significant information such as name, current place of employment, job title, Twitter handle, follower count, and links to other social profiles. Encourage her to get to know the conference participants before she shows up to the party. Don't be afraid to reach out before, during, or after a presentation with a friendly @mention thanking speakers for their insight. The responses are often surprisingly delightful.

Use event hashtags.   Use event hashtags as often as possible. This is not limited to tweets! Stick that hashtag in the title of a blog post that covers an event or conference session. Just make sure it gels (for example, "25 Groundbreaking Takeaways from #IndustryConferenceX 2012"). When the CM or any other interested community member rebroadcasts/retweets the post, it will milk the exposure of that hashtag in a non-spammy way (because hey, your post *is* about #IndustryConferenceX, is it not?).

Interviews

On aimClear Blog, we love hosting interviews with prominent conference speakers and thought leaders across the online marketing industry. Many of them also happen to be our pals, thanks to years covering the conference circuit, speaking, blogging, and live tweeting.

The benefits of hosting interviews are many. They're exciting, and they're all worthy of exclamation points!

- Populate your company blog with rich, unique, informative content that you *pretty much* had written for you. The meat of the post is the interviewee's responses!

- Showcase expertise and best practices straight from credible sources (interviewees) the community looks up to, right in your company blog!

- Learn more about what makes your favorite folks tick, become better acquainted with them through the interview process, and build a professional friendship!

- Make interviewees feel all warm and fuzzy—the spotlight's on them!

- Leverage the interviewee's built-in audience. The more prestigious and well liked, the more friends and fans he or she will bring to read the Q&A (in other words, traffic to your company blog)!

- Start a dialogue among your social community around the interviewee across various social platforms, linking back to the mothership where the interview lives!

- Establish your company as a collator of luminary insight, devoted to sharing others' knowledge with the community. Establish the community manager (or whomever happens to be hosting and publishing the interview) as the Johnny Carson of your industry!

Click on over to www.aimclearblog.com/category/interviews for a look at the rich content this relatively effortless tactic yields. All the CM/blogger/interviewer need do is reach out to the potential interviewee to gauge his or her interest in participating, and then shoot over 5 to 7 well-crafted questions for answering. Anyone worth interviewing will ship back deep, eloquent responses rich in both quantity and quality. Pass it off to the company blogmaster for formatting, add a thoughtful introduction and a headshot, hit publish, and let the fun begin.

Guest Posts

Guest posts are similar to interviews, except the guest author writes the whole thing. Hosting guest posts on the company blog is an equally fantastic way to introduce fresh, quality content to your brand's blog without exhausting your in-house team of writers. Great publications aren't hurting for content; great publications have people competing to write blog posts for them. That said, sometimes you still want a formal letter of invitation to send out to guest bloggers, welcoming them to the table.

Strategic blogger outreach is, in and of itself, a fine art with sensitive thresholds, and it depends on whom you're inviting and how well you know him or her. Sanitize the invite too much and it may appear mechanical and impersonal, like a canned email sent to a billion email addresses in search of free goods. Make the invite too friendly and you risk creeping out the recipient.

Here's a run through some best practices we live by at aimClearBlog.com:

- Hands down, the best blog post outreach is among people with whom you have already a relationship.

- Look inside your own industry. Identify the people you're *actually* friends with, either on Twitter, Facebook, LinkedIn, or in real life.

- Spambot mechanical outreach letters for guest blogging is *so* 2010. It still works, *sometimes*, but the best reason to do blogger outreach is to get closer with your already existing friends.

- Nothing's free! Gently incentivize potential guest bloggers by offering one or two links to content of their choosing (within reason) within their post.

Self-Promotion without Spamming

The secret of selling in social media is to give more than you take and offer value to customers at every turn, to the point where they love to participate with your business. To understand how to market in social, we must first understand what marketing is, which parts of the classic definition don't jive with social, and what exactly social media spam is.

Figure 2.32 shows Merriam-Webster's definition of marketing.

Figure 2.32 Merriam Webster's definition of marketing, from
www.merriam-webster.com/dictionary/marketing

This description of marketing is fairly hardcore, all about selling, purchasing, and distributing. It's also how many marketers think about their jobs. Being a social media marketer must mean you sell things, right? On the other hand, social media participants are coming to the community to participate. To varying degrees, Facebook, Twitter, LinkedIn, and every community tolerate commercial activity or not. Sometimes this is mostly not!

Social hates aggressive marketers. We learned this the hard way back in 2007. aimClear was publishing blog posts about how StumbleUpon was an incredibly fertile marketing environment. The posts included lots of advice for marketers about giving more to StumbleUpon than we take. We talked about maximizing StumbleUpon marketing by lifting up the community and giving. Sounds great, right? Not! Even though marketers were active contributors and valuable StumbleUpon community members, the natives absolutely despised us. Do not ever forget this poignant lesson: Communities ultimately bury spammers.

What is considered spam anyway? Obviously it's not a very big leap to say that social media marketers should not spam community members. To fully understand how to behave without spamming, let's take a look at what clearly crosses the line as spam. While there are many spammer techniques, there are some classic examples of social spam that crosses the line.

Don't lie to gain friendship. As an example, LinkedIn has semi-strict requirements for how a user can reach out to request friendship. You must actually be friends (able to provide an email address) or have been colleagues in the past. Figure 2.33 shows a LinkedIn invitation received that flat-out lies. Michael is gaming LinkedIn for the ability to reach out in friendship. Why does he think it works to start a new relationship with a flat-out falsehood to game the system? What kind of friend will he make? Note the response, just before I pressed the delete button.

RE: Join my network on LinkedIn

 Marty Weintraub · Co Owner & Founder of aimClear® Online Marketing Agency
To: **Michael David**
Date: April 27, 2012

Michael,
Your invitation notes we are colleagues at TastyPlacement.com. I must be having a middle aged moment. I don't remember working there. Please remind me :).

On April 26, 2012 8:18 AM, Michael David wrote:

Let's be super best friends on LinkedIn.

Figure 2.33 Spammy LinkedIn friend request

Never mine email addresses from users' social media profiles for sending email blasts. Many businesses and individuals list email addresses and phone numbers on their social media profiles. Dude, that's *not* your personal marketing list. Figure 2.34 shows a spam email from Pokerchips.com. Making things worse, Pokerchips.com is grubbing for paid links, a total no-no in the online marketing world. #FAIL!

Figure 2.34 Email spam generated from social, asking for illegal (according to Google) paid links

Don't follow users just to splash your sales pitch across many profiles. Figure 2.35 shows a spam follow from @ReplicaWatches. At first you might think it's just one marketer following another. However, after checking out @ReplicaWatches, it's clear that they're splashing spam follows all over the place as self-promotion. The correct response is to block @ReplicaWatches and report them to Twitter.

Figure 2.35 Spam follow in Twitter

Here are other examples of spam and what not to do:

- Be aware of the norm in channels you frequent and participate in appropriate ways. Don't overpost with an inappropriate volume of posts.

- Avoid overt selling unless users specifically subscribe to sales feeds.

- Don't act too familiar or be a creepy stalker.

- Don't make lists of your friends' friends and systematically approach them.

- Don't jump into threads in any channel with irrelevant propaganda and other junk.

- Don't be abusive or a troll of any kind.

Figure 2.36 offers further input from our tweeps on what not to do.

Figure 2.36 What our friends say about social spam

Giving and the Art of Non-Salesy Sales Tactics

Now that we've had a look at what spam is (that is, what not to do), let's outline acceptable tactics for selling in social media. The American Marketing Association (AMA) takes a much fluffier position on what marketing means than Merriam-Webster. The AMA states that "marketing is the activity, set of institutions, and processes for creating, communicating, delivering, and exchanging offerings that have value for customers, clients, partners, and society at large" (October 2007) http://www.marketingpower.com/AboutAMA/Pages/DefinitionofMarketing.aspx. This is a great blueprint for social media marketing.

Placing rigorous focus on "creating, communicating, delivering, and exchanging offerings that have value for customers" is what community management is all about.
—American Marketing Association

It's interesting to think of value exchanges between a brand and its customers as the bedrock of marketing—although when you think about it, customers give value to brands too. In addition to paying for products and services, customers evangelize products they like. It works in reverse too. When customers don't like their purchases, they return things and even say bad things about the brand. Yep, that's right. Customers provide value back to brands, both positive and negative. Keep your wits about you in social marketing, make friends, and avoid the wrath of angry natives.

Ask not what your community can do for you. Ask what you can do for your community! Those of us old enough (or who studied politics) know that this headline evokes John F. Kennedy's immortal inaugural address of January 20, 1961. His words ring true today with astounding clarity and resonate throughout the fabric of society as an entitled generation of global citizens selfishly asks, "What's in it for me?" Nowhere is this clearer than in social media circles, where an icky minority of self-centered users muddy the waters for the authentic.

What unique value does your business bring to the table? How do your community manager's actions lift up those who are less experienced, breathless in excitement to learn? Exactly how hard are you willing to work? How much time are you available to unselfishly invest to bookmark content and network? Do you prove that community matters to you by deeds, not words? Do you race, with quickened pulse, for the privilege of submitting your favorite blog's post, crucial to what your customers need to know, which just rolled in the door by way of a Facebook post? Does your CM spend hours a day healthily engaged in social activities?

Examples of Great Social Media Marketing

aimClear was cited as one of the top 100 places to work in Minnesota. The recognition was run by *Minnesota Business* magazine and promoted largely by amplifying what was published in the paper magazine and website through social media. Out of the 6,000 companies that entered, many generated thousands of tweets, dozens of blog posts, and lots of amazing ballyhoo.

A tremendous amount of awareness was raised for the businesses that participated, to the financial benefit of the magazine. They sold hundreds of banquet seats, earned many links, and generated those coveted social signals so crucial to visibility in search and social these days. Blog posts they published earned lots of traffic because the information was exciting and interesting to businesses competing for the honor.

Minnesota Business offered the community serious value in return. Through a best-place-to-work designation, which is of tremendous value to any of the businesses that won, they achieved excellent balance and gave at least as much or more than they received in return. This is classic social media marketing, an excellent mash-up of outreach, content, community service, and *Minnesota Business's* self-serving interests (Figure 2.37).

Figure 2.37 Minnesota Business's announcement of the best 100 companies to work for

"How to Build a Reputation Monitoring Dashboard" was the most successful post in the history of aimClear Blog. We were the first to evangelize use of free RSS readers, like iGoogle, to monitor filtered reputation monitoring feeds. You'll learn more about reputation monitoring and conversation alerts in Chapter 5.

We charged clients about $3,000 each to install dozens of these over the course of about a year. When it became apparent that a spate of inexpensive products were about to hit the market offering similar and enhanced functionality, we took quick action by ceasing to offer the service commercially and publishing detailed instructions that empowered our readers to easily contract the dashboard. It was one of the smartest moves we ever made (Figure 2.38).

Figure 2.38 Groundbreaking reputation-monitoring dashboard blog post

We estimate that the loss in revenue was between $30,000 and $50,000. When potential clients called, we directed them to the post. We taught the techniques at conferences. aimClear Blog got many links and, for nearly two years, we enjoyed the nonpersonalized organic #1 in Google and Bing for the keyword "Reputation Monitoring." Priceless! There were (and still are) thousands of tweets, Facebook posts, and action in multiple social channels about the blog post and technique, which are still relevant years later. #ForTheWin!

What's amazing about the tactic is that the revenue was going to evaporate anyway. However, by giving away something that was still valuable, aimClear solidified its place among the tip-top thought leaders in the space. We were much more interested in higher-priced jobs to help companies react to what they learned from monitoring. We sold by giving. Classic!

We love this next example (Figure 2.39). Our friends at Search Engine Journal (SEJ), a respected blog, pinged prominent companies with an incredibly unselfish offer. SEJ ran a series of blog posts, along with collateral support in social channels (Twitter, Facebook, etc.) featuring the charities that companies support. The results were astonishing for SEJ, the companies, and the charities supported.

Figure 2.39 Search Engine Journal's charity blog post series

The articles gave priceless links and lent tons of buzz to charities. Each article incited hundreds of tweets. The businesses won too, with enhanced status as philanthropists, which is always a good thing. SEJ won big. They're a marketing blog. Charities and businesses have marketing departments. It is probable that SEJ gained audience shares from the effort. Win, win, win!

It's interesting to note that our examples include blog posts as epicenters of social media marketing outreach. We're a big believer in focusing social marketing on content that we own on sites we control. The concept of releasing content around which to center all promotion, including social, is fundamental.

Mashing Online CM with On/Offline Events

As mentioned earlier in this chapter, social media can be thought of as personal and/or citizen journalism. That classic approach can be organized in beautiful ways as coverage to take advantage of events taking place in business such as trade shows, meetings, gatherings, press conferences, public events, and anything congruent with the community manager's business mission.

Think about it. When covering events, the blogger/Tweeter/Facebooking community manager

- Says the name and/or business participating. They find out about the citation from Google Alerts and other methods.
- Uses tons of keywords important to the businesses, which is important for SEO.
- Establishes the blog and social profiles as experts, thought leaders in the space, and worldly.

- Gives fantastic information to members of the community that could not attend the event.

- Makes friends with the event organizers, which can pay dividends in many ways, including media passes and speaking gigs.

Figure 2.40 shows an example of aimClear's blog coverage of a mainstream industry conference. Our coverage of SMX East and other popular online marketing events is valuable, for reasons mentioned. Conference speakers and the companies they work for share it in communities they frequent. Events coverage is the epitome of social media marketing. Everybody wins. The marketer's position is one of giving.

Figure 2.40 aimClear covers SMX East 2012

CMs should always be on the lookout for public events that might warrant coverage in the classic publishers' sense. Over the years, aimClear Blog has received thousands of high-quality links, comments, and tweets, and made many friends from our conference coverage.

We approach it seriously, sending one- to four-person teams into the field with plenty of preproduction, interviews with speakers and attendees in advance, live-on-the-street tweets, and multiple blog posts each day of the event. It is safe to say that, out of all the components of our company's growth, this is the most crucial social media component.

We publish posts to set expectations (Figure 2.41). Again, note that our event coverage, reaching out with hands extending in giving, is centered on (you guessed it) content that we own posted on a site we control.

Figure 2.41 aimClear's conference coverage setup post

Crowd-sourcing, which means asking followers for input, is another great way to sell in social. For this chapter, we asked our Twitter friends to chime in about spam and appropriate social selling. Our friends were excited about the request, because they know that great comments will make it into the book. Look at all the mutual wins here:

- We got great insights quickly for this book. Our friends are really smart folks.

- We publicized that there is a new book coming. Most likely friends we quoted will buy the book and tell others about it. Crowd-sourcing is a big buzz generator. Some friends found out about the new book for the first time.

- Those quoted are promoted in the book, which is great for anyone. They will think it's cool and be proud.

Figure 2.42 shows my request for input from friends; Figure 2.43 shows responses. Win, win!

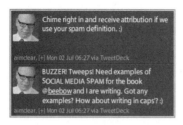

Figure 2.42 Twitter crowd-sourcing request

John F. Kennedy understood that actual power is deep-rooted in our harmony, optimism, and inspiration. Bring more to the table than you take. Ask what you can do for your community.

Figure 2.43 Twitter crowd-sourcing request responses

13 Utterly Annoying Behaviors to Avoid

For years, we've been counseling clients to practice these fundamentals of non-gratuitous social media behavior. Lovely conduct that endears users to other community members and earns respect is actually quite easy. Still, some professionals present terribly irritating habits. Marketers may or may not agree, but here's our stored-up rant featuring aggravating tactics employed by social media players who, in our opinion, just don't get how things work in the sandbox.

1. Pushy Follow Grubbing   Yep, this is the digital birdcage liner of social media. Come on! Provide value and most users will consider following your brand. Unless there's a good reason, please don't tweet, DM in Facebook, beg, send an email, or try to shame folks into following. Literally, we've seen a user give someone crap in public because the request recipient did not follow back or answer a follow-grubbing inquiry within a few minutes or hours. Don't program your post scheduler to tweet your follow-me begging to hashtags every hour on the hour. Grossness showcased in Figure 2.44.

Figure 2.44 Don't be a n00bzor. Earn your followers.

2. Mindless Mechanical Thanking   Thanks for the follow, thanks for the mention, thanks for the link, thanks for thanking me, blah, blah, blah, blah. Empower the brand community manager to act like she's been there before. Some folks say thanks for everything and it just adds noise to feeds. Say the same thing over and over and it begins to lose its meaning. Above all, do not automate messages of thanks for any reason. It's trite and fake. Better to tender actual thanks that mean something by not overdoing it as mechanical standard operating procedure. If your CM is going to thank people over and over, have her do it in private (DM of some kind) so it feels special to the recipient. Avoid being among the likes of those in Figure 2.45.

Figure 2.45 Mindless mechanical thanking

3. Gratuitous Gushing Praise.   If a person you do not know well approached you in person with over-the-top praise, you might feel uncomfortable. Social media praise can be perceived the same way. It is certainly OK to lay well-placed admiration on a fellow community member, but just don't gush. Offer up the same type of feedback that would not creep out the recipient if you were face to face. Be appropriate and measured.

4. Boilerplate Branding as a Social Media "Visionary" or "Guru"   Gandhi was a guru. Einstein was a visionary. Robert H. Goddard was an expert. Really, are you a "guru" to your LinkedIn connections? Are you really a "social media visionary?" Do you lead thinking to such a great extent that you are truly a spiritual teacher? SRSLY? If you really are a pro, don't cheapen your intellect with such a tacky, supercilious, self-imposed title (Figure 2.46).

Figure 2.46 Oh, you're a guru? Really?

5. Spammy Self-Promotion Look, if @SoAndSo is an actual acquaintance, then an occasional sales approach is reasonable. If professionals and companies want to approach a user in LinkedIn to lay some stupid self-promotional spam, they should prepare to be reported as such. The frustrated recipient of your spam may even publish the stupid DM in a book (Figure 2.47).

Figure 2.47 Spammy DMs in LinkedIn? No, thank you!

6. Fake Familiarity Ever meet someone at a party who acted as if they knew you a little *too* well? Did it creep you out? Social media mirrors physical life and the same peer-to-peer (P2P) rules apply. If you don't know someone well, don't act as if you know him or her well. Yes, it's cool to make new friends and work to get closer. That said, frame the context of the communication. Say something like, "We only met last week, but I want to reach out to [purpose of reaching out]. Perhaps you're interested. If that's not what you're into, then no problem, it's good to be casually connected, and thanks for all you give to the community. Ciao!"

7. Selfish Overposting There was recently a study that suggested that Facebook Page owners shouldn't post more than once every three hours. Our friend Dan Zarrella found that users don't like it when a brand spams the feed. To me, this includes personal brands, but the amount of posting that is deemed OK is up in the air. All I know is that I don't want to be constantly pinged in my newsfeed over and over by a single friend who shares a common group or page with me. I know a so-called thought leader who way overdoes it. This person participates in nearly every thread, posts every day repeatedly, and totally spams my news feed. Hey, you know who you are! Take a chill pill and quit trying to dominate the feed. It does not make you a thought leader to overpost; it makes you annoying.

8. Channel-Inappropriate Profiles   Unless your last name is actually "SEO Master," don't say it's your name (Figure 2.48). It's a lie, in the name of optimization, and it does not recommend you in any way. Yeah, like anyone's going to hire you even if you do end up ranking for "SEO of the SEO at SEO." Ick. LinkedIn and Facebook people profiles are supposed to be about people. Don't be a spam-wad hack. If you want to call yourself HoneyBunnyBoo, then get a StumbleUpon or Twitter profile where it's more appropriate to operate under a pseudonym.

Figure 2.48   Hmm, something tells me that's not the name your mama gave you.

9. Gutless Observers   The Arab Spring proved for the gazillionth time that a single idea, from a person with heart and guts, can start a process that can change the world. Be that hero. If in real life you see someone getting mugged in the park, you call 911. When you observe an injustice at work, it's appropriate to report the incident or otherwise stand up for the victim, keeping your own safety prudently in mind. If you see a social media community member being mauled verbally or otherwise bullied by a maleficent provocateur, stand up for what you know is right. Jump in the thread. Contact the person in private to support. Don't be a spineless wimp.

10. Hair-Trigger Anger   I am guilty of this one myself. I tend to try to solve things in public first using a large hammer as opposed to more delicate diplomacy. Sometimes that's a good thing, but more often than not, there are better ways. Try to solve problems in quiet ways that foster the perception that you are a good citizen. Nobody likes a mean old grouch. Save the big stick for when more measured and patient approaches fail. Then, nuke 'em in Twitter or buy Facebook Ads on their brand terms, only if you can stand the heat and have full confidence that you've taken a legal and righteous position.

11. Lies to Game Friendship Mechanisms   Some sites restrict who can friend you. For instance, LinkedIn wants users you approach to be in the same group, current or former colleagues, friends, or other criteria. Don't fib to game the friending criteria (Figure 2.49). It's not a good start to a relationship. And on the note of LinkedIn, always use the message field to your advantage by giving context to why you're connecting. It's a nice touch.

12. Promotion Requests from Idiotic Strangers   Enough said. See Figure 2.50. Grrrrr.

13. Horrendous Ad Targeting   The stupidity of some ad targeting in Facebook and LinkedIn just blows my mind. What could justanswer.jp be thinking here (Figure 2.51)?

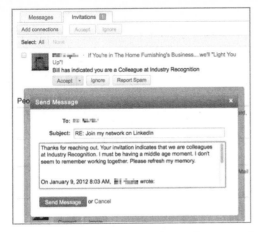

Figure 2.49 Be genuine in your outreach to people you want to befriend.

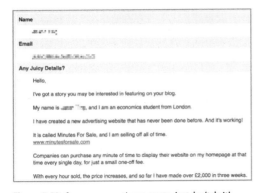

Figure 2.50 Spammy promotion requests. Just don't do it!

Figure 2.51 Come on. We're not going to click on that ad. I don't even know where to begin.

There are so many cool ways to hang in social media. Rebroadcast with added editorial value, ask reasonable questions, don't sell or spam, share delightful content bits, and tastefully thank people. These are wonderful tactics. Be magnanimous and act in ways that would fit in the physical world.

The best way to get likes is to do likable things. The best way to make friends is to be friendly. Follow these simple rules and it's less likely that you'll annoy the snot out of people.

Hit the Ground Running!

This chapter explores the business nature of social media and how to create a scope of work (SOW)/budget-request from the basics you gathered in Chapter 1, "The Social Media Community Manager's Role." We'll explore the terminology used to create such documents, which can be used to sell social media to the boss. Then we'll take a deep dive into the variety of social media channels in which you can implement the tactics as laid out in the SOW.

3

Chapter Contents
First-Step Essentials
Installing Profile Management Tools
The Galactic Guide to Social Media Channels

First-Step Essentials

Social media communities are just that: communities. They're destinations where users, from everyday to fanatical, gather around mutually shared interests and subject matter online. Whether a community manager represents himself/herself outside of work (user), represents a business concern (company), or represents an agency representing companies, social media means big business to someone.

If you're a rank and file user (just some schmo on Twitter, LinkedIn, a blog, or Facebook), business means those community owners are monetizing *you*, the user. Facebook sells ads and Twitter has promoted tweets. Facebook, Twitter, Google, YouTube, StumbleUpon, and even vaunted Wikipedians all sell out users *somehow* to make money. Ka-freakin'-ching! Before you object, users really don't have much to complain about. In order to use Facebook's free software, users submit to the rules by accepting FB's terms of services (TOS). The same type of TOS holds true in pretty much every social channel users can use for free.

If you're the company community manager (CM), then ultimately the business that matters most to you is making money. Don't get all hoity-toity on us now. Think about it. Like it or not, even 501(c)(3) charitable organizations (like the United Way and Men as Peacemakers) all need money.

The good news is that skillful participation by companies in social media can result in positive, even superlative, business results without bothering users much. To companies, skillful participation means community managers report measurable metrics illustrating how social media efforts contribute to the success of the company's overall marketing. This much must be as empirical as possible.

Whether you're a solo entrepreneur or work for a large enterprise, the first step to winning is to know what you're shooting for. It's a time to set goals, objectives, and metrics targets:

- What do you intend to get done here and how will you measure it?
- Which parts are ongoing and fixed-length campaigns within? Who maintains the master calendar?
- How will those KPIs help the company be profitable?
- Who will do what and how much will each piece cost in time and money?
- In reality, do initiatives require outside expertise, and if so, what role should they play?
- Consider granular specifics, from psychographic targeting to landing pages/mash-up experiences

By far, the largest common #FAIL denominator we see among social marketers is a lack of a cohesive framework to define the scope of what's going to happen next or in the next budget cycle. Heck, most CMs we meet don't know questions to ask, let alone systematic intake to budget components of ongoing and fixed-length campaigns. Creating adequate scope descriptions can be a daunting task to community managers who should expect that management will hold them accountable. Creating the next SOW will likely fall on the professional community manager.

Selling Your Boss: A Sample CM SOW/Budget Request

In Chapter 1, we discussed tools for organizing your SOW. Let's review the order of the intake document:

- Preproduction! What are you marketing?
- Demographic research
- Strategy and KPIs
- ROI modeling
- Channel tactics, creative, and testing
- Reporting and optimization
- Team and responsibilities

Grab the questionnaire answers from Chapter 1 and saddle on up! An important thing to keep in mind is that data from the process of questioning is integral to these marching orders.

Social media marketing costs money and time. That makes sense, right? The old adage is that you have to spend money to make money. Someone has to invest. And every investment has stakeholders, maybe even you. No matter what the boss's role connotes in your company's structure, spending time and money requires somebody's approval and expectation of your performance.

The nitty-gritty of making money means we CMs have to undertake some combination of activities. Those activities can be described in a SOW, which describes what will be done. The SOW document makes a super budget-request template, because it plans what will happen in logical format.

This subchapter is annotated with the √ mark, meaning you can head over to www.aimclear.com/cm/chapter3 and grab the sample CM budget-request template for your own use. It's printed here with a lot more explanation. Download the zipped file and open that little guy up. As always, test out the process applied to a real-life or role-played case study of your own. Modify the language to be reflective of your unique company and distribute the tool. The methodology that follows is straight-up language from aimClear's SOW-building process.

Each area of the SOW/budget-request document has various options. Having the company's template master interview the CM while taking notes is the best method by which to create the SOW. Of course, the process is easily self-administered, which works great and takes a little longer. The output from this process is a SOW/budget request, suitable for presentation to procure the engagement.

You know you're good when you can effectually blueprint what's going to happen in advance, say what you're going to spend, and project earnings. A well-constructed SOW is the high-level framework of a marketing plan suitable for the budgeting process.

CMs should be so powerful that they lead management through the budget planning process. Use the language in this section to scope out your own SOWs.

Divide your budget request/SOW into the following major areas. We'll dig into them one at a time with options to consider for each while correlating to the questionnaire. First come listening, research, and strategy:

- Reputation monitoring
- Social research (including competitive analysis and psychographic persona modeling)
- Strategy, KPIs, and a multichannel marketing plan

Next come channel tactics, both organic and paid. Later in this chapter, we'll take a deep dive into social media channels. The Galactic Guide to Social Media Channels is the definitive guide to every social network under the sun, including microblogging, business, health, tech, travel, photos, and pretty much any other type of social site you can think of. Channel tactics include the following:

- Data-driven community management/profile management
- Social advertising and paid organic amplification
- Landing page/experience build
- Campaign analytics audit, monitoring, and consulting
- Social display ads banner design
- Public relations mash-up
- Link building mash-up
- Content creation

Let's go through each of the major SOW areas one at a time. Budget how much time you think each task will take over a given time period. We usually plan in 3–6-month intervals, revisiting strategy and KPIs. Also, SOWs are usually added and/or subtracted during the planned-for period. Verbiage that is part of the template is boxed off for quick reference.

Reputation Monitoring: __ Hours and/or $__

If you're going to be the eyes and ears of the brand, then you'd better watch and listen. Most marketers would agree that listening to customers, also known as reputation monitoring, is a first step that can't go wrong. Consider first listening steps a part of social research.

You'll need the entire intake questionnaire to get a sense of what should be monitored, at least initially. Keep in mind that setting up the mechanics of your listening system may be a great investment with a third party, such as an agency or consultant. Most folks who are not pros at reputation monitoring miss a lot.

- Set up real-time email alerts and monitor conversations behind login walls to the greatest extent reasonably possible using current public and proprietary technology.

- The following RSS feeds, unavailable by commercial services, will be created by data extraction to feed technology. Consult legal counsel to ensure that automated monitoring of some channels does not violate that channel's terms of services.

- Build an executive dashboard to view the most recent __ items per keyword/ station/vertical.

- Monitor brand terms, category keywords, key employee names, and other critical conversations and keywords. The system will check channels every __ minutes or as we mutually agree with technology provided by [monitoring company].

- Listening stations will be distributed by territory. For instance, Portugal can monitor Portuguese news, Twitter, YouTube, and other verticals (channels) anywhere in the world whereas Mexico might monitor Spanish in North America at the same time Spain monitors Spanish everywhere else globally.

- Your listening team, comprised of [individuals' names], will monitor and be prepared to execute a prudent response plan for applicable situations. Alert community management team to engage, as prudent, in relevant conversations expeditiously.

Research and Psychographic Persona Modeling: __ Hours and/or $__

OK. Now let's take answers from the demographic research part of the marketing plan questionnaire and allot time to undertake research as part of this module. Budget the time required for social research. As a boilerplate number, this process takes between 15 and 20 hours per vertical. Sometimes it takes much more or much less time.

Demographics are only the half of it. As an industry, we have finally arrived in the holistic-user-targeting future! We consider demographics to be any attribute of a person, available by traditional web analytics. *Psychographic* research is now the gold standard by which to hold marketers accountable because they include Facebook interests, YouTube searches, keywords, LinkedIn data via social, and more. Now and forever, best-in-class execution means paid and organic campaigns that deliver seriously sliced and tagged traffic by empirical social attributes across social and search. Haven't heard of psychographics? Well, you will. Google "aimClear psychographic" and have a little fun!

Psychographic variables are any attributes connecting users' personalities, values, attitudes, interests, and lifestyles. Some intellectuals also refer to them as IAO (interests, activities, and opinions) variables. Psychographic variables complement and contrast classic demographic variables (like gender and age), behavioral attributes (like loyalty and usage habits), and psychographic variables (such as industry, seniority, and functional area). Psychographics are deeper and should not be confused with classic demographics. For example, the age of a user is not just defined by years. Perspective is also gleaned by psychographic attributes like mind-sets and cultural criteria.

The multichannel psychographic process requires intuition, guile, and determination. We've been talking about similar values focused on Facebook since late 2007. With Google and proprietary retargeting schemes, the concept of whole-customer psychographic targeting has gone mainstream, baby. Here's the language for the SOW. Perform Google Display, YouTube, Facebook, Twitter, LinkedIn, blogs/blogger, media, and competitive psychographic research focused on identifying multichannel contextual market segments with a reasonable likelihood of being susceptible to the missions of the KPIs, sufficiently divided so as to be industry consensus best practices.

- Mine any available organic analytics, pay-per-click (PPC), social analytics, and conversions for insight into market segments and any available history.

- Strategy, KPIs, and a holistic multichannel marketing plan: __ Hours and/or $__

Cull strategy and KPIs from the demographic research section of the marketing plan questionnaire. Options here are about setting various KPIs, as advised by those answers. Essentially, this is the marketing plan in which goals are set and projected ROI is specified.

- Create a holistic social marketing plan. Set strategies and KPIs (goals).
- [If determining the cost per action (CPA), requires testing first] Work to establish reasonable and prudent mutually agreed-upon KPIs and a controlling strategy to guide channel tactics that support the marketing plan.
- [If you know the targeted CPA] The goal is to grow traffic and conversion at an agreed-upon and reasonably attainable CPA, which we define as $____ per KPI conversion. The KPIs may include the following and/or others:
  - Direct response leads/sales CPA
  - PR, media outreach
  - Community-building
  - Branding

Data-Driven Community Management/Profile Management: __ Hours and/or $__

Now that we're done planning, it's time to get into the meat and potatoes. Every item that follows is considered a tactic, which means how we're going to get things done.

Tactics can be paid and/or organic. They can be in one channel or multiple. Consider the marketing plan answers from the Channel Tactics, Creative, and Testing module. Here we go on our tactical wonder tour.

- [Name/agency] will "man the wall," providing eyes, ears, and voice for [company's] social media welcoming and outreach tactics, as prescribed by the marketing plan.

- Approximately __ hours per month community management, undertaking active participation as the brand in social media channels, according to the strategic plan. Engage through nongratuitous, magnanimous social behavior. Channels include

  - [Fill in channels such as Facebook, Twitter, YouTube, and Google+ here]

  - Niche topical communities such as blogs and forums as discovered by psychographic research

- Streamline complementary and noncompetitive discovery of content to share.

- Build an up-to-the-minute expert-content RSS dashboard. (In Chapter 4, "Content, Reputation, and Hardcore Listening Hacks," we'll discuss the process of automating researching for sharing content. This clause is key.

- Map keyword research to social; identify, vet, and document conversations that surround conversion semantics. Interact with relevant and authority users. (In Chapter 5, "Find Themed Conversations: The Superior CM's Edge," there's a cool section on mapping keywords to conversations. Essentially, it means finding themed threads where interested users are having public conversations about keywords that matter to your brand.)

- Work in harmony with the publication calendar. Provide research and input, as requested, to support the content team, including target briefings, demographic research, ideas, and recommendations.

- Provide input and feedback on the content team's created sharing materials, including videos, audio, and infographics, to support the team in creating social media assets that the team leader believes will work.

- Participate in weekly production team check-in phone meetings, inbound/outbound briefings to/from partner agencies to review topline results from the previous week's and the upcoming week's production schedule, and monthly meetings at the executive level to review the previous month's results. Handle inevitable modifications of the team's priorities.

- Perform weekly and monthly KPI reporting.

  - Reporting will be derived via Facebook Insights standard output, Google Analytics standard output, and other tools as the team leader determines are appropriate.

Social Advertising and Paid Organic Amplification: ___ Hours and/or $___

When it comes to social, paid ads are your best friend. Because social ads can be set up to enable organic features that search engines and social platforms only make available to advertisers, PPC is an essential arrow in the community manager's quiver. We believe that it's best for CMs to handle many aspects of social PPC, especially as it pertains to distribution of socially promoted content.

- As prescribed by the marketing plan, [name/agency] will pilot and prove social display ad channels as mutually agreed upon, including ad copy, to reach an aggressive and reasonably attainable target CPA. Paid advertising channels uses may include Google and Bing display ads, YouTube search/display ads, Facebook Ads, LinkedIn Ads and/or additional channels upon which we agree. Conduct multivariate targeting, ad message, and landing experience testing. The objective is to determine a grid of targets and marketing messages that drive users to landing pages at or below a mutually agreed-upon target CPC. Deploy, pilot, manage, and report on multichannel ads campaigns.

- Organic amplification ads: As applicable in the field, [name/agency] will deploy the following organic amplification paid ad units:
  - Facebook page post ads
  - Facebook page post like sponsored stories
  - Facebook page like sponsored stories
  - Twitter promoted tweets
  - Twitter promoted accounts
  - Twitter sponsored hashtags (requires Twitter account representative)
  - Twitter sponsored trends (requires Twitter account representative)
  - Premium [channel] ad units (if budget warrants)

- Perform weekly and monthly KPI reporting.
  - Reporting will be derived from output from each ad platform's standard output, Google Analytics standard output, and/or as mutually agreed.

Landing Page/Experience Build: ___ Hours and/or $___

Landing pages are a sticky wicket because there are so many technical minefields to traverse. Also, the term "landing pages" applies to interesting mash-up pages. They could be in social or on your website. They could be your blog post, embedded on a Facebook wall, or in a YouTube video on your site's page. You need to ask the following questions first:

- Are you committing to designing and deploying landing pages?
- Or, are you committing to support the team's internal build process, and you build at your sole discretion?

- Are assets strictly in social or are they freestanding on team's site? (Or are they mashed up?)

Here are the options we usually choose from. Some of them are technical. Some of them are simple. Most landing page/experience situations are covered. Remember that these are either/or.

- Design and development:
  - Support the team in adapting the design of existing or creating new landing pages. At the community manager's discretion, an agency may be retained to design and code new landing pages if we deem that they are required.
  - Adapt the design of existing landing pages or create new ones.
- Location of landing page:
  - Landing pages may be freestanding on our website and/or in-social channel experiences.
  - Landing pages will be freestanding on the team's website.
  - Landing pages will be in-social channel experiences in the following channels: [fill in channels such as Facebook, YouTube, and/or Twitter here].
- Delivery of landing page:
  - Landing pages will be delivered to the team as [layered or flat] PNG files for the team to deploy and script.
  - Landing pages will be delivered to the team as PHP files with associated image files for the team to deploy and script.
  - Landing pages will be delivered to the team as PHP files with associated image files, scripted to the team's CRM or sales system. The team agrees to provide the team leader with any relevant technical information, including, but not limited to, form variable names and field types, character limitations, form validation requests, and other information that may be required for scripting. The team agrees to provide the team leader with a qualified team-side technical contact to facilitate the process. The parties agree that the team leader will not archive form submissions or any other aspect of user submissions.
  - Landing pages will be delivered to the team as PHP files with associated image files, with a form scripted to team leader–authored email script for delivery to the team. The team agrees to provide the team leader with form variables, character limitations, form validation requests, notification email recipients' email addresses, and other information that relates to the notification emails. The parties agree that the team leader will not archive notification emails.
- Team leader–provided landing pages may not be deployed without the team's approval.

Campaign Analytics Audit, Monitoring and Consulting: __ Hours and/or $__

This one's easy and speaks to keeping eyes on the campaigns.

- Provide ongoing monitoring of multichannel analytics.
- Perform daily monitoring and weekly analytics reporting, and provide monthly high-level recommendations.
- Flag anomalies and recommend a prudent response plan as often as reasonably necessary.

Social Display Ads Banner Design: __ Hours and/or $__

Some social advertising channels, like Google's Display Network, can use banners of different sizes. Also, many sites run their own banners on pages receiving social traffic. This portion of the SOW is where community managers request and receive banner design. Again, there are various options.

- [Select one:]
  - Create custom-designed banners.
  - Modify the design of the team's existing banners.
- Each banner will be designed to fit the following format(s): 450×50, 480×70, 300×50, 120×600, 728×90, 200×200, 160×600, 250×250, 320×50, 425×600, 300×600, 336×280, 300×1050, 300×250, 488×60 [select relevant sizes]
  - No banner's file size may exceed __ MB.
- Creative ideas for the banners will be culled from [team's input/team's preapproved branding claims, messages, and images/source art and images approved by team] and licensed by the team leader.
- Prior to design production, the team leader will submit proposed text copy and art to the team for review, input, and approval. Once the copy and art are approved, the team leader will design the banners and submit them to the team for review, input, and approval. The team agrees to review the materials in a responsive and timely manner, and approvals may not be unreasonably withheld.
- Delivery to team will be by zipped directory of flat JPEG and/or GIF files of sufficient compression to meet the file size limitations. Layered source files will remain the property of the team leader. The team leader will provide the transfer of single-use licenses to the team, sufficient for using the embedded source art for public advertising purposes. The team will reimburse the team leader for any image licenses, provided the expense is mutually approved.

Public Relations Mash-up: __ Hours and/or $__

Social media marketing is especially powerful for media outreach by using both paid and organic social marketing methods. This section speaks to the community manager's integration with PR folks, as specified in the publication calendar.

- The team leader provides new and traditional PR strategies that are designed to reach journalists, bloggers, news organizations, and the public.
- Our PR efforts are geared to leverage the content in search and social, as well as traditional periodicals, to generate hundreds of millions of impressions in dozens of channels, ad networks, and social communities.
- The team leader works to pilot creative messaging via holistic paid and organic distribution networks using cutting-edge techniques.
- Our goal is to run PR campaigns that achieve measurable results both online and offline.

Link Building Mash-up: __ Hours and/or $__

Link building is an objective that is often served by social. Here are methods commonly included in social media scope documents.

- Link building remains an essential search engine optimization (SEO) tactic in order to attain organic prominence. The team leader will undertake link-building outreach efforts by
  - Placing content in other publications
  - Using classic PR outreach to garner reviews, articles, and other media placements
  - Retaining interviews for team representatives and/or proxies
  - Using virtual conferences and other aggregation tactics
  - Using other white-hat tactics
- The goal is to attain ___ high-quality (___+ mozRank homepage) and ___ moderate-quality (___+ mozRank homepage) links per month. (As defined by SEOmoz, "MozRank represents a link popularity score. It reflects the importance of any given web page on the Internet. Pages earn MozRank by the number and quality of other pages that link to them. The higher the quality of the incoming links, the higher the MozRank.")

Content Creation: __ Hours and/or $__

Describing content marketing components can be a daunting task. This section divides up the content marketing universe by measureable deliverables.

- It may be that your company/client has an editorial team and calendar already developed. If so, use this: development of a social content editorial calendar that demonstrates how the existing content plan will be executed in social channels based on strategy.

- Approximately __ hours per month production, __ content blocks per week (authors will use pseudonyms or, if agreed to by team, their bylines). Reasonable/prudent to use external writers.
- Minimum of three features, 450–900 words, well researched, targeted, and so on
  - Edutainment
  - Infographics
  - Human interest
  - Topical and niche
  - Noneditorial reviews
  - Other
- 1 to 2 serialized convention posts, designed to engage 5 to 8 targets each by aggregating content with added value
  - Link roundups
  - Video roundups
  - Important and complementary news items
  - Conference coverage (travel and other expenses not included)
  - Featured bloggers, communities, and companies (with the team's preapproval)
  - Other, as team concurs
- "Package" (write setup, headlines, etc.) and release team-created sharing materials
- Rewritten releases, linking to the original PR web and/or other releases
- Collateral promotions materials

Attaining Interdepartmental Stakeholder Buy-In

Once the SOW/budget document is complete, we don't recommend sending it along to your boss without a meeting. If it's important to share, then only send the headlines (the part where you specify hours and dollars). That may be enough. If not, save the detail for a one-on-one meeting, leaving time to explain. A good rule of thumb is to first present the highest part of the outline and costs. Then, if needed, introduce the next level of granularity. Rinse and repeat.

Also, be sure to reword what we've outlined in the language that your audience will best understand. Always keep in mind that not everyone is a seasoned community manager and needs things presented clearly and simply. Our trick with this is to think about community management as if you had never heard of it or knew little, and then write for this audience. Also, be sure to keep your whole team in the loop and take the time to explain all the details and gain buy-in.

OK, now as promised, let's look at a comprehensive list of channels and what they're good for. We suggest getting a nice coffee, tea, or wine (in abundance), because you're going to be doing some serious reading!

Installing Profile Management Tools

There are oodles of online tools floating around in cyberspace that can benefit your company on its social media mission. Listening tools for reputation management, social customer relationship management (SCRM) tools to manage content and its performance, and user-powered directories for deadeye social demographic research are powerful assets for every CM's toolkit. But a core foundation of all these applications, and of any business's social media presence in general, is its branded profile, or, in many cases, profiles.

As you're about to discover in our Galactic Guide to Social Media Channels, target audiences don't always confine themselves to one social media platform (for example, Facebook). Savvy brands and community managers should be prepared to have a presence (profile) on any social channel where their target customers congregate.

That said, (wo)manning separate social media profiles on Facebook, Twitter, Google+, Pinterest, Foursquare, or any other combination of social platforms can be one heck of an undertaking. And if you're working for an agency responsible for community management for multiple clients across multiple platforms, watch out! That can get extremely convoluted and massively time-consuming. So many sites to log into, so many passwords to remember!

The wise and multitasking CM, mindful of blood pressure and professional obligation, leverages powerful profile management tools to streamline day-to-day social media profile maintenance. At a high level, what characterizes a modern profile management tool is the ability to manage multiple social media profiles across a variety of networks, including multiple accounts *within* one network, in an organized dashboard. In other words, profile management tools allow the CM to administer social media avatars in one or more Twitter accounts, one or more Facebook Pages, one or more LinkedIn accounts, and so forth, all in a single, comprehensive desktop-based, web-based, or mobile dashboard.

In this section, we'll explore some widely embraced profile management tools that can make daily social media community management more efficient and enjoyable. Each glance at a profile management tool includes a bulleted list of basic (free) features, as well as a look at premium features accessible to paying customers, as well as complementary mobile apps. As a special bonus, we've also provided words of wisdom (read: warning) on automating the art of social media. Saddle up, we're off!

TweetDeck

Let's start our journey with a look at TweetDeck, a widely-embraced social dashboard.

Features of the basic app:

- Free!
- Owned by Twitter
- Desktop app available for download
- Web UI client available
- Web app for Chrome
- Mobile app for iPhone, iPad, and Android
- Mobile web browser compatible with Windows Mobile, BlackBerry, Symbian, and web OS handsets
- Ability to arrange feeds with customizable columns (see Figure 3.1)
- Advanced filters that let you focus column content
- Ability to schedule tweets in advance
- Ability to monitor and manage unlimited accounts
- Integration with Facebook, LinkedIn, Foursquare, and MySpace
- Optional inline media previews (view videos and images directly in TweetDeck)
- Ability to create, edit, and delete lists, and to remove members from lists (directly in TweetDeck)
- Enhanced Mentions column, featuring alerts when you're @mentioned, followed, retweeted, favorited, or added to a list
- Old and new retweet formats (see Figure 3.2)

Figure 3.1 TweetDeck at a glance

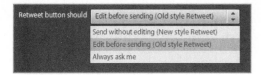

Figure 3.2 Retweet options in TweetDeck

Seesmic

Next up, Seesmic—similar to TweetDeck, with subtle differences.

Features of basic app:

- Free!
- Up to 10 posts per day
- Up to 3 accounts for posting
- Free Windows Desktop app
- Free mobile apps

Seesmic Plus:

- $4.99/month
- Up to 50 posts per day
- Up to 10 accounts for posting
- No feature limits
- Free mobile apps
- Free Windows Desktop app
- Ability to submit support tickets

Seesmic Pro:

- $49.99/month
- Unlimited posts per day
- Unlimited accounts for posting
- No feature limits
- Free mobile apps
- Free Windows Desktop app
- 24-hour response time on submitted support tickets

HootSuite

HootSuite offers a robust web UI, and its paid packages come with some nifty features.

Features of basic app:

- Free!
- Web interface plus mobile apps for iPhone, iPad, Android, BlackBerry, and Keitai
- Ability to manage up to five social profiles and two RSS/Atom feeds (free package)
- Ability to schedule messages and tweets
- Ability to track brand mentions
- Ability to create search streams
- Ability to search by @mentions
- Ability to search by hashtag
- Ability to filter by geolocation, Klout, keyword, and language
- Ability to create search streams based on any keyword
- Ability to create smart queries for multiple terms
- Social media traffic analysis
- Native Ow.ly URL shortener, which allows for shortened links and file sharing, as well as tracking click-throughs and site visits

HootSuite Pro:

- $9.99/month
- Ability to manage unlimited social profiles
- One free enhanced analytics report
- Google Analytics integration
- Facebook Insights integration
- Unlimited RSS feeds
- Bulk CSV uploader for messages

HootSuite Enterprise:

- Geared toward larger social media marketing campaigns
- Advanced social analytics
- Industry-leading security controls

- Increased collaboration, allowing companies to build CM teams from 10 to 500,000-plus
- Exclusive integrations and apps, including access to LinkedIn company pages, Google+ pages, SocialFlow, Adobe Genius, and more
- Branded URL shorteners, geo- and language targeting on Facebook, and the ability to archive tweets
- Enterprise customer support
- Ability to opt out of ads

No public pricing information is available on HootSuite Enterprise. Check out `http://hootsuite.com/enterprise` to submit a request to learn more.

SocialEngage

SocialEngage is a somewhat new kid on the block, spawned from CoTweet, another social dashboard application.

- CoTweet's Enterprise edition (CoTweet for free no longer exists)
- Web UI
- Geared toward companies, not individuals
- Ability to maintain a "unified inbox" to manage all your Twitter and Facebook accounts from a single user interface
- Ability to archive communications for the lifetime of the customer
- Ability to categorize tweets with tags and assign tasks to team members/customer service
- Rich analytics and reporting for reach, engagement, and influence
- Ability to stay connected 24/7 with the iPhone and Android mobile app
- Ability to track bit.ly custom short domains
- RSS integration
- Editorial workflow for approving and publishing content

Involver

Next up: Involver.

- Scalable social marketing management platform
- Ability to monitor conversations and post to Facebook and Twitter
- Ability to deploy applications on Facebook Pages
- Ability to design pages and social apps
- Multiuser functionality with roles and permissions; great for comprehensive marketing teams (marketers, creative, and developers)
- Ability to track engagement with custom parameters and organized reporting

Sprout Social

Sprout Social is another groovy platform.

- Ability to publish and schedule posts across multiple social channels
- RSS/Atom feed integration
- Ability to monitor brand-centric and competitors' chatter across social channels and the Web
- Ability to leverage discovery tools to hone in on your target audience
- Robust analytics and reporting for measurable ROI
- Simple collaboration across teams with task and permission tools
- Sprout Social for mobile available
- Deep CRM dashboard, which lets you add notes to contacts, set reminders per contacts, view contacts' social media presence, and archive all past history with contacts

Buffer

Last but not least, Buffer offers super streamlined content scheduling.

- Free!
- Web UI, mobile app for iPhone
- Emphasis on scheduling posts in advance that the app posts throughout the day (see Figure 3.3)
- Option to upgrade to support an additional team member and up to five social accounts for just $10/month

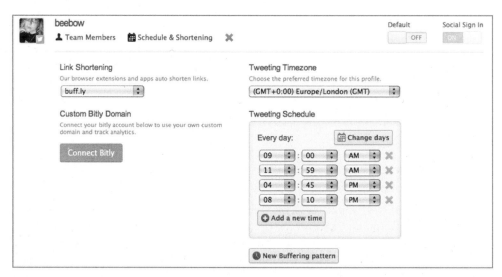

Figure 3.3 A look at scheduling and shortening options in Buffer

A Word about Automation

The automation features offered by many of these desktop, mobile, and web social media dashboards are lifesavers. Happy is the CM who can schedule content in advance across Twitter, Facebook, LinkedIn, Google+, and more, and have them fire effortlessly at a specified time. Automating tedious, repetitive, time-consuming, or no-brainer social media tasks frees up pockets of the community manager's schedule, affording her more time to take on other in-house or client responsibilities. Win-win!

However, as with any facet of data-driven community management, there are best practices to abide by. Social media automation tools, though beneficial and rewarding, are no excuse for a "set it and forget" mentality. CMs who schedule content to publish throughout the day better be prepared to check in on their social communities from time to time (read: at least four times each day, or a certain amount of time after each post fires) to ensure things are running smoothly and to engage where appropriate. At aimClear, we're a fan of the widely embraced "80/20" rule when it comes to automation. If clients choose to leverage social media automation tools, we strongly advise them to keep automation to 20 percent of a social media campaign, and have an active, calculating, and charming community manager (wo)manning the wall, handling the other 80 percent of tasks and responsibilities.

The Galactic Guide to Social Media Channels

Let's play a little word association. When we say "social media," you say...? Odds are it starts with an "F" and rhymes with Shmacebook. We find that so many brands are eager to hop on the FB bandwagon because they believe that's what it means to be social. "Everyone's on Facebook! It's the largest social network in the world. OMG, 900 million people, we gotta be there, too! If we're not on Facebook, we're nothing!"

Whether your company is attacking social media from the organic side, paid side, or both, the channel in which your CM is operating should be selected thoughtfully and purposefully, with a strong emphasis on the *quality* of the users and less so on quantity. In other words, you *don't* have to be on *any* social network just because it appears to have the largest user base. You *should* be where your target audience gathers, gabs, shares, and listens.

Naturally, this requires a bit of research.

Consider a community manager sent by her boss, the CEO of a kitty couture company, into Facebook in order to befriend folks who like cats. A quick peek at the Facebook Ads platform will reveal a cool 480,000 people who like cats so much they went the extra mile to disclose this via some amalgamation of keywords on their profiles. That's great! Plenty of cat lovers for the CM to cozy up to, either by way of some clever organic maneuvering or a deadeye Facebook Ads campaign. But is it the right channel for this brand? OK, it's certainly not the *wrong* channel, but is there a better fit?

Thirty seconds of social demographic research reveals a bevvy of niche social networks dedicated exclusively to cats, catering completely to the crazy cat lady (or gentleman) in all of us (Figure 3.4). Put on your data-driven CM hat and drill down a little deeper.

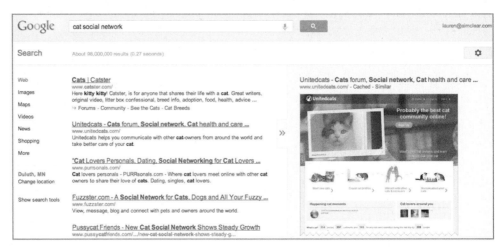

Figure 3.4 A quick Google search reveals a variety of cat-themed social networks. It's not all about Facebook!

UnitedCats.com, for example, is a network with more than 750,000 registered users, and they seriously freakin' love cats, so much so that they went the extra billion miles to create an account and set up a profile on this niche social network. When they're logged on to UnitedCats, users are in a feline frame of mind, and anything you have to say to them about cats stands a strong chance of resonating deeply.

Now, that's not necessarily the case when users hop on Facebook. FB is a mainstream social network that blends together all interests, thus making users fair game for other CMs and paid marketers who may speak to their other interests. Companies on Facebook have the single largest pool of people to target, but they're competing against other marketers who have other products for that same demographic.

The same goes for any vertical you can imagine: fashion, tech, food, travel, health, photography, video, charity, education—the list goes on. Facebook is not the undisputed epicenter of social media, and it won't be the most effective channel for every marketer. Niche social networks can be compact, concentrated pots of gold. The smaller the site, the tighter the community, the better the network and the more likely users will convert.

As we settled down to create The Galactic Guide to Social Media Channels, we thought of our friends at KnowEm (http://knowem.com), a website where people or brands can find out if their names are available across a plethora of social networking sites. Co-founders Michael Streko and Barry Wise have assembled a gigantic database of every social network you've ever heard of and every one you haven't. (In fact, hat-tip to Michael for the UnitedCats.com example. Meow!) From mainstream to obscure, Barry and Michael have compiled one heck of a directory and generously made it available to the masses through KnowEm.

Convinced of the awesome value of this directory, we've collated all of that information for your perusing pleasure. You can download the complete Galactic Guide to Social Media Channels at www.sybex.com/go/communitymanager for detailed ranks and tags on over 300 sites. But for now, read on for our favorite highlights culled from cyberspace. We want to open your eyes to the dozens of social networks in existence beyond the realm of Facebook. Have fun!

Some notes on navigating the guide:

- Sites are broken out across the following categories:
  - Blogging
  - Bookmarking
  - Business
  - Community
  - Design
  - Entertainment
  - Health
  - Information
  - Microblogging
  - Music
  - News
  - Photo
  - Tech
  - Travel
  - Video
- Each category features top sites for that vertical.
- Each listing features a brief description, assorted metrics (Social Media Relevance Rankings), and similar tags users of that community use to illustrate cross-pollinated interests.
- The Social Media Relevance Rankings describe the relevance of each site in relation to the estimated 600 social media networks KnowEm tracks. A site with a score of 1 is in the lowest percentile for that metric; a site with a score of 100 is in the highest.
- Each ranking, as explained by KnowEm:
  - Alexa Rank: A reflection of the Alexa rank for the domain
  - Compete Rank: A reflection of the Compete rank for the domain

- Compete Volume: Based on the monthly traffic volume Compete reports for the site
- Referring Domains: The number of unique domains that refer to the site with incoming links as reported by Majestic SEO
- Majestic Links: How many incoming links Majestic SEO reports for the domain
- Some sites feature a Bonus Primary Value, courtesy of our pals over at SEOmoz (http://www.seomoz.org). There are social media marketers in it *now* to promote link-worthy content, garner strong profile rankings, and hone in on direct link sources. As such, we've pulled out communities with these values featured in the venerable SEOmoz directory and placed them atop the otherwise alphabetical listings.

Blogging

Consistently churning out fresh, engaging, relevant content is fabulous practice for any company hungry for online success. Business blogging is where it's at! From sites that allow you to create your own blogs to forums dedicated to content management system (CMS) chatter, this section is your go-to directory for communities of casual bloggers and professional writers alike.

Blogger

- Website: www.blogger.com
- Description: Blogger is a free blog publishing tool from Google for easily sharing your thoughts with the world.
- Bonus Primary Value: Direct link sources
- Alexa Rank: 100
- Compete Rank: 100
- Compete Volume: 1
- Referring Domains: 100
- Majestic Links: 100
- Similar Tags: SEO, Social Media, Social Media Marketing, Blogging, Internet Marketing, Search Engine Optimization, Marketing, Photography, Web Design, Technology, Music, Travel, Social Networking, Branding, Advertising, Internet, Real Estate, Web Development, SEO Professional, SEM, Art, Design, Media, Search Engine Marketing, Business, Online Marketing, Social Media Consulting, Education, Web Marketing, Movies

Tribe

- Website: http://tribe.net
- Description: An online community, based in several cities throughout the United States and in Canada. Users create a network of friends and join or create tribes for common interests.
- Bonus Primary Value: Strong profile rankings
- Alexa Rank: 97
- Compete Rank: 100
- Compete Volume: 1
- Referring Domains: 43
- Majestic Links: 6
- Similar Tags: Social Media, SEO, Marketing, Search Engine Optimization, Blogging, Travel, Internet Marketing, Social Media Marketing, Social Networking, Web Design, Photography, Search Engine Marketing, Technology, Advertising, Digital Marketing, Music, PPC, Startups, Web Development, Business, Ecommerce, Entrepreneurship, Fitness, Small Business, Affiliate Marketing, Art, Cars, Finance, Media, SEM

Tumblr

- Website: www.tumblr.com
- Description: Tumblr makes it effortless to share text, photos, quotes, links, music, and videos.
- Bonus Primary Value: Direct link sources
- Alexa Rank: 100
- Compete Rank: 100
- Compete Volume: 1
- Referring Domains: 100
- Majestic Links: 100
- Similar Tags: Social Media, SEO, Internet Marketing, Social Media Marketing, Search Engine Optimization, Technology, Blogging, Marketing, Music, Web Design, Travel, Photography, Social Networking, Web Development, Internet, Web Marketing, Art, Advertising, SEM, SEO Professional, Design, Entrepreneurship, Movies, Search Engine Marketing, Online Marketing, Real Estate, Business, Branding, Email Marketing, News

WordPress

- Website: http://wordpress.org
- Description: A semantic personal publishing platform with a focus on aesthetics, web standards, and usability.
- Bonus Primary Value: Direct link sources
- Alexa Rank: 100
- Compete Rank: 100
- Compete Volume: 1
- Referring Domains: 100
- Majestic Links: 100
- Similar Tags: Social Media, SEO, Social Media Marketing, Internet Marketing, Blogging, Social Networking, Technology, Travel, Search Engine Optimization, Marketing, Music, Web Design, Photography, Internet, Real Estate, Business, SEM, Web Development, Social Media Consulting, Advertising, Movies, Search Engine Marketing, Design, Media, Health, Online Marketing, SEO Professional, Art, Branding, Entrepreneurship

Bookmarking

Social bookmarking is a term to describe the marking, saving, and archiving of certain websites. Users can use social bookmarking tools to track and organize their favorite websites and access them from any computer hooked up to the Internet. Over the past few years, social bookmarking sites have become increasingly popular and have created their own niche communities around the bookmarking functionality.

A1-Webmarks

- Website: www.a1-webmarks.com
- Description: A1-Webmarks is a free service that combines the convenience of a personal webmark server with the power of social webmarking.
- Bonus Primary Value: Direct link sources
- Alexa Rank: 98
- Compete Rank: 100
- Compete Volume: 1
- Referring Domains: 12
- Majestic Links: 3
- Similar Tags: SEO, Social Media, Search Engine Optimization, Blogging, Photography, Used Car Dealer, Art, Bible Commentary, Computers, Email Marketing, Fashion, Fotografie, Honda Certified, Honda Civic, Honda Dealer,

Honda Vehicles, London, Marketing, Shopping, Texas, UK, Weight Loss, Accord, AdWords, Affiliate Marketing, Android, Beachfront Homes For Sale Costa Rica, Beachfront Property Costa Rica, Best Anti Aging Wrinkle Cream, Business Credit

Delicious

- Website: http://delicious.com
- Description: Keep, share, and discover the best of the Web using Delicious, a leading social bookmarking service.
- Bonus Primary Value: Strong profile ranking
- Alexa Rank: 100
- Compete Rank: 100
- Compete Volume: 1
- Referring Domains: 100
- Majestic Links: 100
- Similar Tags: Social Media, SEO, Social Media Marketing, Blogging, Technology, Internet Marketing, Photography, Music, Travel, Marketing, Search Engine Optimization, Web Design, Internet, Social Networking, Web Development, Advertising, SEM, Entrepreneurship, Online Marketing, Design, Movies, Search Engine Marketing, Art, Branding, SEO Professional, Sports, Web Marketing, Fitness, Social Media Consulting, Business

Folkd

- Website: www.folkd.com
- Description: Save your bookmarks online and share them with your friends.
- Bonus Primary Value: Promote link-worthy content
- Alexa Rank: 99
- Compete Rank: 100
- Compete Volume: 1
- Referring Domains: 85
- Majestic Links: 100
- Similar Tags: SEO, Social Media, Internet Marketing, Travel, Search Engine Optimization, Blogging, Marketing, Social Media Marketing, Web Design, Business, Photography, SEO Professional, Real Estate, Search Engine Marketing, SEM, Social Networking, Music, Cars, SEO Services Company, Entrepreneurship, Startups, Technology, Web Development, Automotive, Car Dealers, Advertising, Affiliate Marketing, Art, Business Development, Car Dealer Reviews

Diigo

- Website: www.diigo.com
- Description: Diigo is a powerful research tool and a knowledge-sharing community.
- Bonus Primary Value: Direct link sources
- Alexa Rank: 100
- Compete Rank: 100
- Compete Volume: 1
- Referring Domains: 100
- Majestic Links: 100
- Similar Tags: Social Media, SEO, Internet Marketing, Search Engine Optimization, Social Media Marketing, Blogging, Travel, Marketing, Technology, Web Design, Photography, Social Networking, Music, Advertising, Business, SEM, Art, Entrepreneurship, Real Estate, SEO Professional, Affiliate Marketing, Design, Web Development, Web Marketing, Online Marketing, Reading, Twitter, WordPress, Branding, Education

Jumptags

- Website: www.jumptags.com
- Description: Jumptags.com is a revolutionary Web 2.0 social bookmarking web service for collecting, storing, sharing and distributing web bookmarks.
- Bonus Primary Value: Promote link-worthy content
- Alexa Rank: 98
- Compete Rank: 100
- Compete Volume: 1
- Referring Domains: 43
- Majestic Links: 82
- Similar Tags: SEO, Social Media, Search Engine Optimization, Internet Marketing, Marketing, Blogging, Travel, SEM, Social Media Marketing, Real Estate, Web Design, Web Marketing, Advertising, Apple, Digital Marketing, Events, Fitness, Gymnastics, Health, iPhone, Mac, Macintosh, OSX, SEO Professional, Social Networking, Startups, Swimming, Used Car Dealer, Web Development, Wedding

Mister Wong

- Website: www.mister-wong.com
- Description: With Mister Wong you can search for the best websites, save them, and share them with others, completely free.

- Bonus Primary Value: Promote link-worthy content
- Alexa Rank: 96
- Compete Rank: 100
- Compete Volume: 1
- Referring Domains: 85
- Majestic Links: 100
- Similar Tags: Internet Marketing, Social Media, SEO, Marketing, Social Media Marketing, Travel, Search Engine Optimization, Technology, Web Design, Social Networking, Blogging, Photography, Advertising, Affiliate Marketing, Online Marketing, Real Estate, SEO Professional, Search Engine Marketing, Business, Automotive, Car Dealer Reviews, Car Dealers, Cars, Digital Marketing, Ecommerce, Email Marketing, Finance, Internet, Movies, Music

My Link Vault

- Website: www.mylinkvault.com
- Description: Online links made easy; this site lets you store your links online.
- Bonus Primary Value: Direct link sources
- Alexa Rank: 97
- Compete Rank: 100
- Compete Volume: 1
- Referring Domains: 18
- Majestic Links: 16
- Similar Tags: SEO, Social Media, Marketing, Internet Marketing, Search Engine Optimization, Advertising, Photography, Real Estate, Blogging, Social Networking, Affiliate Marketing, Digital Marketing, Travel, Social Media Marketing, Business, Entrepreneurship, Search Engine Marketing, Startups, Technology, Art, Ecommerce, Fitness, Music, Web Design, Web Development, WordPress, Automotive, Car Dealers, Cars, Dealership

Squidoo

- Website: www.squidoo.com
- Description: Popular (free) site for creating single web pages on your interests and recommendations. You can even earn money for charity or yourself.
- Bonus Primary Value: Direct link sources
- Alexa Rank: 100
- Compete Rank: 100
- Compete Volume: 1
- Referring Domains: 100

- Majestic Links: 100
- Similar Tags: Social Media, SEO, Social Media Marketing, Blogging, Search Engine Optimization, Internet Marketing, Marketing, Web Design, Travel, Technology, Photography, Social Networking, Advertising, Real Estate, Web Development, Business, Music, Web Marketing, Online Marketing, SEM, Search Engine Marketing, Affiliate Marketing, Branding, Digital Marketing, Health, Social Media Consulting, Design, Entrepreneur, Entrepreneurship, Network Marketing

StumbleUpon

- Website: www.stumbleupon.com
- Description: StumbleUpon discovers websites based on your interests, learns what you like, and brings you more.
- Bonus Primary Value: Strong profile rankings
- Alexa Rank: 100
- Compete Rank: 100
- Compete Volume: 1
- Referring Domains: 100
- Majestic Links: 100
- Similar Tags: Social Media, SEO, Social Media Marketing, Internet Marketing, Blogging, Search Engine Optimization, Marketing, Music, Web Design, Social Networking, Technology, Travel, Photography, Web Development, Entrepreneurship, Design, Online Marketing, SEM, Art, Internet, Web Marketing, Advertising, SEO Professional, Search Engine Marketing, Social Media Consulting, Business, Real Estate, Social Media Strategy, Branding, Cooking

Pinterest

- Website: http://pinterest.com
- Description: Pinterest is one of the hottest sites in social media. It is a place to pin images of everything you're interested in and share these boards with your friends, family, and anyone else who happens to be using Pinterest.
- Bonus Primary Value: Promote link-worthy content
- Similar Tags: Blogging, SEO, Social Media, Travel, Affiliate Marketing, Internet Marketing, Photography, Search Engine Optimization, Entrepreneurship, Marketing, Social Media Marketing, Advertising, Art, Blogger, Education, Email Marketing, Gardening, Media, Online Marketing, SEO Professional, Animals, Australia, Branding, Business, Charity, Copywriting, Design, Development, Digital Marketing Consulting, Family

Business

I say "social media," you say "Facebook!" I say "business + social media," you probably say "LinkedIn!" There's a whole universe of professional social networks out there, LinkedIn included. This section features social media channels that cater specifically to business folk around the world.

Epinions

- Website: www.epinions.com/
- Description: Epinions helps people make informed buying decisions. It is an online consumer reviews platform that gives users the ability to comment, advise, review, and evaluate products from every corner of the earth. Before you buy something, visit epinions.com.
- Bonus Primary Value: Strong profile rankings
- Alexa Rank: 99
- Compete Rank: 100
- Compete Volume: 1
- Referring Domains: 100
- Majestic Links: 42
- Similar Tags: Social Media, SEO, Search Engine Optimization, Travel, Internet Marketing, Marketing, Social Media Marketing, Technology, Blogging, Web Design, Entrepreneurship, Social Networking, PPC, Web Marketing, Search Engine Marketing, Web Development, Cars, Consulting, Photography, SEM, Startups, Twitter, Advertising, Automotive, Business, Computers, Design, Digital Marketing, Email Marketing, Family

Get Satisfaction

- Website: http://getsatisfaction.com/
- Description: Get Satisfaction brings customers and company employees together to make things better for everyone. Great answers and ideas can come from anywhere; Get Satisfaction just does its part to get them to the people who can do something about it.
- Bonus Primary Value: Direct link sources
- Alexa Rank: 100
- Compete Rank: 100
- Compete Volume: 1
- Referring Domains: 41

- Majestic Links: 100
- Similar Tags: Social Media, SEO, Technology, Social Networking, Blogging, Social Media Marketing, Web Design, Search Engine Optimization, Music, Web Development, Photography, Internet Marketing, Marketing, Entrepreneurship, Web Marketing, Real Estate, Advertising, Design, Internet, SEO Professional, Travel, Twitter, Computers, Cooking, Gadgets, Startups, Games, Search Engine Marketing, Sports, WordPress

Kaboodle

- Website: www.kaboodle.com
- Description: Kaboodle is a fun shopping community where people recommend and discover new things.
- Bonus Primary Value: Promote link-worthy content
- Alexa Rank: 99
- Compete Rank: 100
- Compete Volume: 1
- Referring Domains: 100
- Majestic Links: 100
- Similar Tags: Social Media, SEO, Internet Marketing, Marketing, Travel, Blogging, Search Engine Optimization, Social Media Marketing, Social Networking, Design, Advertising, Technology, Entrepreneurship, Photography, Art, Digital Marketing, PPC, Cooking, Fitness, Real Estate, SEO Professional, Web Design, Automotive, Finance, Internet, Startups, Business, Car Dealer Reviews, Car Dealers, Cars

LinkedIn

- Website: www.linkedin.com
- Description: LinkedIn strengthens and extends your existing network of trusted contacts. LinkedIn is a networking tool that helps you discover inside connections.
- Bonus Primary Value: Strong profile rankings
- Alexa Rank: 100
- Compete Rank: 100
- Compete Volume: 1
- Referring Domains: 100
- Majestic Links: 100
- Similar Tags: Social Media, SEO, Social Media Marketing, Blogging, Internet Marketing, Technology, Marketing, Search Engine Optimization, Social

Networking, Music, Photography, SEM, Web Design, Travel, Web Development, Online Marketing, Social Media Consulting, Design, Entrepreneurship, SEO Professional, Web Marketing, WordPress, Branding, Real Estate, Advertising, Social Media Strategy, Business, Internet, Search Engine Marketing, Website Design

Community

This section features online communities that truly emphasize the "community" element. Each site speaks to its own niche, but the core purpose is to connect humans with like-minded humans.

Facebook

- Website: www.facebook.com
- Description: Facebook is a social media platform connecting people all over the world with their friends, families, co-workers, and classmates. Facebook also allows you to interact with your favorite bands, brands, and local shops by sharing photos, comments, and questions.
- Bonus Primary Value: Strong profile rankings
- Alexa Rank: 100
- Compete Rank: 100
- Compete Volume: 1
- Referring Domains: 100
- Majestic Links: 100
- Similar Tags: Social Media, SEO, Social Media Marketing, Blogging, Marketing, Music, Technology, Internet Marketing, Web Development, Social Networking, Web Design, Photography, Travel, Search Engine Optimization, Graphic Design, Online Marketing, Internet, Web Marketing, Website Design, Design, SEM, Social Media Consulting, Art, SEO Professional, Sports, Movies, Real Estate, Writing, Reading, Branding

Multiply

- Website: http://multiply.com
- Description: Users can create, share, and discuss blogs, photos, videos, and music with others as well as post reviews of movies and books, or share a calendar of events.
- Bonus Primary Value: Strong profile rankings
- Alexa Rank: 100
- Compete Rank: 100

- Compete Volume: 1
- Referring Domains: 100
- Majestic Links: 100
- Similar Tags: Social Media, SEO, Social Media Marketing, Travel, Blogging, Music, Social Networking, Marketing, Search Engine Optimization, Internet Marketing, Web Design, Photography, Real Estate, Online Marketing, Technology, Advertising, Cars, Design, Entrepreneurship, Internet, SEO Professional, Web Development, Art, Automotive, Digital Marketing, Search Engine Marketing, SEM, Twitter, Business, Movies

SlideShare

- Website: www.slideshare.net
- Description: SlideShare is a presentation sharing community. Share publicly or privately, and add audio for webinars.
- Bonus Primary Value: Strong profile rankings
- Alexa Rank: 100
- Compete Rank: 100
- Compete Volume: 1
- Referring Domains: 100
- Majestic Links: 64
- Similar Tags: Social Media, Social Media Marketing, SEO, Internet Marketing, Blogging, Marketing, Search Engine Optimization, Social Networking, Travel, Web Design, Technology, Web Development, Music, Photography, Advertising, Online Marketing, Social Media Consulting, Search Engine Marketing, Entrepreneurship, Internet, Real Estate, Art, Business, Design, Social Media Strategy, Web Marketing, Media, SEM, Email Marketing, PPC

Xanga

- Website: www.xanga.com
- Description: Xanga is a community where you can start your own free blog, share photos and videos, and meet new friends.
- Bonus Primary Value: Direct link sources
- Alexa Rank: 99
- Compete Rank: 100
- Compete Volume: 1
- Referring Domains: 100

- Majestic Links: 100
- Similar Tags: Social Media, SEO, Internet Marketing, Marketing, Technology, Blogging, Travel, Social Media Marketing, Photography, Business, Music, Social Networking, Media, Reading, Search Engine Optimization, Art, Movies, Web Design, Advertising, Email Marketing, Online Marketing, Politics, Sports, Automotive, Computers, Design, Internet, Search Engine Marketing, Twitter, Video

Yelp

- Website: www.yelp.com
- Description: The site provides user reviews and recommendations of top restaurants, shopping, nightlife, entertainment, services, and more.
- Bonus Primary Value: Strong profile rankings
- Alexa Rank: 100
- Compete Rank: 100
- Compete Volume: 1
- Referring Domains: 1
- Majestic Links: 1
- Similar Tags: Travel, Social Media, Blogging, Marketing, SEO, Entrepreneurship, Social Networking, Cooking, Fitness, Internet Marketing, Photography, Search Engine Optimization, Social Media Marketing, Sports, Used Car Dealer, Web Design, Web Development, Web Marketing, Affiliate Marketing, Business, Ecommerce, Golf, Online Marketing, Startups, Technology, Advertising, Cars, Dealership, Deals, Design

Design

One of a few geek-chic sections in this massive directory, here you'll find social media channels dedicated to members of the design community, both print and digital. From storybook illustrators to graphic artists, there's a creative crowd across these networks.

DeviantART

- Website: www.deviantart.com
- Description: This site provides a community of artists and those devoted to art: digital art, skin art, themes, wallpaper art, traditional art, photography, and poetry/prose.
- Bonus Primary Value: Direct link sources
- Alexa Rank: 100

- Compete Rank: 100

- Compete Volume: 1

- Referring Domains: 100

- Majestic Links: 100

- Similar Tags: SEO, Social Media, Photography, Social Media Marketing, Internet Marketing, Web Design, Music, Social Networking, Blogging, Search Engine Optimization, Web Development, Art, Marketing, Design, Entrepreneurship, SEO Professional, Technology, Travel, Video, Web 2.0, Games, Graphic Design, Internet, Movies, Branding, Media, Online Marketing, Real Estate, Search Engine Marketing, SEO Services Company

Behance

- Website: www.behance.net

- Description: The site provides a platform for the creative professional community.

- Alexa Rank: 100

- Compete Rank: 100

- Compete Volume: 1

- Referring Domains: 37

- Majestic Links: 15

- Similar Tags: Social Media, SEO, Blogging, Marketing, Art, Design, Photography, Video, Social Networking, Web Design, Branding, Internet Marketing, Technology, Music, Web Development, Advertising, Cooking, Development, Digital Marketing, Graphic Design, Internet, Social Media Marketing, Web 2.0, Web Marketing, Business, Ecommerce, Entrepreneurship, Gymnastics, iPhone, KnowEm

Jimdo

- Website: www.jimdo.com

- Description: You can create a free website with Jimdo's website builder. With 500 MB storage, you can drag and drop to make a website, upload over 12,500 pictures, and use Jimdo's beautiful layouts or make your own.

- Alexa Rank: 100

- Compete Rank: 100

- Compete Volume: 1

- Referring Domains: 100

- Majestic Links: 54
- Similar Tags: SEO, Search Engine Optimization, Blogging, Social Media, Social Media Marketing, Social Networking, Affiliate Marketing, Art, Digital Marketing, Internet Marketing, Web Development, Advertising, Bedbugs, Blogger, Bugs, Business, Community, Company, Creative, Custom Website Design, Design, Design Cloud Nine, Entrepreneurship, Exhibition, Facebook for Business, Farmersburg, Fashion, Graphic Design, Indiana, Insects

Entertainment

Humor sites, gossip sites, games, fashion, celeb sightings, and yes, those beloved LOLCats galore. The goal? Fun. And possibly the slow decay of brain cells.

Fanpop

- Website: www.fanpop.com
- Description: Fanpop is a network of fan clubs for fans of television, movies, music, and more to discuss and share photos, videos, news, and opinions with fellow fans.
- Bonus Primary Value: Promote link-worthy content
- Alexa Rank: 100
- Compete Rank: 100
- Compete Volume: 1
- Referring Domains: 37
- Majestic Links: 5
- Similar Tags: Social Media, SEO, Internet Marketing, Social Networking, Marketing, Blogging, Entrepreneurship, Affiliate Marketing, Search Engine Optimization, Social Media Marketing, Startups, Technology, Business, Digital Marketing, Ecommerce, KnowEm, Laminate Flooring, Photography, Real Estate, Search Engine Marketing, SEO Professional, Shopping, Web Marketing, Advertising, Cars, Cooking, Design, Development, Education, Entrepreneur

Stylehive

- Website: www.stylehive.com
- Description: The goal is to connect stylish people.
- Bonus Primary Value: Strong profile rankings
- Alexa Rank: 96
- Compete Rank: 100
- Compete Volume: 1

- Referring Domains: 19
- Majestic Links: 7
- Similar Tags: Social Media, Marketing, SEO, Internet Marketing, Search Engine Optimization, Travel, Technology, Advertising, Automotive, Blogging, PPC, Social Networking, Art, Ecommerce, Photography, Real Estate, Social Media Marketing, Video, Affiliate Marketing, Car, Car Dealer Reviews, Car Dealers, Cars, Dealership, Digital Marketing, Entrepreneurship, Fitness, KnowEm, Sales, Shopping

Cracked.com

- Website: www.cracked.com/
- Description: This is a website filled with funny videos, pictures, articles, and a whole bunch of other funny stuff.
- Alexa Rank: 100
- Compete Rank: 100
- Compete Volume: 1
- Referring Domains: 43
- Majestic Links: 11
- Similar Tags: SEO, Social Media, Social Media Marketing, Search Engine Optimization, Social Networking, Automotive, Car Dealer Reviews, Car Dealers, Dealership, Holidays, Internet Marketing, Marketing, Web Design, Auto, Automobiles, Blogging, Business, Car, Car Dealer Check, Cars, Dealer, Deals, Digital Marketing, Finance, Honda, Texas, Travel, Used Car Dealer, AdWords, Asset Management

Ebaumsworld

- Website: www.ebaumsworld.com
- Description: This site offers funny pictures and videos, Flash games, and jokes.
- Alexa Rank: 100
- Compete Rank: 100
- Compete Volume: 1
- Referring Domains: 78
- Majestic Links: 14
- Similar Tags: SEO, Social Media, Laminate Flooring, Marketing, Social Media Marketing, Social Networking, Affiliate Marketing, Akiles, Binding, Cooking, Cutters, Fellowes, Gbc, Ibico, Laminating, Laminator, Martin Yale, Mybinding, Paper Shredder, Proclick, Report Covers, Sales, Shredder, Trimmer, Vancouver, Basketball, Blogging, Digital Marketing, Entrepreneurship, Internet Marketing

Cheezburger

- Website: http://icanhascheezburger.com/
- Description: Cheezburger offers a humorous look at cats and other animals through hilarious user-generated photo and video content.
- Alexa Rank: 99
- Compete Rank: 100
- Compete Volume: 1
- Referring Domains: 41
- Majestic Links: 16
- Similar Tags: Social Media, SEO, Marketing, Travel, Blogging, Internet Marketing, Technology, Games, Search Engine Optimization, Social Networking, Music, Internet, Sports, Advertising, Art, Online Marketing, Photography, PPC, Social Media Marketing, Automotive, Business, Car Dealer Reviews, Car Dealers, Cars, Digital Marketing, Ecommerce, Entrepreneurship, Facebook, It, KnowEm

Popsci

- Website: www.popsci.com
- Description: Aggregators for news stories pertaining to new technology and futuristic concepts.
- Alexa Rank: 98
- Compete Rank: 100
- Compete Volume: 1
- Referring Domains: 53
- Majestic Links: 14
- Similar Tags: Used Car Dealer, Honda Certified, Honda Civic, Honda Dealer, Honda Vehicles, Search Engine Optimization, Accord, Crystal Awards, Crystal Gifts, Crystal Plaques, Dealership, Entrepreneurship, Hamilton, Honda, Laminate Flooring, New Cars, New Jersey, Pilot, Printing, SEO, Used Cars, Weight Loss, Weight Loss Program, AdWords, Akiles, Americas Got Talent, Analytics, Asset Management, Asset Management IT, Asset Management Technology

TMZ

- Website: www.tmz.com
- Description: TMZ is a website where you can read and discuss the latest gossip in the world of entertainment. See celebrities at their best and worst on TMZ. Photos, videos, interviews, and much more from your favorite celebrities are available.

- Alexa Rank: 1
- Compete Rank: 1
- Compete Volume: 1
- Referring Domains: 1
- Majestic Links: 1
- Similar Tags: SEO, Social Media, Android, API, App Stores, Apps, Arcade Games, Basketball, Cable TV Deals, Comcast Deals, Condos for Rent Hawaii, Counter Surveillance, Counterespionage, Daenemark, Danmark, Denmark, Development, Downloads, Eavesdropping Detection, Entertainment, Eve Zaremba, Facebook Games, Ferien, Ferienhaus, Ferienhausvermietung, Ferienwohnung, Finance, Focus, Free Games, Gastric Band

Yardbarker

- Website: www.yardbarker.com
- Description: Yardbarker provides sports news gossip and discussion.
- Alexa Rank: 98
- Compete Rank: 100
- Compete Volume: 1
- Referring Domains: 21
- Majestic Links: 21
- Similar Tags: SEO, Social Media, Web Marketing, Agent, Android, Android Apps, App Community, App Development, App Store, App Stores, Apps, Arcade Games, Art, Auction, Auction Site, Auction Sites, Auctions, Bank Owned Foreclosures, Beezid, Best Apps, Blade, Bootstrapping, Branding, Build an App, Cataract, Chabluk, Chris Powell, Chris Powell Diet, Chris Powell Diet Plan, Chris Powell Meal Plan

Health

Whether you're in the medical field or like selling crunchy granola bars to nature-nuts, this section showcases a variety of social apps and communities where health-conscious users congregate.

Active

- Website: www.active.com
- Description: Active.com is the leading online community for people who want to discover, learn about, share, register for, and ultimately participate in activities about which they are passionate.

- Alexa Rank: 99
- Compete Rank: 100
- Compete Volume: 1
- Referring Domains: 90
- Majestic Links: 39
- Similar Tags: Entrepreneurship, SEO, Travel, Used Car Dealer, Blogging, Dealership, Marketing, Startups, Auto, Automobiles, Automotive, Best Anti Aging Wrinkle Cream, Car, Car Dealer Check, Car Dealer Reviews, Car Dealers, Cars, Cheap Holidays, Community, Dealer, Deals, Digital Marketing, Entrepreneurs, Finance, Holidays, Honda, Kids Insoles, New Cars, Search Engine Optimization, Service

dailymile

- Website: www.dailymile.com
- Description: This site lets you share your training with friends and stay motivated. Find training partners, local events, routes, and groups as well as social training for runners, triathletes, and cyclists.
- Alexa Rank: 94
- Compete Rank: 100
- Compete Volume: 1
- Referring Domains: 4
- Majestic Links: 2
- Similar Tags: Social Media, Marketing, SEO, Blogging, Search Engine Optimization, Business, Entrepreneurship, Social Networking, Travel, Ecommerce, Real Estate, Finance, Fitness, Internet Marketing, Mobile, PPC, Twitter, Used Car Dealer, Car Dealer Reviews, Car Dealers, Cars, Golf, Online Marketing, Photography, Sports, Startups, Technology, Video, Affiliate Marketing, Automotive

Families

- Website: www.families.com
- Description: This site lets you meet other parents to share tips and ask advice.
- Alexa Rank: 88
- Compete Rank: 100
- Compete Volume: 1
- Referring Domains: 20
- Majestic Links: 8

- Similar Tags: Social Media, Search Engine Optimization, SEO, Travel, Entrepreneurship, Marketing, Blogging, Used Car Dealer, Business, SEO Professional, Social Networking, Startups, Technology, Web Design, Dealership, Development, Finance, Holidays, Internet Marketing, iPhone, Laminate Flooring, Mobile, Photography, Real Estate, Social Media Marketing, Venture Capital, Web Marketing, Accord, AdWords, Affiliate Marketing

43Things

- Website: www.43things.com
- Description: 43Things is a social networking site where users create accounts and then share lists of goals and hopes.
- Alexa Rank: 95
- Compete Rank: 100
- Compete Volume: 1
- Referring Domains: 37
- Majestic Links: 14
- Similar Tags: Social Media, SEO, Marketing, Social Media Marketing, Blogging, Social Networking, Entrepreneurship, Internet Marketing, Photography, Search Engine Optimization, Technology, Travel, Real Estate, Startups, Web Design, Web Development, Web Marketing, Cooking, Fitness, Advertising, Branding, Cars, Digital Marketing, KnowEm, Music, Online Marketing, Search Engine Marketing, SEM, SEO Professional, Automotive

Mapmyrun

- Website: www.mapmyrun.com
- Description: Plot maps of where you've run and where you want to run. Record varied statistics, including calories burned.
- Alexa Rank: 94
- Compete Rank: 100
- Compete Volume: 1
- Referring Domains: 13
- Majestic Links: 8
- Similar Tags: SEO, Search Engine Optimization, Travel, Social Media, Business, Entrepreneurship, Holidays, Marketing, Photography, Weight Loss, AdWords, Basketball, Blogging, Business Development, Cheap Holidays, Ecommerce, Kids Insoles, Martial Arts, Sales, Startups, Venture Capital, Web Development, Weight Loss Program, Advertising, Airports, All Inclusive Holidays, All Nighter, Alternate Energy, Analytics, Android

SparkPeople

- Website: http://sparkpeople.com/
- Description: SparkPeople.com is a free online diet and healthy living community with over 3 million members who provide support and motivation to each other.
- Alexa Rank: 99
- Compete Rank: 100
- Compete Volume: 1
- Referring Domains: 24
- Majestic Links: 13
- Similar Tags: Blogging, Marketing, Photography, Social Media, Technology, Cataract, Healthcare, Management, Pay Per Click, Real Estate, Sales, Search Engine Optimization, SEO, Absence Management, Accord, AdWords, Affiliate Marketing, Air Compressors, API, Art, Art History, Autobiography, B2B, B2C, Beading, Biography, Blade, Blog Development, Blogger, Bluray Authoring

Information

The answers to every question you ever had, as well as every question you never knew to ask—an inquisitive bunch linger in these social nooks and crannies. Do you have the answers to their burning questions? Step inside, listen to the chatter, and consider reaching out with some insight.

Scribd

- Website: www.scribd.com
- Description: Scribd is a social publishing site, where tens of millions of people share original writings and documents.
- Bonus Primary Value: Promote link-worthy content
- Alexa Rank: 100
- Compete Rank: 100
- Compete Volume: 1
- Referring Domains: 100
- Majestic Links: 100
- Similar Tags: Social Media, SEO, Social Media Marketing, Blogging, Social Networking, Marketing, Internet Marketing, Search Engine Optimization, Music, Technology, Travel, Web Design, Photography, Entrepreneurship, Search Engine Marketing, Real Estate, SEO Professional, Web Development, Advertising, Online Marketing, Social Media Consulting, Web Marketing, Art, Business, Games, Internet, Startups, Design, Media, News

Wikipedia

- Website: www.wikipedia.org
- Description: Wikipedia is a free encyclopedia with millions of articles contributed collaboratively using wiki software in dozens of languages.
- Bonus Primary Value: Strong profile rankings
- Alexa Rank: 100
- Compete Rank: 100
- Compete Volume: 1
- Referring Domains: 100
- Majestic Links: 100
- Similar Tags: SEO, Internet Marketing, Social Media, Blogging, Music, Art, Search Engine Optimization, SEM, Social Media Marketing, Social Networking, Web Development, Web Marketing, Google, Photography, PHP, SEO Professional, Technology, Anime, Auto Insurance, Cooking, Copywriter, Design, Digital Art, Entrepreneurship, Games, Health, Internet, Linux, Marketing, News

Yahoo!

- Website: www.yahoo.com
- Description: Yahoo! lets you quickly find what you're searching for, get in touch with friends, and stay in the know with the latest news.
- Bonus Primary Value: Promote link-worthy content
- Alexa Rank: 100
- Compete Rank: 100
- Compete Volume: 1
- Referring Domains: 100
- Majestic Links: 100
- Similar Tags: Social Media, Social Media Marketing, SEO, Social Networking, Internet Marketing, Music, Marketing, Photography, Blogging, Search Engine Optimization, Web Design, Technology, Travel, Web Development, Design, Search Engine Marketing, Web Marketing, SEO Professional, Social Media Consulting, Real Estate, SEM, Art, Entrepreneurship, Internet, Online Marketing, Sports, Web 2.0, Advertising, Family, Fashion

about.me

- Website: http://about.me
- Description: about.me lets you create a unique website that's all about you and your interests. Upload a photo, write a short bio, and add your favorite social networks to show the world what you're all about.

- Alexa Rank: 99
- Compete Rank: 100
- Compete Volume: 1
- Referring Domains: 33
- Majestic Links: 23
- Similar Tags: Social Media, Blogging, SEO, Search Engine Optimization, Social Media Marketing, Social Networking, Photography, Web Design, Internet Marketing, Marketing, SEO Professional, Technology, Travel, Art, Internet, Fashion, Business, Entrepreneurship, Finance, Real Estate, Web Development, Commercial Vehicle, Computers, Design, Eicher Trucks Dealers, Entrepreneur, Music, News, Shopping, Startups

Answers

- Website: www.answers.com
- Description: The site provides Q&A combined with a free online dictionary, thesaurus, and encyclopedias. Ask important questions and receive quick, educated answers.
- Alexa Rank: 100
- Compete Rank: 100
- Compete Volume: 1
- Referring Domains: 100
- Majestic Links: 100
- Similar Tags: Search Engine Optimization, Social Media, Entrepreneurship, SEO, Blogging, Photography, Startups, Web Design, Internet Marketing, Search Engine Marketing, Social Media Marketing, Travel, Web Development, Backpacking, Business, Camping and Adventures, Computers, Hiking, Holidays, Indiana, LinkedIn, News, Outdoors, SEO Professional, Shopping, Social Networking, Used Car Dealer, Venture Capital, Video Marketing, Weight Loss

Netvibes

- Website: www.netvibes.com
- Description: Netvibes was the first personalized dashboard-publishing platform for the Web. The site focuses on digital life management, widget distribution services, and brand observation rooms.
- Alexa Rank: 100
- Compete Rank: 100
- Compete Volume: 1
- Referring Domains: 100

- Majestic Links: 100
- Similar Tags: Social Media, SEO, Blogging, Social Media Marketing, Web Design, Internet Marketing, Marketing, Chabluk, Darren Chaluk, Dinar, Dinars, Drdinar, Internet, Iraq Dinar, Iraqi Dinar, Search Engine Optimization, Photography, SEO Professional, Technology, Art, Design, SEO Services Company, Social Media Consulting, Social Networking, Web 2.0, Web Development, Cars, Consulting, Digital Marketing, Email Marketing

Suite101

- Website: www.suite101.com
- Description: Suite101 is a place to publish, discuss, and discover ideas on any topic. It provides a network of writers, bloggers, experts, and teachers sharing their knowledge, opinions, and experiences.
- Alexa Rank: 100
- Compete Rank: 100
- Compete Volume: 1
- Referring Domains: 100
- Majestic Links: 17
- Similar Tags: Search Engine Optimization, Social Media, SEO, Social Media Marketing, Social Networking, Web Design, Web Development, Art, Blogging, Digital Marketing, Ecommerce, Entrepreneurship, Golf, Marketing, Online Marketing, Sales, Search Engine Marketing, SEO Professional, Used Car Dealer, Accents, Accessories, Advertising, AdWords, Affiliate Marketing, Akiles, Analytics, Artist, Auction, Auction Site, Auction Sites

wikiHow

- Website: www.wikihow.com/Main-Page
- Description: wikiHow is a wiki-based collaboration whose goal is to build the world's largest, highest-quality how-to manual. Its multilingual how-to manual has free step-by-step instructions on how to do all types of things.
- Alexa Rank: 100
- Compete Rank: 100
- Compete Volume: 1
- Referring Domains: 73
- Majestic Links: 12
- Similar Tags: SEO, Internet, Social Media, Entrepreneurship, Search Engine Optimization, Startups, Blogging, Business, Marketing, Social Networking,

Used Car Dealer, Web Design, Cms, Dealership, Digital Marketing, Ecommerce, Holidays, Honda, Music, Sales, Travel, Venture Capital, Active Inverter, Art, Asset Management, Asset Management IT, Asset Management Technology, Auto, Auto Insurance, Automobile

Microblogging

Microblogging is like blogging, only smaller! Microbloggers are usually on-the-go, in the field, ready to roll, and quick to engage. And yes, there *are* platforms aside from Twitter that they use.

Plurk

- Website: www.plurk.com
- Description: Plurk is a social journal for your life. If you're tired of your existing social networks, share your life easily with friends, family, and fans on Plurk.
- Bonus Primary Value: Strong profile rankings
- Alexa Rank: 100
- Compete Rank: 100
- Compete Volume: 1
- Referring Domains: 42
- Majestic Links: 70
- Similar Tags: Social Media, SEO, Social Media Marketing, Search Engine Optimization, Marketing, Travel, Technology, Blogging, Internet Marketing, Music, Photography, Social Networking, Web Design, Web Development, SEM, Online Marketing, Internet, Search Engine Marketing, Web Marketing, Advertising, Design, Entrepreneurship, Real Estate, SEO Professional, Art, Education, Automotive, WordPress, Business, Digital Marketing

Twitter

- Website: http://twitter.com
- Description: Twitter is a free social network that allows messaging, or "tweets" of up to 140 characters. Twitter is all about real-time events and updates. Jokes, news, photos, quotes, and inspirational messages can be found every second on Twitter. Aside from connecting with and following friends on Twitter, users can explore tweets from artists, celebrities, brands, athletes, and musicians.
- Bonus Primary Value: Promote link-worthy content
- Alexa Rank: 100
- Compete Rank: 100
- Compete Volume: 1

- Referring Domains: 100
- Majestic Links: 100
- Similar Tags: Social Media, SEO, Social Media Marketing, Internet Marketing, Blogging, Marketing, Music, Social Networking, Web Design, Technology, Search Engine Optimization, Travel, Photography, Web Development, Design, Internet, Art, Online Marketing, Advertising, SEM, Branding, Web Marketing, Business, Social Media Consulting, Entrepreneurship, Sports, Movies, Search Engine Marketing, SEO Professional, Writing

formspring

- Website: www.formspring.me
- Description: Formspring allows you to create a box where friends can ask questions anonymously, or you can answer random questions from the community. Post your responses to Tumblr, Twitter, Facebook, or your blog.
- Alexa Rank: 100
- Compete Rank: 100
- Compete Volume: 1
- Referring Domains: 65
- Majestic Links: 79
- Similar Tags: Social Media, SEO, Social Media Marketing, Blogging, Marketing, Photography, Web Design, Internet Marketing, Music, Social Networking, Web Development, Search Engine Optimization, Art, Sports, Technology, Travel, Design, Internet, Reading, SEO Professional, Web Marketing, Entrepreneurship, Online Marketing, Startups, Affiliate Marketing, Business, Computers, Ecommerce, Email Marketing, Fashion

Foursquare

- Website: http://foursquare.com
- Description: Foursquare is the premiere geolocation application for your smart phone. It allows you to "check in" to physical places to visit. It also doubles as an online social network. Foursquare gives you and your friends new ways to explore your city, earn points, and unlock badges by experiencing new things.
- Alexa Rank: 100
- Compete Rank: 100
- Compete Volume: 1
- Referring Domains: 44
- Majestic Links: 25

- Similar Tags: Social Media, Social Media Marketing, Blogging, SEO, Marketing, Technology, Music, Internet Marketing, Photography, Travel, Web Design, Web Development, Social Networking, Search Engine Optimization, Entrepreneurship, Internet, SEM, Twitter, Web Marketing, Facebook, Online Marketing, Business, Media, Movies, SEO Professional, Affiliate Marketing, Design, Gadgets, Reading, Startups

FriendFeed

- Website: `http://friendfeed.com`
- Description: Allows you to build a customized feed comprised of content your friends on other collaborative sites have shared, including news articles, videos, photos, and more.
- Alexa Rank: 100
- Compete Rank: 100
- Compete Volume: 1
- Referring Domains: 100
- Majestic Links: 100
- Similar Tags: Social Media, SEO, Blogging, Social Media Marketing, Internet Marketing, Technology, Travel, Marketing, Music, Social Networking, Photography, Web Design, Search Engine Optimization, Web Development, Internet, Design, Art, Advertising, SEM, Web Marketing, Entrepreneurship, Real Estate, Search Engine Marketing, Twitter, Web 2.0, Cooking, Online Marketing, Business, Games, Movies

identi.ca

- Website: `http://identi.ca`
- Description: identi.ca is a social microblogging service similar to Twitter, built on open source tools and open standards. Identi.ca has a great community with very helpful and insightful members.
- Alexa Rank: 98
- Compete Rank: 100
- Compete Volume: 1
- Referring Domains: 67
- Majestic Links: 75
- Similar Tags: Social Media, SEO, Travel, Social Media Marketing, Marketing, Internet Marketing, Search Engine Optimization, Blogging, Technology, Music, Social Networking, Photography, Web Design, SEM, Web Development,

Advertising, Web Marketing, Design, Entrepreneurship, Internet, Real Estate, Search Engine Marketing, Online Marketing, Sports, Art, Education, News, Startups, Automotive, Business

Music

Tune in, turn on, drop out! These music-centric social networks attract rock stars from all corners of the world: artists, songwriters, record producers, or just straight-up fans. Hunt around and have fun.

last.fm

- Website: www.last.fm
- Description: This online music catalog offers free music streaming, videos, photos, lyrics, charts, artist biographies, concerts, and Internet radio.
- Bonus Primary Value: Strong profile rankings
- Alexa Rank: 100
- Compete Rank: 100
- Compete Volume: 1
- Referring Domains: 100
- Majestic Links: 100
- Similar Tags: Social Media, SEO, Marketing, Social Media Marketing, Blogging, Music, Social Networking, Web Design, Internet Marketing, Search Engine Optimization, Technology, Travel, Photography, Internet, Web Development, Web Marketing, Design, Entrepreneurship, Art, Movies, PPC, Games, Online Marketing, SEM, Video, Web 2.0, Writing, Fitness, SEO Professional, Advertising

8tracks

- Website: http://8tracks.com/
- Description: Personalized Internet radio created by the user. 8tracks has music from numerous genres, including hip-hop, indie, rock and roll, pop, top 40, and anything else you could possibly think of.
- Alexa Rank: 98
- Compete Rank: 100
- Compete Volume: 1
- Referring Domains: 7
- Majestic Links: 2
- Similar Tags: SEO, Marketing, Social Media Marketing, Blogging, Social Media, Social Networking, Art, Business, Design, Digital Marketing, Entrepreneurship,

Holidays, Internet Marketing, SEO Professional, Startups, Travel, Animals, Asset Management, Asset Management IT, Asset Management Technology, Auto Insurance, Automotive, Blogger, Business Credit, Business Credit Builder, Car Dealer Reviews, Car Dealers, Cheap Holidays, Credit, Designer

BLIP.fm

- Website: http://blip.fm
- Description: Become a DJ and discover new music or share the music you love with a large and ever-growing audience. BLIP.fm lets you listen to a continuous stream of songs played by any of its members, or you can be the DJ and gain fans based on your selections.
- Alexa Rank: 96
- Compete Rank: 100
- Compete Volume: 1
- Referring Domains: 18
- Majestic Links: 73
- Similar Tags: Social Media, SEO, Blogging, Social Media Marketing, Music, Marketing, Social Networking, Internet Marketing, Technology, Photography, Travel, Search Engine Optimization, Art, Entrepreneurship, Twitter, Facebook, Affiliate Marketing, Design, Internet, Online Marketing, Reading, Web Design, Movies, News, Politics, SEM, Video, Automotive, Cooking, Real Estate

DatPiff

- Website: www.datpiff.com
- Description: DatPiff is a hip-hop social network that lets users listen to free music, new mixes, and hot artists' tracks. Users can download free mix tapes.
- Alexa Rank: 99
- Compete Rank: 100
- Compete Volume: 1
- Referring Domains: 18
- Majestic Links: 9
- Similar Tags: Entrepreneurship, Search Engine Optimization, Social Media, Travel, Asset Management, Asset Management IT, Asset Management Technology, Basketball, Cheap Holidays, Computers, Family, Grappling, Holidays, Investment Management Cloud, Investment Management Reporting, Investment Management Technology, Mobile Marketing, Music, SEO, Social Media Marketing, Startups, Wealth Management, Weight Loss, Weight Loss Program, Advertising, AdWords, Agent, Ajax, Akiles, All Inclusive Holidays

ReverbNation

- Website: www.reverbnation.com
- Description: ReverbNation allows independent bands to create a formidable web presence. Bands can also upload their music to iTunes and sell their record. Bands can easily connect to other social network platforms like Facebook and Twitter.
- Alexa Rank: 100
- Compete Rank: 100
- Compete Volume: 1
- Referring Domains: 76
- Majestic Links: 44
- Similar Tags: Social Media, SEO, Internet Marketing, Marketing, Real Estate, Social Networking, Entrepreneurship, Karen Briggs, Music, Paul Dateh, PPC, Social Media Marketing, Buying Property Abroad, Search Engine Optimization, Startups, Art, Black Violin, Blogging, Buy Overseas Property, Buy Property, Daniel D, Design, Development, Digital Marketing, Disaster Recovery, Ecommerce, Emaily Wells, Entrepreneurs, Facebook, Golf

SoundCloud

- Website: http://soundcloud.com
- Description: SoundCloud is a large community of musicians, fans, producers, record labels, and journalists who come together to hear new music, demo tracks, and experimental works in progress. User-generated content is key at SoundCloud.
- Alexa Rank: 100
- Compete Rank: 100
- Compete Volume: 1
- Referring Domains: 100
- Majestic Links: 68
- Similar Tags: Social Media, SEO, Search Engine Optimization, Marketing, Technology, Music, Photography, Travel, Art, Real Estate, Automotive, Entrepreneurship, Internet, Social Media Marketing, Dealership, Search Engine Marketing, Social Networking, Startups, Used Car Dealer, Web Design, Advertising, Blogging, Car, Car Dealer Reviews, Car Dealers, Computers, Design, Gadgets, Games, Holidays

News

Extra! Extra! Read all about it! These niche social networks are bringing the news to their communities—politics, celeb gossip, breaking stories, and everything in between. Hint: Scour the comment threads for the juiciest goods from passionate community members.

Fark

- Website: www.fark.com
- Description: Fark provides interesting, bizarre, and amusing news stories, along with regular photo manipulation contests.
- Bonus Primary Value: Promote link-worthy content
- Alexa Rank: 99
- Compete Rank: 100
- Compete Volume: 1
- Referring Domains: 100
- Majestic Links: 100
- Similar Tags: Social Media, Internet Marketing, Travel, SEO, Search Engine Optimization, Social Networking, Blogging, Technology, Marketing, Social Media Marketing, Search Engine Marketing, Web Marketing, Art, Entrepreneurship, Music, Photography, Web Design, Automotive, Business, Car Dealer Reviews, Car Dealers, Cars, Design, Movies, SEM, SEO Professional, Sports, Web Development, Development, Finance

Newsvine

- Website: www.newsvine.com
- Description: Register to read recent news, add a news story, comment, or write a column. Newsvine is an open source community news service that lets its members customize the news.
- Bonus Primary Value: Promote link-worthy content
- Alexa Rank: 99
- Compete Rank: 100
- Compete Volume: 1
- Referring Domains: 100
- Majestic Links: 100
- Similar Tags: SEO, Social Media, Marketing, Blogging, Internet Marketing, Travel, Social Media Marketing, Search Engine Optimization, Social

Networking, Technology, Web Design, Business, Entrepreneurship, Internet, Photography, Cars, Music, SEM, Startups, Web Development, Web Marketing, Cooking, Email Marketing, Online Marketing, PPC, Web 2.0, Advertising, Automotive, Branding, Car Dealer Reviews

NowPublic

- Website: www.nowpublic.com
- Description: NowPublic is a Vancouver-based information platform for participatory news-gathering. Find global posts of news, photos, video, and more.
- Bonus Primary Value: Promote link-worthy content
- Alexa Rank: 97
- Compete Rank: 100
- Compete Volume: 1
- Referring Domains: 39
- Majestic Links: 28
- Similar Tags: Social Media, Marketing, SEO, Internet Marketing, Technology, Blogging, Social Media Marketing, Travel, Business, Development, Ecommerce, KnowEm, Photography, PPC, Search Engine Optimization, Social Networking, Affiliate Marketing, Entrepreneur, Entrepreneurship, iPhone, Mobile, Online Marketing, Real Estate, Search, Social Media Optimization, Sports, Video, Web Design, WordPress, Adventure

Reddit

- Website: www.reddit.com
- Description: Reddit collects user-generated news links. User votes promote stories to the front page or knock them down. The Reddit community is large and educated and loves its online news.
- Bonus Primary Value: Direct link sources
- Alexa Rank: 100
- Compete Rank: 100
- Compete Volume: 1
- Referring Domains: 100
- Majestic Links: 100
- Similar Tags: Social Media, SEO, Internet Marketing, Social Media Marketing, Marketing, Search Engine Optimization, Technology, Travel, Web Design, Social Networking, Blogging, Photography, Music, Web Development, Internet,

Web Marketing, Advertising, SEM, Entrepreneurship, Fitness, Search Engine Marketing, SEO Professional, Art, Design, Health, Online Marketing, Business, Cars, Games, News

Technorati

- Website: http://technorati.com
- Description: Technorati provides real-time search for user-generated media by tag, keyword, or phrase. Technorati also provides popularity indexes.
- Bonus Primary Value: Strong profile rankings
- Alexa Rank: 100
- Compete Rank: 100
- Compete Volume: 1
- Referring Domains: 100
- Majestic Links: 100
- Similar Tags: Social Media, SEO, Social Media Marketing, Internet Marketing, Blogging, Web Design, Social Networking, Technology, Marketing, Photography, Search Engine Optimization, Music, Travel, Advertising, SEM, Web Marketing, Design, Internet, Web Development, SEO Professional, Entrepreneurship, Art, Business, Branding, Online Marketing, Movies, Search Engine Marketing, Web 2.0, Affiliate Marketing, News

Gawker

- Website: http://gawker.com
- Description: Gawker prides itself on bringing all celebrity news, rumors, gossip, and ridiculous news from around the nation. From the bright lights of Broadway to the Hollywood Hills, you are not safe from Gawker and its investigative rumors and gawks.
- Alexa Rank: 100
- Compete Rank: 100
- Compete Volume: 1
- Referring Domains: 100
- Majestic Links: 100
- Similar Tags: Social Media, SEO, Marketing, Photography, Technology, Internet, News, Real Estate, Social Media Marketing, Social Networking, Sports, Art, Blogging, Cooking, Dogs, Facebook, Fitness, Laminate Flooring, Lasik, Management, Music, Politics, Programming, Sales, Video, Web Design, Apartments, Asia, Carpet, Ceramic Flooring

Huffington Post

- Website: www.huffingtonpost.com
- Description: Arianna Huffington's Internet newspaper, the Huff Post offers syndicated columnists, blogs, and news stories with moderated comments.
- Alexa Rank: 100
- Compete Rank: 100
- Compete Volume: 1
- Referring Domains: 100
- Majestic Links: 100
- Similar Tags: Social Media, SEO, Marketing, Travel, Blogging, Entrepreneurship, Internet Marketing, Search Engine Optimization, Web Design, Social Networking, Design, KnowEm, Photography, Real Estate, Social Media Marketing, Technology, Advertising, Affiliate Marketing, Art, Cars, Digital Marketing, Search Engine Marketing, Startups, Business, Car Dealer Reviews, Car Dealers, Internet, News, Social Media Optimization, Used Car Dealer

MyAlltop

- Website: http://my.alltop.com/
- Description: MyAlltop is an online news collective. Users share the top stories floating around the Web. Started by Guy Kawasaki, this site is one of the top online news providers in the business.
- Alexa Rank: 99
- Compete Rank: 100
- Compete Volume: 1
- Referring Domains: 21
- Majestic Links: 17
- Similar Tags: Social Media, SEO, Blogging, Marketing, Social Media Marketing, Internet Marketing, Travel, Search Engine Optimization, Social Networking, Web Design, Art, Entrepreneurship, Music, Photography, Advertising, Automotive, Business, Design, SEO Professional, Technology, Used Car Dealer, Cars, Email Marketing, Internet, Marketing Communications, PPC, Real Estate, Sports, Web Development, Web Marketing

Photo

Photo enthusiasts of the world, unite! These social communities are fertile playgrounds for photographers and everyone else who just likes taking and sharing pics online. One, two, three, smile!

23HQ

- Website: www.23hq.com
- Description: 23HQ makes photo sharing easy for beginners and advanced users. Share private or public with photo albums, tags, storage, slideshows, photoblogs, and subscriptions; send photos; and much more.
- Bonus Primary Value: Direct link sources
- Alexa Rank: 86
- Compete Rank: 100
- Compete Volume: 1
- Referring Domains: 15
- Majestic Links: 16
- Similar Tags: Social Media, SEO, Entrepreneurship, Search Engine Optimization, Art, Design, Photography, Startups, Used Car Dealer, Artist, Blogging, Community, Dealership, Holidays, Honda, Internet, Social Networking, Texas, Travel, Venture Capital, Web Design, Active Inverter, AdWords, Asset Management, Asset Management IT, Asset Management Technology, Auto, Automobiles, Automotive, Basketball

Flickr

- Website: www.flickr.com
- Description: Show off your favorite photos and videos to the world with Yahoo! hosted Flickr. Flickr lets users share photos with just their friends or with the public.
- Bonus Primary Value: Strong profile rankings
- Alexa Rank: 100
- Compete Rank: 100
- Compete Volume: 1
- Referring Domains: 100
- Majestic Links: 100
- Similar Tags: Social Media, Photography, SEO, Social Media Marketing, Blogging, Travel, Internet Marketing, Web Design, Search Engine Optimization, Social Networking, Technology, Music, Marketing, Web Development, Art, Internet, Design, Entrepreneurship, Movies, SEM, Games, Video, Web Marketing, Facebook, Fitness, Graphic Design, Media, Online Marketing, Social Media Consulting, Twitter

DailyBooth

- Website: http://dailybooth.com
- Description: Snap a photo of yourself every day and share them with your friends.
- Alexa Rank: 98
- Compete Rank: 100
- Compete Volume: 1
- Referring Domains: 21
- Majestic Links: 9
- Similar Tags: Social Media, SEO, Social Networking, Search Engine Optimization, Social Media Marketing, Technology, Photography, Travel, Internet Marketing, Marketing, Blogging, Affiliate Marketing, Web Design, Web Marketing, Art, Business, Web Development, Advertising, Cars, Design, Entrepreneurship, Fitness, Internet, Search Engine Marketing, Twitter, Automotive, Facebook, Music, Politics, Sports

Instagram

- Website: http://instagram.com
- Description: This site lets users snap a photo, add a filter, add a hash tag with categories and locations, and share with their Instagram community.
- Similar Tags: Social Media, SEO, Social Networking, Search Engine Optimization, Social Media Marketing, Technology, Photography, Travel, Internet Marketing, Marketing, Blogging, Affiliate Marketing, Web Design, Web Marketing, Art, Business, Web Development, Advertising, Cars, Design, Entrepreneurship, Fitness, Internet, Search Engine Marketing, Twitter, Automotive, Facebook, Music, Politics, Sports

Photobucket

- Website: http://photobucket.com
- Description: This site lets users store, create, and share their photos and videos.
- Alexa Rank: 100
- Compete Rank: 100
- Compete Volume: 1
- Referring Domains: 100
- Majestic Links: 100
- Similar Tags: Social Media, Social Media Marketing, Art, Social Networking, Travel, Blogging, Internet Marketing, Photography, SEO, Entrepreneurship,

Basketball, Design, Holidays, Internet, Marketing, SEO Professional, Video Marketing, Web Design, Advertising, Affiliate Marketing, Animals, Designer, News, Search Engine Optimization, Swimming, Video, Website Design, Writing, Active Inverter, Artist

Tech

Polish your specs and insert your pocket protectors. These tech-tastic communities are the perfect attractions for digitally savvy users.

DotNetKicks

- Website: www.dotnetkicks.com
- Description: DotNetKicks.com is a community-based news site edited by its members. It specializes in .NET development techniques, technologies, and tools, including ASP.
- Bonus Primary Value: Promote link-worthy content
- Alexa Rank: 82
- Compete Rank: 100
- Compete Volume: 1
- Referring Domains: 22
- Majestic Links: 45
- Similar Tags: Search Engine Optimization, Social Media, Entrepreneurship, Marketing, SEO, Real Estate, SEO Professional, Social Networking, Web Marketing, Website Design, Cars, Internet Marketing, Search Engine Marketing, Social Media Marketing, Startups, Web Design, Auto, Automobiles, Automotive, Blog Development, Blogging, Business Development, Car, Car Dealer Check, Car Dealer Reviews, Car Dealers, Cataract, Cheap Holidays, CMS, Community

Slashdot

- Website: http://slashdot.org
- Description: This site is a source for technology-related news, with a heavy slant toward Linux and open source issues.
- Bonus Primary Value: Promote link-worthy content
- Alexa Rank: 100
- Compete Rank: 100
- Compete Volume: 1
- Referring Domains: 100

- Majestic Links: 100
- Similar Tags: Social Media, SEO, Marketing, Social Networking, Internet Marketing, Blogging, Internet, Music, Search Engine Optimization, Social Media Marketing, Technology, Games, SEM, Web Design, Apple, Automotive, Business, Mac, Real Estate, Social Media Optimization, Web Development, Advertising, Art, Car, Car Dealer Reviews, Car Dealers, Cars, Computers, Design, Development

bitly

- Website: `http://bitly.com/`
- Description: Bitly is a bookmarking site that offers URL redirection service with real-time link tracking. It allows users to collect and share various links with the world.
- Alexa Rank: 100
- Compete Rank: 100
- Compete Volume: 1
- Referring Domains: 100
- Majestic Links: 100
- Similar Tags: Social Media, Social Media Marketing, SEO, Internet Marketing, Social Networking, Advocacy, Blogging, Search Engine Optimization, SEM, SEO Professional, Entrepreneurship, Music, Travel, Web Design, Consultancy, Marketing, Photography, Search Engine Marketing, Social Media Consulting, Startups, Web Development, Actmind, Advertising, Affiliate Marketing, Asset Management IT Awareness, Basketball, Education, Email Marketing, Environment

Gizmodo

- Website: `http://gizmodo.com/`
- Description: Gizmodo is a technology blog about consumer electronics. It's known for up-to-date coverage of the technology industry and the personal, humorous, and sometimes very inappropriate writing style of the contributors.
- Alexa Rank: 100
- Compete Rank: 100
- Compete Volume: 1
- Referring Domains: 100
- Majestic Links: 100

- Similar Tags: SEO, Social Media Marketing, Social Media, Blogging, Social Networking, Web Design, Internet, Internet Marketing, Marketing, SEO Professional, Digital Marketing, Entrepreneurship, Facebook, Programming, Search Engine Optimization, Social Media Optimization, Software, Video, Web Development, Advertising, Branding, Business, Computers, Copywriting, Education, Email Marketing, Fitness, Gadgets, Games, Graphic Design

Sourceforge

- Website: http://sourceforge.net/
- Description: This open source applications and software directory offers fast, secure, and free downloads.
- Alexa Rank: 100
- Compete Rank: 100
- Compete Volume: 1
- Referring Domains: 100
- Majestic Links: 100
- Similar Tags: Social Media, Blogging, Basketball, Marketing, Search Engine Optimization, Video, Best Anti Aging Wrinkle Cream, Entrepreneurship, Gadgets, Music, Photography, Project Management, Sales, SEO, Shopping, Social Networking, Swimming, Website Design, WordPress, AdWords, Agrandamiento Del Pene, Agrandar El Pene, Americas Got Talent, Android Apps, Anfrohel, Anti Aging, Anti Aging Face Care, Anti Aging Skin Care Cream, Anti Aging Supplements, Art

Travel

Pack your bags—we're off on a quest to identify travel lovers! These social media channels welcome users who love to travel, share their experiences, gain feedback or advice, swap travel pics and stories, and more.

CouchSurfing

- Website: www.couchsurfing.com
- Description: This is a volunteer-based worldwide network connecting travelers with members of local communities who offer free accommodation, activities, and advice on exploring their local area.
- Bonus Primary Value: Direct link sources
- Alexa Rank: 1
- Compete Rank: 100

- Compete Volume: 1
- Referring Domains: 19
- Majestic Links: 3
- Similar Tags: Social Media, Travel, SEO, Marketing, Search Engine Optimization, Internet Marketing, Social Media Marketing, PPC, Social Networking, Art, KnowEm, Search Engine Marketing, Web Design, Web Marketing, Affiliate Marketing, Basketball, Blogging, Cars, Ecommerce, Entrepreneurship, Music, Real Estate, SEO Services Company, Small Business, Staffing, Technology, Video, Website Marketing, AdWords, Airline Cheap Fares

Loggel

- Website: www.loggel.com
- Description: Loggel is an online diary for travelers who spend their time all over the world.
- Alexa Rank: 100
- Compete Rank: 100
- Compete Volume: 1
- Referring Domains: 1
- Majestic Links: 1
- Similar Tags: Marketing, Social Media, Travel, SEO, Holidays, Social Networking, Asset Management, Asset Management IT, Asset Management Technology, Automotive, Blogging, Business, Car Dealer Reviews, Car Dealers, Cheap Holidays, Digital Marketing, Finance, Investment Management Cloud, Investment Management Reporting, Investment Management Technology, Marketing Services, Texas, Vacations, Wealth Management, Weight Loss, Weight Loss Program, ADP, Adventure, Advertising, Agent

Lonely Planet

- Website: www.lonelyplanet.com
- Description: Lonely Planet is as collective of travel guides, forums, and unique travelers from all over the world who band together to share their experiences and help future travelers have a better trip.
- Alexa Rank: 100
- Compete Rank: 100
- Compete Volume: 1
- Referring Domains: 100

- Majestic Links: 38
- Similar Tags: SEO, Social Media, Travel, Holidays, Marketing, SEO Professional, Social Media Marketing, Social Networking, Blogging, Business, Internet Marketing, Skiing, Blogger, Entrepreneurship, Finance, Internet, Real Estate, Startups, Web Design, Advertising, Affiliate Marketing, Asset Management, Asset Management IT Asset Management Technology, Basketball, Cheap Holidays, Digital Marketing, Downloads, Ecommerce Positioning, Entrepreneur

Qype

- Website: www.qype.co.uk
- Description: UK-based Qype users post about restaurants, hotels, and exciting travel destinations all over the world.
- Alexa Rank: 97
- Compete Rank: 100
- Compete Volume: 1
- Referring Domains: 11
- Majestic Links: 100
- Similar Tags: SEO, Social Media, Blogging, Travel, Search Engine Optimization, Social Media Marketing, Social Networking, Entrepreneurship, Marketing, Affiliate Marketing, Internet Marketing, Real Estate, Advertising, Business, Development, Ecommerce, Holidays, PPC, Search Engine Marketing, Startups, Technology, Used Car Dealer, Video, Web 2.0, AdWords, Art, Basketball, Cars, Consulting, Cooking

Video

These sites are perfect for videographers, filmmakers, or ordinary people who like to watch videos of people falling down or cats doing hilarious things.

YouTube

- Website: www.youtube.com
- Description: Google-owned YouTube is a place where people come to watch videos with friends, share their own videos, comment on videos, watch television shows and movies, create playlists, and create their own YouTube channel. Founded in February 2005, YouTube allows billions of people to discover, watch, and share originally created videos. YouTube provides a forum for people to connect, inform, and inspire others across the globe. YouTube also acts as a distribution platform for original content. You can even make money from YouTube by allowing advertisements to run on your YouTube videos.

- Bonus Primary Value: Strong profile rankings
- Alexa Rank: 100
- Compete Rank: 10
- Compete Volume: 1
- Referring Domains: 100
- Majestic Links: 100
- Similar Tags: Social Media, SEO, Blogging, Social Media Marketing, Marketing, Internet Marketing, Social Networking, Music, Travel, Photography, Search Engine Optimization, Web Design, Technology, Design, Advertising, SEM, Web Development, Internet, Entrepreneurship, Online Marketing, Reading, SEO Professional, Art, Movies, Social Media Consulting, Search Engine Marketing, Web Marketing, Fitness, Branding, Health

Blip

- Website: http://blip.tv/
- Description: Blip is a site that simplifies video podcasting and vlogging by using its own software through a web-based interface. Users share thoughts on politics, sports, TV, or movies or create original content such as web-based TV shows.
- Alexa Rank: 99
- Compete Rank: 100
- Compete Volume: 1
- Referring Domains: 100
- Majestic Links: 51
- Similar Tags: Marketing, SEO, Social Media, Social Media Marketing, Social Networking, Blogging, Digital Marketing, Entrepreneurship, Startups, Basketball, Holidays, Internet, Marketing Services, Online Marketing, Search Engine Optimization, SEO Professional, Texas, Travel, Venture Capital, Video, Web Design, Advertising, Android, Asset Management, Asset Management IT, Asset Management Technology, Automotive, Branding, Business, Car Dealer Reviews

Dailymotion

- Website: www.dailymotion.com
- Description: Dailymotion is about finding new ways to see, share, and engage your world through the power of online video. Users can upload personal videos to share.
- Alexa Rank: 100

- Compete Rank: 100
- Compete Volume: 1
- Referring Domains: 100
- Majestic Links: 100
- Similar Tags: Social Media, Internet Marketing, Marketing, Social Media Marketing, SEO, Social Networking, Technology, Travel, Blogging, Advertising, Search Engine Optimization, Music, Web Design, Entrepreneurship, Internet, Photography, Real Estate, Cars, Coaching, Games, Health, Network Marketing, Automotive, Car Dealers, Interactive Marketing, Media, Movies, News, Online Marketing, Video

Funny Or Die

- Website: www.funnyordie.com
- Description: Funny or Die is a collective of funny videos featuring celebrities, comedians, and users from all over the world. The site was started by Will Ferrell, Adam McKay, and Chris Henchy.
- Alexa Rank: 100
- Compete Rank: 100
- Compete Volume: 1
- Referring Domains: 57
- Majestic Links: 14
- Similar Tags: Social Media, Travel, Marketing, SEO, Entrepreneurship, Internet Marketing, Search Engine Optimization, Social Networking, Technology, Automotive, Blogging, Car Dealer Reviews, Car Dealers, Cars, KnowEm, Photography, Startups, Used Car Dealer, Video, Art, Business, Car, Holidays, Music, SEO Professional, Auto, Automobiles, Car Dealer Check, Dealership, Entrepreneur

Hulu

- Website: www.hulu.com
- Description: Hulu is a website that offers commercial-supported streaming video of TV shows and movies from NBC, Fox, ABC, and many other networks and studios. Hulu videos are currently offered only to users in the United States.
- Alexa Rank: 100
- Compete Rank: 100
- Compete Volume: 1
- Referring Domains: 63
- Majestic Links: 16

- Similar Tags: Social Media, Social Media Marketing, Marketing, SEO, Music, Photography, Search Engine Optimization, Cleaning, Colon Cleanse, Detox Diet, Fast Weight Loss, Internet Marketing, Lemonade Diet, Master Cleanse, Social Networking, Travel, Blogging, Web Design, Web Development, Cooking, Entrepreneurship, Movies, Finance, Internet, Media, Reading, Technology, Advertising, Art, Business

Metacafe

- Website: www.metacafe.com
- Description: One of the world's largest video sites in the Web, Metacafe serves up short-form videos, funny movies, clips, sports videos, and video game information.
- Alexa Rank: 100
- Compete Rank: 100
- Compete Volume: 1
- Referring Domains: 100
- Majestic Links: 94
- Similar Tags: Social Media, Internet Marketing, Marketing, SEO, Social Media Marketing, Blogging, Online Marketing, Social Networking, Search Engine Optimization, Travel, Advertising, Business, Digital Marketing, Entrepreneurship, Internet, Photography, Real Estate, Technology, Art, Automotive, Startups, Design, Music, Network Marketing, Web Design, Affiliate Marketing, Car Dealer Reviews, Car Dealers, Cars, Education

Vimeo

- Website: www.vimeo.com
- Description: Vimeo is a respectful community of creative people who are passionate about sharing the videos they make.
- Alexa Rank: 100
- Compete Rank: 100
- Compete Volume: 1
- Referring Domains: 100
- Majestic Links: 100
- Similar Tags: Social Media, Marketing, Social Networking, SEO, Social Media Marketing, Search Engine Optimization, Travel, Music, Photography, Blogging, Design, Internet Marketing, Technology, Web Design, Advertising, News, Entrepreneurship, Online Marketing, Web 2.0, Internet, Affiliate Marketing, Branding, Business, Games, Search Engine Marketing, SEO Professional, Sports, Web Development, Web Marketing, Art

Content, Reputation, and Hardcore Listening Hacks

This chapter looks at one of the pillars of community management: content. Everything that publishers publish and users generate is content. Every single tweet, blog mention, Facebook post, magazine citation, YouTube comment, Wikipedia article, and ripoffreport.com rant is content. All sorts of players crank out content. Well-spun official brand content is doggedly earned by PR agency placements, and everyday users publish at will in social media. Content includes brand mentions, products, and people. Pretty much anything any person might say can and will be mentioned online by somebody. In this chapter, you'll learn how to listen to content for the purpose of reputation monitoring, sharing, and creating your own content. Let's rock this out.

4

Chapter Contents

The Importance of Content
Publishing Content on Websites You Own
Building RSS Dashboards Powered by Business Rules
Outlook Dashboard Building Tutorial
Sourcing Feeds

The Importance of Content

Content published on the Internet is important to brands for many reasons:

- Obviously, any time something is published mentioning your brand terms, it's important. Listening to brand-specific content, including real time in social channels, is generally referred to as reputation monitoring.

- Many types of content, published on a website or mentioned in social, will be indexed by Google, Bing, and other search engines. Customers who search for your brand may discover this content.

- Listening to other keywords matters to community managers (CMs) too. If you're the manufacturer of specialized running belts, you might want to monitor content that speaks to running shoes technology and marathon running, because running belts are a great compliment to those products.

- Of course, mentions of competitors' brand terms are important listening points for CMs. We want to know what's happening out there.

- Staying in tune with content about the industry or category of your products and services can be a crucial aspect of creating your own content.

Community management is all about listening, publishing valuable content that connects with our audience in a human way, engaging with the community, and managing our reputation. So how do all of these work together? Serving up our own content, as well as curating third-party content for sharing, is a big part of our job as marketers. But doing this most effectively requires programmatic listening so we gain access to the right buzz about our brand at the right time.

There is little difference between how we listen to content and conversations about interests versus listening to content and conversations about our brand terms and those of our competitors. Listening to third-party content and chatter surrounding words representing our brand's trademarked and copyrighted assets is called *reputation monitoring*.

The mechanics involved in staying abreast of salient content to share with the community are the same as those related to reputation monitoring. We set up dashboards that check channels for mentions of important keywords. The system sends us alerts when vital keywords are triggered. Reputation is simply another type of third-party content to zero in on.

Also, others are listening to you. Creating great and targeted content is the total inverse of monitoring third-party content and should be undertaken with a firm understanding that others are listening and may react. Several skills of community management are the most important to master; we need to be able to create informed content for others to hear and publish it properly, all while we are listening to third-parties react to our brand, and while we are staying completely tuned in so we can hear tightly related third-party content offerings.

Publishing Content on Websites You Own

Above all, the most important thing to do in online marketing is driving traffic to sites you own for conversion and/or subscription. Subscriptions should result in or assist future conversions. If conversion metrics seemingly don't justify your participation in social, then look to attribution models to see how social traffic assists conversions. All of this holds true across both paid and social. Does the traffic yield or assist conversions? Ask this over and over again. We believe that social media content strategy ultimately needs to somehow be about building traffic and conversions to websites we own.

Importance of Owning Your Content

Fundamentally, your content should be hosted on domains, pages, and applications your brand controls, and then shared out for amplification in social to draw in fans and new users. Next, the content should be shared across your channels as appropriate. Such timed content releases have been standard since the *Mad Men* days. That sounds so familiar. In this sense, social media as a list building/subscription/conversion marketing channel changes nothing as to how things have always been.

Facebook is a double-edged sword because you don't own Facebook. Facebook can decide to kick you out to varying degrees whenever it wants. This is no different than before. Google can kick you out, too. Furthermore, Facebook is the one deciding what you can do with your fans, not you. Facebook owns Facebook. You own whatever FB lets you own, even among the fruits of your community-building labor. And even then, nothing's for certain.

Though goal-oriented conversions (KPIs) can certainly take place in Facebook, marketers have the least control, and they never truly own the process. This is true for most, if not all, social networks. LinkedIn leads are gathered by LinkedIn's system. We're always beholden to data points and terms of service platforms placed on the APIs that reflect data structure they want us to see. We can be restricted at any time, including to further monetize the social community.

The best Facebook strategy results in channeling new brand awareness by way of content to a growing psychographic segment that likes and follows back to root content on the brand's website.

Twitter is pretty much the same in terms of API worries and business justification for being in the channel. Sure, Twitter's cool and social and stuff. But how much do you really own by building even a tightly focused and highly functional Twitter list? Arguably, you have a neat list and a mechanism with which to market it. Still, how do you monetize and measure Twitter? This much can be debated, but one thing's for sure: Driving traffic to convert over time on your own website is always a KPI that deserves prioritization.

Of course, social has tons of benefits outside of conversion. Twitter and Facebook profiles index and rank prominently in Google organic search engine results. New friends can be made, customer support tendered, and all sorts of gorgeous stuff.

Most social channels also rock for building lists of fans and followers who essentially opt in to listen to a brand's feed. Just be mindful when it comes to where you share your content goodies.

Tactics to Own the Benefits of Buzz and Engagement

The always-on premise of jigging campaigns to promote websites we own is subject to the creativity of the marketer, not the idiosyncrasies of distributing content on any particular social channel. A great marketing idea is a great marketing idea, no matter which channel it is executed in. The *how* of focusing any campaign's ultimate gain on building brand.com's website is a marketing conundrum, not a distribution method question. Here lies yet another reason to judge social media success by measuring traffic and contribution to conversions on sites we own.

Think of your site as a real-world street address storefront, where you sell, say, hockey equipment. Your goal is to get people to the store. What could you say to get those parents and rink rats in the family car and get them to drive to your hockey store? The most important marketing question is: What reason do our customers have for coming to our store?

Answers to that age-old marketing question are only as creative as the marketer. Sure, the hockey store can offer high-quality skate sharpening for free with complimentary hot chocolate while new customers wait in the lovely store, strolling around looking at all the groovy inventory for a fair price.

Another classic tactic to bring foot traffic home is to earn trust by offering resources. For instance, the hockey site could host a free nutrition best-practices seminar by the respected local sports physician who serves the University of Minnesota Duluth Bulldogs women's hockey team. This approach can work with proper promotion. When the hockey families come through the store by any method, direct them to resources on your blog to aid in the gear-buying decision or healthy eating. The point is that people will do whatever it takes, even walk places (with their feet!), to receive something they perceive as valuable. You want traffic to assets you own? Create value, and then distribute and promote it properly.

These metaphors all apply to social media as well. The hockey store in the online metaphor is the home site, brand.com. The goal is to promote awareness of the wonderful resources placed on your site, whether they are physical or virtual events, sales, tools, applications, contents, or whatever, so social users who receive an impression (reach) click on the content object and come to your site. That means you need to a) create content that compels users to do so, and b) make sure the content sees the light of day. It's crucial to make sure that enough eyeballs see the content to give it a shot.

Leveraging an Editorial Calendar

Google loves fresh content. Social media loves fresh content. Publishing fresh content on a schedule is everything. Having a system in place that spans progression of creating content objects is essential. This is about creating a schedule and winning the marketing game by having a higher level of organization. Use editorial calendars; they are cool because great planning increases your chances for success. Every client and in-house department has various cycles to honor. The ongoing process of choosing topics, researching, writing, approving, and publishing in a number of social channels requires organization. Time is a variable as well. Interview requests go out, and writing is scheduled and coordinated with stakeholders.

According to Wikipedia:

An editorial calendar is used by bloggers, publishers, businesses, and groups to control publication of content across different media, for example, newspaper, magazine, blog email newsletters, and social media outlets like Twitter and Facebook fan pages. They are an extremely efficient way to control publication of content across diverse media outlets over time.

As you bring content to market, transforming your website into a publication, focus content creation on drawing in all parts of the organization. Ask what seasonal activities, events, and initiatives are taking place in all corners of the company and when key industry trade conferences take place. Put that all on the editorial calendar. Be prepared to support it with content. Think of your site as a feed, a place where the public life of your company is reflected.

Create your "mechanicals." There are some forms of content that are inherently viral as vanity bait, as discussed in Chapter 2, "Timeless Tenets of Non-Gratuitous Social Behavior." Link roundups, video roundups, editorial reviews, interviews, featured bloggers, communities, and companies are great examples. They draw in by design and require very little work (for you). Put these on the editorial calendar along with due dates for each step of the process. Make your own library based on your content and layers of approval. Later you'll include content amplification tactics to trail content releases with stepped support. For now, it's cool to know what's going to be published when, with a great plan in place.

Here are some examples of language for an editorial calendar that covers content production organization. How many of these you use depends on the level of approval and processes required. The steps may differ if you are writing in-house or for yourself, as opposed to in an agency environment. Think of your editorial calendar as a refrigerator and these snippets as magnetic poetry to arrange as marketing orders by date.

Topics Selected, Submitted For Approval	Receive Feedback From Team
	Implement Tweaks From Feedback
Topics Approved	Submit Draft Two For Final
Research Post	Review
Write Post	Stage Post In Blog
Research & Write Post	Publish Post
Submit Post For Approval	

After the mechanicals are slotted on the calendar, schedule the premium content, such as release of research, features, and editorial regarding important news items, press release teases, and event marketing. If you know there is going to be an important event in the company, from new-product launches to the latest community program, plan it ahead of time. Put the run-up on the calendar as far ahead as possible. Include layers of approvals and any unique steps your situation dictates, including compliance steps in regulated verticals such as pharmaceuticals and banking.

Be prepared for opportunities to present themselves and require damage control. It's not possible to plan all content, that's for sure. However, it is entirely possible to plan much of the freshly created content everybody loves. Oh, and be sure to schedule the day you are to create the next editorial calendar.

Editorial Calendar Template

 Head over to aimclear.com/cm/chapter4 and grab the sample editorial calendar template (as shown in Figure 4.1) for your own use. It includes a snippet library to get you started, and a tab with a sample. Import our template into Excel or Google Docs and have at it planning your publication.

@aimClear®

February, 2012

	Monday	Tuesday	Wednesday	Thursday	Friday	Saturday
	13	14	15	16	17	18
Production	Feature Posts #3 & #4 Topics Selected & Approved. **Serialized Post #1** Returned with Feedback	Feature Posts #3 & #4 Researched & Written	Serialized Post #2 Topic Selected & Approved. **Link Round Up #2** Post Selected	Feature Posts #3 & #4 Submitted for Review. **Serialized Post #2** Researched & Written	Feature Posts #3 & #4 Returned with Feedback. **Link Round Up #3** Topic Selected. **Serial Post #2** Submitted for Review	
Publication & Promotion	Link Round Up #1 Researched, Written, Staged, & Published	Publish Feature Post #1	Publish **Serialized Post #1**	Publish Feature Post #2	Link Round Up #2 Researched, Written, Staged, & Published	
	27	28	29			
Production	Feature Posts #5 & #6 Topics Selected & Approved. **Serialized Post #2** Returned with Feedback	Feature Posts #5 & #6 Researched & Written	Serialized Post #3 Topic Selected & Approved. **Link Round Up #4** Post Selected	Feature Posts #5 & #6 Submitted for Review. **Serialized Post #2** Researched & Written	Feature Posts #5 & #6 Returned with Feedback. **Link Round Up #5** Topic Selected. **Serial Post #3** Submitted for Review	
Publication & Promotion	Link Round Up #3 Researched, Written, Staged, & Published	Publish Feature Post #3	Publish **Serialized Post #2**	Publish Feature Post #4	Link Round Up #4 Researched, Written, Staged, & Published,	
Notes:						

Figure 4.1 Sample editorial calendar

Why Personal Dashboards Rule

We know that listening is listening, whether we're monitoring trademarked or registered keywords or picking up a thread about organic weed eradication in a blog post somewhere about lawnmowers. The tools we listen with are dashboards.

If you think about it, all of us consume our email in a dashboard and we use it as such every day. Google Apps, Outlook, and Lotus email user interfaces (UIs) are all dashboards. In these dashboards we flag and open messages in, reply to, delete, mark as spam, forward, forward based on keyword rules in the email subject and body, and mark as read. The channel is email. The usage is to monitor our inbound and outbound email feed, react, and handle.

The secret to understanding power dashboarding is to treat Really Simple Syndication (RSS) feed items (objects) like email. The email subject is analogous to the RSS headline and the email body to the RSS body. Most of the cool channels we listen to (Google, Facebook, Twitter, blogs, etc.) are available as RSS feeds. The ones not available can often be scraped and set to custom feed, including automated login by proxy.

The dashboard we'll show you how to create in this chapter will serve you forever in concept, because no matter how sophisticated the feed you subscribe to, you can dashboard it with all your other sources. Other sources range from all of Google to a single user in a single community you are watching. Get Google Alerts? Dashboard them here. You'll aggregate true multinational, multilingual feed segmentation via Sysomos. Log in to that central trade forum of 35,000 users that matter most to you on earth, search it, and feed that.

Great dashboards handle RSS from any inbound channel you're listening to, processed by the same business metaphors as email. Dashboards aggregate feeds from many channels, including boutique aggregators. Consider this. Facebook, Google, Twitter—every channel—is somehow an aggregator. The output can be fed by RSS in most cases. You can build a dashboard to aggregate the aggregators and take charge of what triggers alerts and what you see when.

The second half of this chapter is a guerrilla tutorial for dashboarding filtered RSS feeds, which are crucial for monitoring one's reputation and content. It can be used to monitor reputation in search, news, social, and other verticals. You'll be able to easily build a tool where nobody can even whisper your business keywords, in a positive or negative light, without your awareness. If you subscribe to advanced tools, you'll be able to aggregate their feeds into whatever else you're listening to, including your email.

Outlook and Applying Business Rules to Feed Objects

There used to be a lot more feed readers out there, but now they're built into iOS and Microsoft Office software. Microsoft has one software title that, to our mind, has not been equaled in mainstream adoption: Outlook. What makes Outlook special is its library of business rules for handling inbound emails as objects. There are many ways to filter inbound emails and act on a specific email with a variety of important actions.

Outlook treats RSS feeds similarly to email, and most of the same rules can be applied to RSS objects. This broke the ground for us, making it possible to create personal dashboards. Even now that we build reputation monitoring dashboard tools, we still use Outlook for various applications.

The business rules in Outlook, combined with the nested hierarchy of feeds, make Outlook more robust than most mainstream solutions. The raw listening power is awesome. The caveat is that Outlook does not provide any analysis, which is interesting because we've always thought that what we monitor is as important as how we monitor. However, sometimes fancy listening tools provide deep analysis on the wrong list of keywords. That said, we've seen sentiment analysis keyword lists in homemade Outlook dashboards that rivaled the biggest players. Sentiment analysis is about the keyword list, not about the dashboard that is listening.

The tutorial in this chapter is set in Windows. Outlook was way cooler for Windows a long time before it was for Mac but we doubt it's still as cool. We're devoted Mac users and use VMware Fusion to run the most current Windows OS live on Mac. It works really well. Please note that we have not tested Outlook for Mac for the processes in the tutorial.

Building RSS Dashboards Powered by Business Rules

The Outlook system (exportable by Outline Processor Markup Language [OPML] and rules) can be used to mine extremely fast alerts from an amazing array of paid and organic channels. In some cases, alerts can be generated much faster than many brands are used to listening to. If you depend on Google Alerts, this chapter could change your life. To advanced readers, you'll enjoy the exercise as a metaphor for what you demand from listening platform providers. Heck, you can dashboard them! This dashboard is a great socket for any custom feed you subscribe to and any guerilla feed you want to hunt down. After the tutorial, there is a list of killer feeds for reputation and content monitoring. We hope you enjoy the show.

Outlook Dashboard Building Tutorial

The entire Outlook dashboard-building tutorial is published in this chapter. It is also available for download here: aimclear.com/cm/chapter4/dashboard. You will need to enter the password **rocketgenius** to get the file.

Choosing Your First Feed

The first order of business is to find something you want to monitor. Our example features the Technology subreddit on Reddit.com, shown in Figure 4.2. After the tutorial, we'll turn you on to tons of cool feeds for dashboard listening.

Figure 4.2 The Technology category on Reddit.com

Reddit's RSS is easy to find—just add `.rss` to the end of the URL. Figure 4.3 shows the RSS code.

Figure 4.3 The code for Technology subreddit RSS feed

Adding the Feed to Outlook

Next, hop into Outlook (note that these instructions are for 2007, although the process will be similar in other versions as well). Right-click on RSS Feeds and choose Add A New RSS Feed (Figure 4.4).

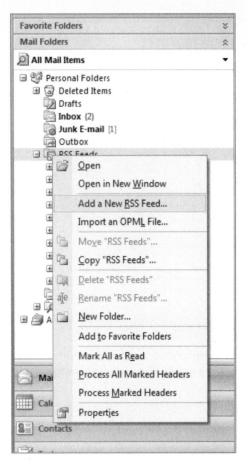

Figure 4.4 The first step in adding an RSS feed to Outlook

When prompted, paste the feed URL into the box (Figure 4.5).

Figure 4.5 Paste the feed URL in the field provided.

Before confirming the subscription, click Advanced, as shown in Figure 4.6. Doing so opens the RSS Feed Options dialog box, as shown in Figure 4.7. Uncheck the bottom check box to enable retrieval faster than the publisher's recommendation. You may also want to check Download The Full Article, which will download each post as an attachment. Figure 4.8 shows the result after adding one RSS feed to Outlook.

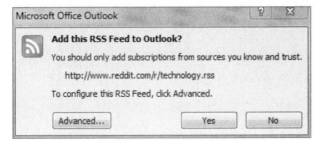

Figure 4.6 Click Advanced in the confirmation box.

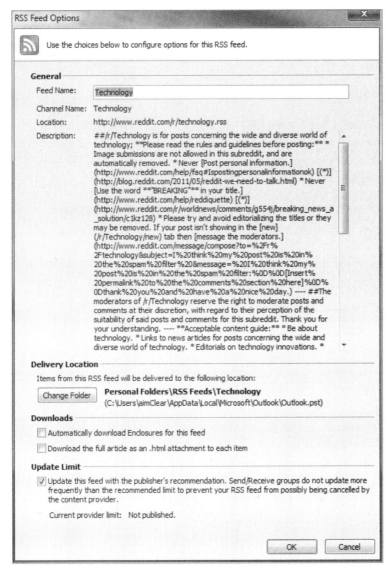

Figure 4.7 The RSS Feed Options dialog box

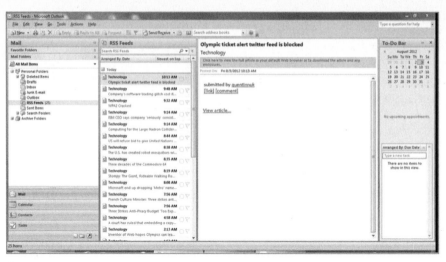

Figure 4.8 You've successfully added your first RSS feed to Outlook.

Reddit's feed only offers the name of the post (as the subject), the post date, the submitter, and the comment count. If you did not check the Download The Full Article check box, you can still click through and download the content for each post individually, as shown in Figure 4.9.

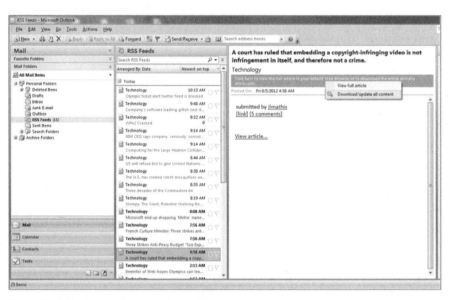

Figure 4.9 Clicking through allows you to download the content.

Figure 4.10 shows what the post looks like as an attachment—the full page, including header, footer, and sidebar information, appears.

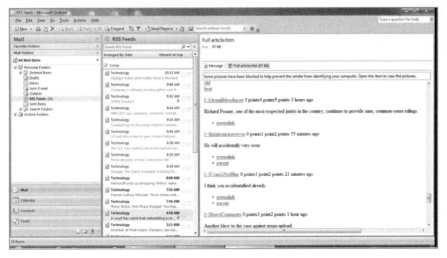

Figure 4.10 Viewing the post as an attachment

Set Send/Receive Interval, Speed as a Variable

Next, you will want to set how often feeds are fetched and mail is sent. Navigate to the Define Send/Receive Groups options by clicking Send/Receive in the toolbar. Then choose Send/Receive Settings from the drop-down menu, as shown in Figure 4.11.

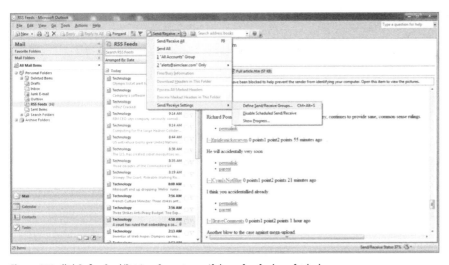

Figure 4.11 Click Define Send/Retrieve Groups to specify how often feeds are fetched.

The default setting is every 30 minutes (Figure 4.12). The maximum frequency Outlook allows is every 2 minutes, which is our preferred setting. This is huge because 2 minutes is fast enough to catch a live conversation somewhere.

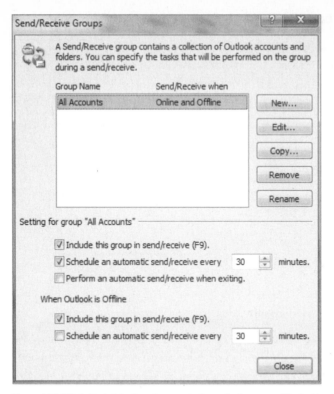

Figure 4.12 This Outlook dialog box allows you to change the frequency of feed retrieval.

Alert! First Business Rule: Filter and Forward

Right now you have a basic RSS reader, but that isn't the fun part. You need to set up email alerts based on certain conditions. In this example, you're going to enable rules to be alerted when certain items are posted.

1. Go to the Rules options by clicking Tools and then selecting Rules And Alerts. Click New Rule (as shown in Figure 4.13).

2. The Rules wizard launches, which allows you to build the rule. Check out Figure 4.14 for a taste. Under Start From A Blank Rule, click Check Messages When They Arrive and click Next.

3. Next you must specify the condition, as shown in Figure 4.15. Check the From RSS Feeds With Specified Text In The Title (or From Any RSS Feed if you will be applying the same rule to all feeds) box.

4. You can now click the blue Specified Text link, and in the RSS Feeds window choose which RSS feeds to search in (Figure 4.16). Click OK.

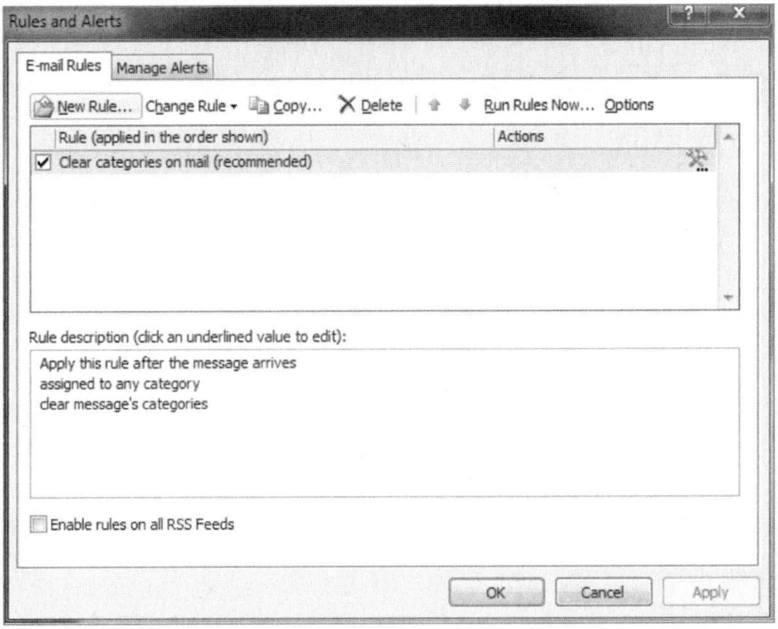

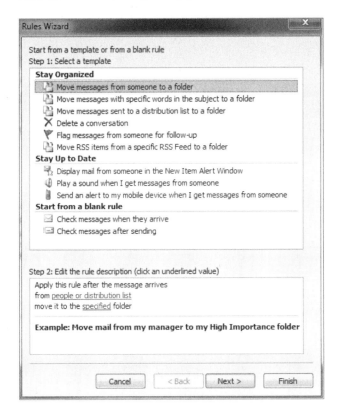

Figure 4.13 Click New Rule to begin setting up email alerts.

Figure 4.14 To set up a new rule, start from a blank rule.

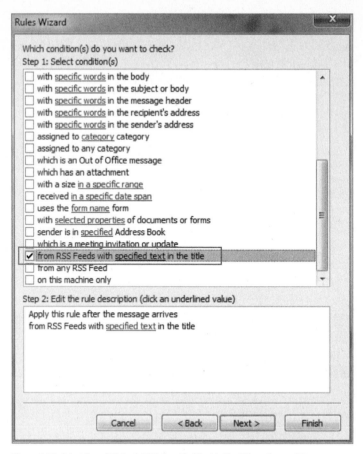

Figure 4.15 Select From RSS Feeds With Specified Text In The Title as the condition.

Figure 4.16 Select the RSS feeds in which to search
for the specified text.

5. The other condition you will use filters out irrelevant posts. As shown in Figure 4.17, check the With Specific Words In The Subject box. Click the blue Specific Words text to bring up the search text box.

Figure 4.17 Check With Specific Words In The Subject to filter by keyword.

6. From the Search Text dialog box, choose which words to include. For the example shown in Figure 4.18, you are looking for posts that mention the United States (or variations of it), so type **u.s.a** in the upper box and hit Add. Continue for any other words and click OK when finished. Click Next.

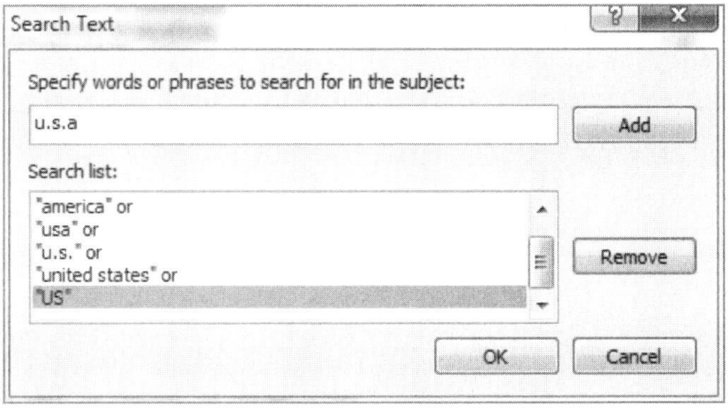

Figure 4.18 Specify words to search for in the post subject.

7. On the next screen, select what to do with messages that match your conditions. Figure 4.19 shows how you forward it to someone monitoring the account (by checking the Forward It To People Or Distribution List), which is our preference.

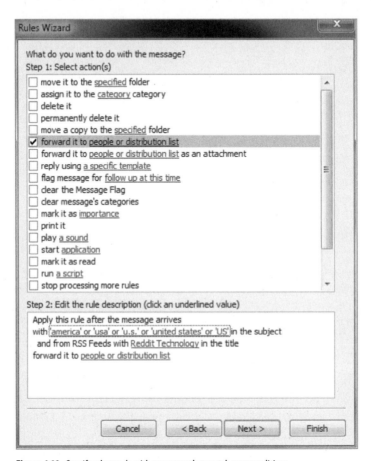

Figure 4.19 Specify what to do with messages that match your conditions.

Clicking the People Or Distribution List link at the bottom brings up your contacts manager (Figure 4.20). Note that the contact must already be in your address book at this point; you cannot add a new address in this step.

8. Click Next again to add exceptions to the rule (Figure 4.21).

In the example shown in Figure 4.22, we're filtering out posts that mention "CISPA" in the title.

9. Name the rule in Step 1, click Turn On This Rule in Step 2, review the description in Step 3, and click Finish (Figure 4.23).

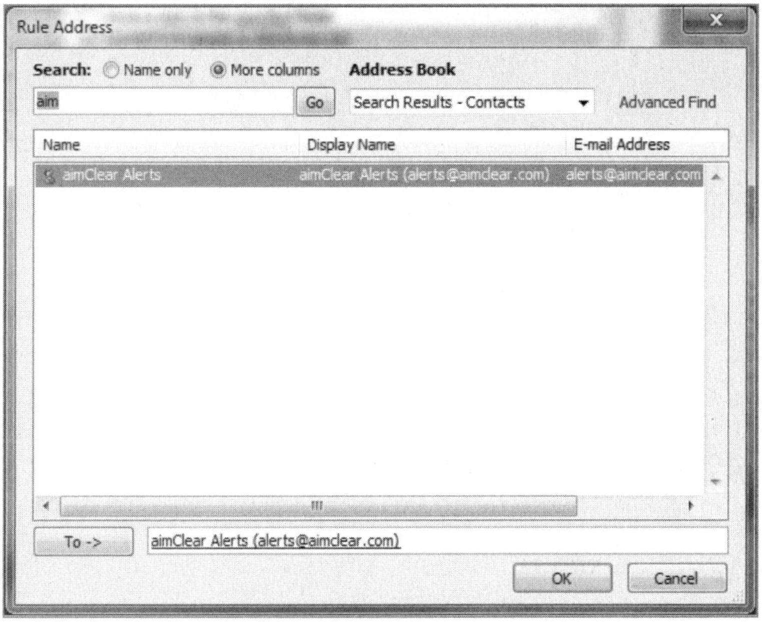

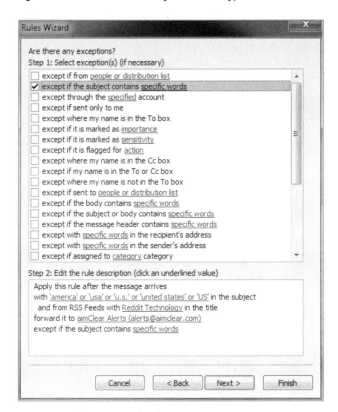

Figure 4.20 Select who to send messages to from among your contacts.

Figure 4.21 Add exceptions to the rule.

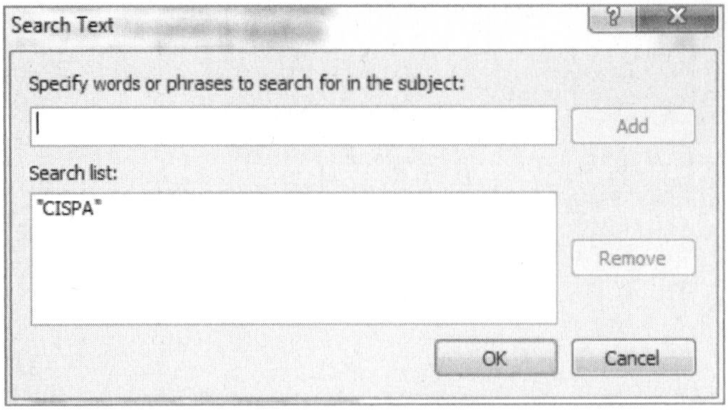

Figure 4.22 Specify keywords to add as an exception to the rule.

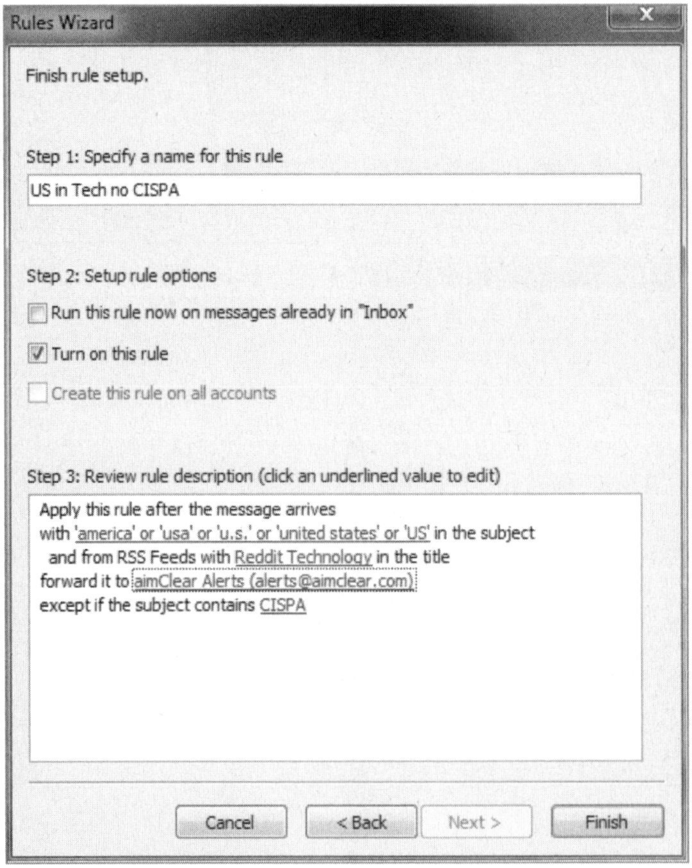

Figure 4.23 Name the rule and click Finish.

OK, Now You're Listening

Phew! That was intense, but we did it. Figure 4.24 illustrates the end result, with our inbox showing messages with technology posts from Reddit relating to the United States.

Figure 4.24 The result of filtering our Reddit Technology RSS feed

Rule: Marking as Read

We recommend adding another rule (optional) to mark all items not matching your conditions as read. Simply create a rule that marks all messages in the specified feed as read, as shown in Figure 4.25.

Rules Wizard

Finish rule setup.

Step 1: Specify a name for this rule

Tech No Rule

Step 2: Setup rule options

☐ Run this rule now on messages already in "Inbox"

☑ Turn on this rule

☐ Create this rule on all accounts

Step 3: Review rule description (click an underlined value to edit)

Apply this rule after the message arrives
from RSS Feeds with Reddit Technology in the title
mark it as read

| Cancel | < Back | Next > | Finish |

Figure 4.25 Create a rule that marks all messages as read.

Move this rule below the previously created rule so that it only affects items not matching any other rules (Figure 4.26).

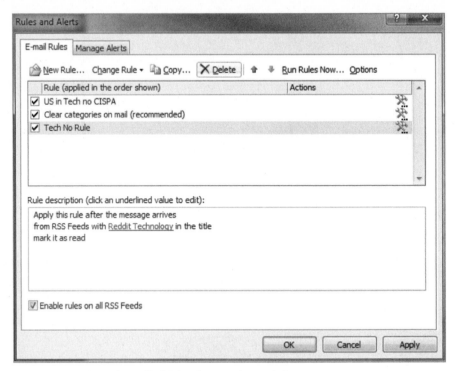

Figure 4.26 Move the "mark as read" rule below the previously created rule.

Rule: Filing Objects

You may also want to adjust your rule to automatically move flagged posts to a new folder for organization purposes, as shown in Figure 4.27.

One thing to watch out for with Reddit RSS feeds is that each time something about the post changes (such as the number of comments), it's treated as a new item and will therefore get cycled through Outlook again. This is effectively alerting you to each new comment, although it can get cumbersome with popular posts that may receive thousands of comments. Use your filter with negative keywords to slow down what you're seeing.

Each channel we deal with will have its own idiosyncrasies. You'll get to know each of the important channels with a little experience. They're all pretty easy.

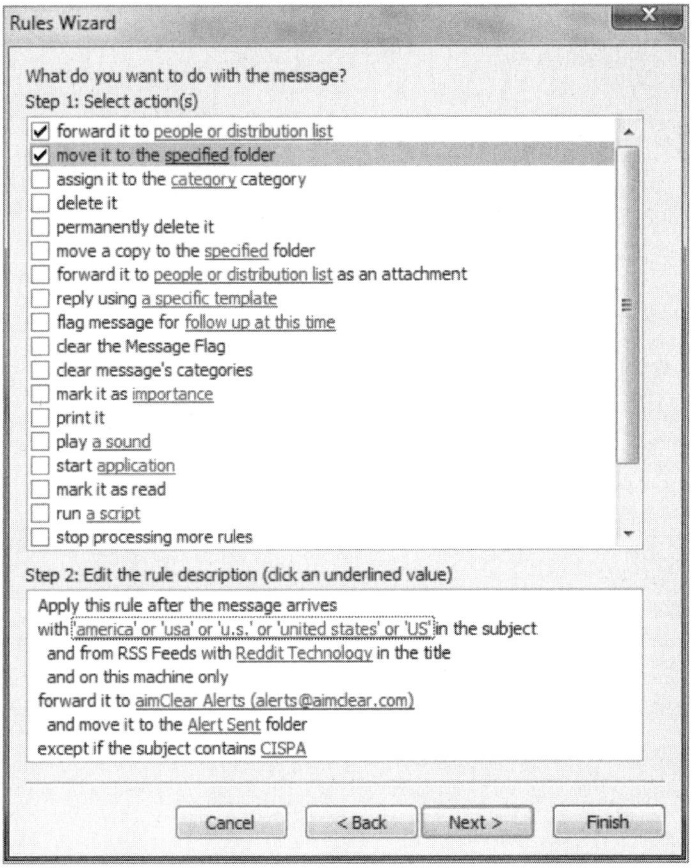

Figure 4.27 Move flagged posts to a specified folder.

Import/Export

You can pilot dashboards on your machine. They can easily be pushed to other Outlook installations. To export a feed for distribution:

1. Click File › Import And Export, as shown in Figure 4.28.

2. On the first page of the Import And Export wizard, choose Export RSS Feeds To An OPML File, as shown in Figure 4.29, and click Next.

3. On the next screen, select the feed(s) you wish to export. All of your Outlook feeds will appear here (Figure 4.30). Click Next when you are done.

4. Choose a location to save the OPML file to (Figure 4.31) and click Next to finish.

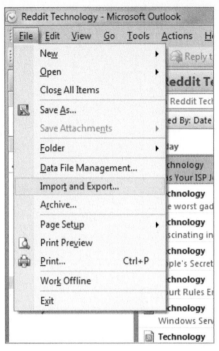

Figure 4.28 Choose Import And Export to export a feed for distribution.

Figure 4.29 Select Export RSS Feeds To An OPML File.

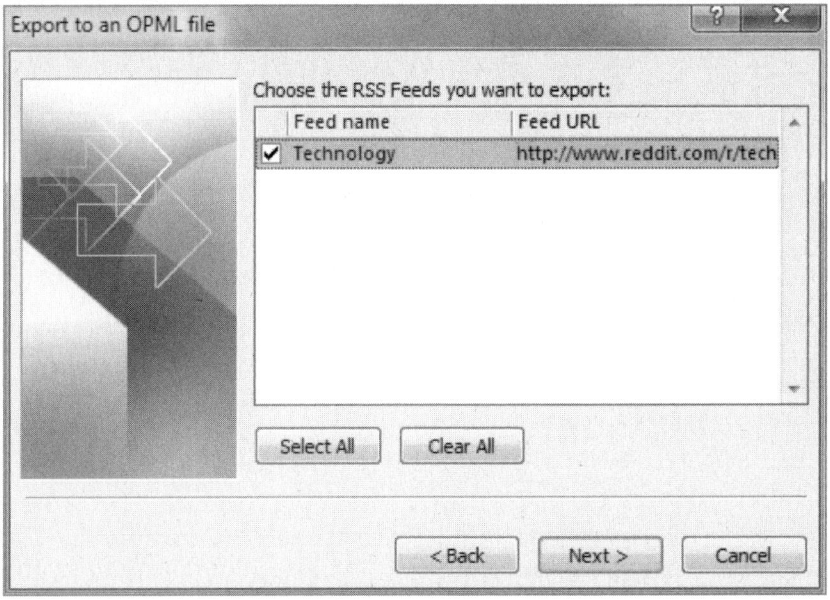

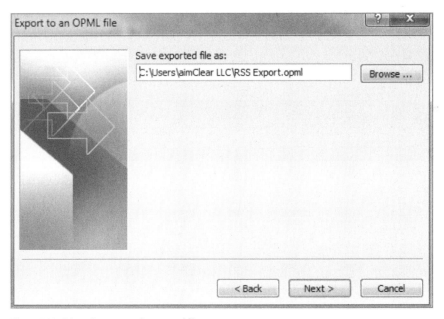

Figure 4.30 Select the feed(s) you'd like to export.

Figure 4.31 Select where to save the exported file.

Importing follows the same steps, but you will choose Import RSS Feeds From An OPML File instead, as shown in Figure 4.32.

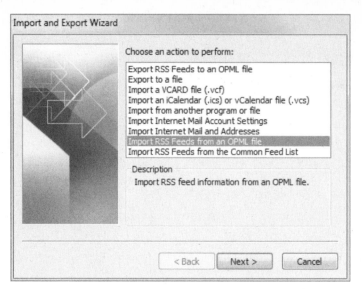

Figure 4.32 To import a feed, select Import RSS Feeds From An OPML File.

To export rules

1. In the Rules And Alerts dialog box (found by clicking Tools in the menu bar and then Rules and Alerts...), on the E-mail Rules tab click Options (Figure 4.33).

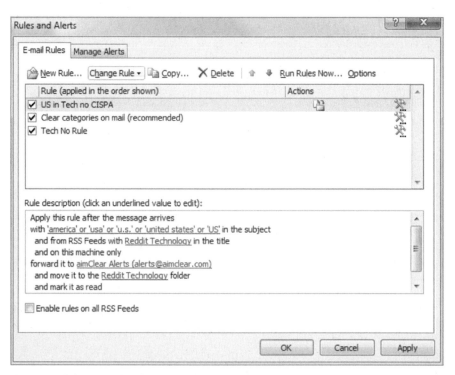

Figure 4.33 Click Options in the Rules And Alerts dialog box to export a rule.

2. In the Options dialog box, click the Export Rules button (Figure 4.34).

Figure 4.34 Click Export Rules.

3. In the Save Exported Rules As dialog box, give your file a name and choose a save location (Figure 4.35). Then click Save.

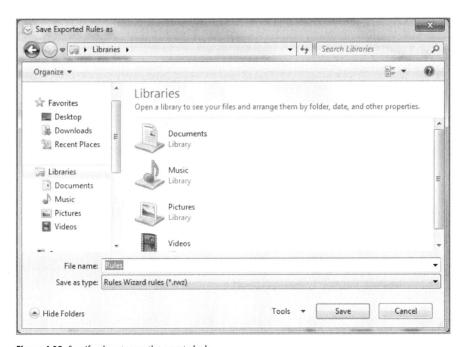

Figure 4.35 Specify where to save the exported rule.

Once again, the steps for importing are exactly the same as exporting, but in the Options dialog box you will choose Import Rules instead (Figure 4.36).

Figure 4.36 Select Import Rules to import a rule.

Sourcing Feeds

By now you get the drill. Listening to content and conversations is fundamental to community management, whether to keep track of content for sharing, competitive intelligence, or straight-up reputation monitoring.

Since you care about brand mentions in every channel, choosing feed sources is important to both content and reputation monitoring. Here are some awesome feed sources to start with. Remember, you can patch in feeds from your expensive tools as well and mash them into these classic sources.

The source feed examples are provided as OPML and Rules export/import. Point your browser to `aimclear.com/cm/chapter4/` to snag the downloads. You'll need the password `firehose`.

Sources

- YouTube full-text search on all videos mentioning `KEYWORD`:
  - `http://gdata.youtube.com/feeds/base/videos?q=KEYWORD&client=ytapi-youtube-search&v=2`.
  - Check out other YouTube feeds at `gdata.youtube.com/demo/index.html`.
  - You can also grab the YouTube feed for Most Recent videos, which will effectively give you all new uploads, at `http://gdata.youtube.com/feeds/api/standardfeeds/most_recent`.
- Social Mention, which cuts a wide swath across blogs, microblogs, bookmarks, comments, events, images, news, video, audit, Q&A, and various networks:
  - `http://api2.socialmention.com/search?q=KEYWORD&t=all&f=rssh`
- Reddit search for `KEYWORD`; includes post title, description, and comments:
  - `www.reddit.com/search/.rss?q=KEYWORD`
  - Or just grab an entire subreddit at `www.reddit.com/r/SUBREDDIT.rss`.

- Facebook fan page for `PAGEIDNUMBER`:
  - `www.facebook.com/feeds/page.php?format=atom10&id=PAGEIDNUMBER`
- BoardReader feed, aggregated from forums all over the Internet, for `KEYWORD`:
  - `www.boardreader.com/rss/KEYWORD.html?p=20&format=RSS2.0`
- AllTop has hundreds of tags to grab feeds from. Search for `KEYWORD` to find tags being used:
  - `http://KEYWORD.alltop.com/rss`

Some companies seem to feel safe under the Google Alerts notification blanket. We don't. It's true that Google Alerts keep reputation managers apprised of content, conversations, news, and so forth, indexed by Google products. However, Google Alerts alone are far from a complete picture of what's going on out there. Social media updates can take days or even weeks to show up, if at all. It's easy to be caught unaware.

Still, it's not unwise to *start* with Google Alerts by RSS. You'll be on par with what most others in America listen to, and you will find out at least as fast as Google emails out keyword alerts.

Google alerts are slightly more complex to add, but still simple. Go to `google.com/alerts` and sign in. Enter your query (you can use any valid search operator such as `site:`). Set the delivery type to Feed, as shown in Figure 4.37.

Figure 4.37 To add Google Alerts to your dashboard, enter your keyword and set the delivery type to Feed.

Clicking Create Alert will now bring you to your dashboard of alerts (Figure 4.38).

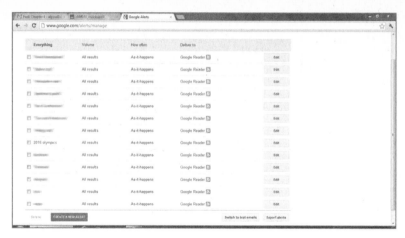

Figure 4.38 Google Alerts dashboard

Click the orange RSS icon, copy the URL, and add it to Outlook. Figure 4.39 shows downloadable examples.

Figure 4.39 Examples of RSS feeds set up in Outlook

Using Mozenda Data Extraction (Scraping) Tools

Sometimes, feeds are simply not available. This is usually because the site's owner doesn't want third parties to be able to mine the data. Issues like these can get very political. Twitter eliminated RSS for searches, and Facebook does not allow feeds for most sections of the site. The answer is Mozenda (Figure 4.40). Although Mozenda is a lightly kept insiders' secret, huge players like Microsoft, Ancestry.com, Harper Collins, IBM, and CTI use it. Visit `http://mozenda.com/` to check it out.

Figure 4.40 Mozenda enables community managers to pull feeds where none are provided by the site.

Mozenda is technically an object-based data extraction tool. With a doable learning curve that is not for the faint of heart, Mozenda empowers community managers to scrape data from almost any public web page, insert it into a database, and crank out the data as a custom RSS feed. Go grab the free Mozenda download and start learning. Mozenda totally rocks and many companies we know use it.

Some major services, including Facebook and Twitter, severely limit our ability to pull feeds down by RSS. The answer is to search and scrape them with Mozenda and create your own RSS feed for use in the dashboard. Of course, check with your closest legal counsel and ask if scraping violates either that channel's terms of services or the law of whatever jurisdiction you're in. Most often, it violates terms of services. However, scraping is a time-tested gray-hat webmaster hack. If you think about it, that's what Google does to your website. Google scrapes the data while crawling websites and reduces data culled to a database. Should we be allowed to scrape Google? We think so, but it's technically against Google's rules.

When scraping big public sites like Bing or Amazon, make sure to be gentle. Mozenda lets operators insert pauses between searches. Some sites, most notably Facebook, are too complex for Mozenda to handle scraping directly. The way around this is to scrape *other* sites that have gained access to Facebook and Twitter. One of our favorite sources for data extraction is IceRocket.com. Using Mozenda to scrape IceRocket, we can pull down Facebook, Twitter, and many other feeds unavailable by standard methods.

Don't worry if IceRocket goes away. There will always be those who scrape mainstream sites that *you can* turn into your scrape food. Scraping Bing gets you special access to Facebook because of Bing's proprietary business arrangement with Facebook which makes the data available. Also, both Google and Bing are awesome to scrape, especially using advanced search operators. Try scraping just Google or Bing news or videos. In fact, it's easy to scrape anything publicly posted by Facebook, Google, Bing, Twitter, and YouTube. Almost everywhere websites are available with no RSS feeds, Mozenda can be leveraged to scrape and bake your own feeds.

Even where there *are* feeds, Mozenda is useful for small but essential parts that are not available by feed. For instance, there are no YouTube comments available anywhere by RSS. Mozenda can easily grab all YouTube comments for any videos returned by any list of keyword searches. It's that powerful.

Finally, community managers can use Mozenda to prewire logins for sites, including username and password. Though it does not work on every site, this function (log in by proxy) is unbelievably mighty. We use it to log into walled-garden forums and niche social sites to automatically search around and feed us data by RSS for inclusion in our dashboards. You can also use it to follow individual users in individual communities. How cool is that?

Firehose and Filter vs. Prefiltering

We'll end this chapter with a housekeeping concept. When you are sourcing feeds for content and reputation monitoring, it's always essential to ask whether the inbound feed is prefiltered by keywords and if it will need any additional filters. The Reddit example was prefiltered in that we used Reddit's ability to output an RSS feed from a subreddit. This essentially means the feed represents an internal Reddit keyword search. The same holds true for Google Alerts mined by RSS feeds pumped into a dashboard. The inbound feed is already prefiltered by keyword. Prefiltering is not always possible. For instance, we can't feed *all* of Google.

The opposite condition is called *firehosing*. An example is taking the entire feed of new YouTube videos and checking it every two minutes. Firehosing is not always possible. Rather it's the full-on blast from YouTube. You can then filter that with Outlook rules. This is cool because, even though the YouTube firehose is on full blast, you only need an instance of the feed and from that firehose, you can filter out what you need for alerts for as many keywords as you like.

In the prefiltered scenario, you need one instance of the feed for each keyword you monitor. When firehosing, you only need one instance of the feed. Ultimately that can require lower overhead, in terms of bandwidth and CPU power running Outlook. Just keep in mind that it's always a tradeoff when you're deciding whether you'll have multiple prefiltered feeds from the same channel or whether you're going to firehose and filter locally using rules.

Most of the nuts and bolts involved in community management essentially surround content and reputation, publishing, and monitoring. Stay with the basics and you'll be successful. Master personal dashboard creation and aggregate feeds, including expensive subscription listening services that offer segments of their data by feed. Be creative when it comes to what feeds you listen to and how to get them.

Most important, publish content on sites you own and radiate the content release out into social channels. Listen carefully to content filtered by keywords important to your endeavor, especially those that include your brand terms for reputation monitoring.

In the next chapter, we'll talk more about using our dashboards to find themed conversations to participate in. Happy dashboarding!

Find Themed Conversations: The Superior CM's Edge

5

This chapter looks at the importance of sharing and how to go about finding content to share with your community. It also delves into finding appropriate users to befriend and conversations to participate in.

Chapter Contents

Best-Content-on-the-Block Sharing

For today's data-driven community manager, the initial jump into social media on behalf of a brand might feel like moving to a new town: fresh start, exciting possibilities, pools of new people to meet, not to mention a curiously overwhelming desire to be accepted, liked, and befriended. Unfortunately, that's not always the easiest task. Yes, it's one thing to be present on the social scene, wherever that may be. Your brand's channel of choice may be Twitter, Facebook, YouTube, or a blended strategy spanning multiple platforms. But it's a separate feat altogether to be accepted, liked, befriended, and, dare we say, evangelized.

Still, there are brands that *do* become evangelized, *do* see incredible ROI from social marketing campaigns, and make it look effortless. What's their secret? One solution to the "mystery" harkens back to kindergarten principles 101: sharing. Sharing what? Content. What kind of content? Amazing content—content that is of significant value to the company's online community. Content that accomplishes a task, such as breaking industry news, answering a question, solving a problem, or making a community member (nearly) pee his or her pants laughing. CMs who circulate wonderful, high-quality, informative, or simply entertaining content are embraced and beloved because they're doing a laudable service for their communities. They're giving people a reason to follow them.

In the upcoming sections, we'll take a close look at several benefits of sharing, along with tips, tactics, resources, and best practices for identifying and segmenting the types of content the data-driven CM could (read: should) be sharing with the world.

Note: Several sections of this chapter draw from various guest blog posts aimClear has contributed to industry publications Search Engine Land and Acquisio Blog. We encourage you to check out those posts in their entirety by navigating to the following URLs:

www.acquisio.com/social/3-surefire-ways-to-become-the-coolest-community-manager-on-the-block/

http://searchengineland.com/3-content-aggregators-for-the-b2b-community-manager-toolkit-125418

http://searchengineland.com/beef-up-b2b-publications-with-rockstar-industry-conference-coverage-112468

Importance of Sharing

What's the big deal about social sharing, anyway? By consistently syndicating relevant and newsworthy content with your community, your company can simultaneously achieve several admirable goals sure to please any member of the C-suite:

- Constantly learn new information pertaining to the company's field and stay up-to-speed on breaking news. (Tip: Have the CM circulate such content to the in-house team, or at least debrief the team once every week or two, so everyone can be kept in the loop.)

- Establish the brand as an industry authority and valuable resource for topical news and become someone the community looks to for the industry 411 or thought-leadership.

- Always be armed with a conduit for social engagement—the CM can start conversations surrounding the content he/she shares. The goal is to disseminate diverse content generating diverse conversations, making for a rich, dynamic, and authentic social media presence.

- Increase social visibility and get on the radar of target customers, future friends, and power users.

At the end of the day, the data-driven community manager's goal is to make friends *who matter*: friends who convert according to established marketing KPIs and translate to some form of ROI. Strategically sharing killer content can help make new-found social buddies who then become word-of-mouth evangelists or paying customers. Either way, these people are priceless byproducts of a CM's non-gratuitous and consistent social sharing. Now, what exactly is that community manager sharing?

Bucketing Content for Sharing

When it comes to the content community managers collate and distribute, we like to lump the material into three separate categories, as listed here (along with percentages that speak to recommended frequency of sharing):

- Third-party, noncompetitive, complementary content (50 percent)
- Strategic personalization and real-time journalism (30 percent)
- Branded, self-promotional content (20 percent)

Read on for a closer look at what comprises each bucket as well as resources for beefing up each so that data-driven CMs are never without something fabulous to share with their communities.

Third-Party, Noncompetitive, Complementary Content

It's nothing new to preach the importance of sharing noncompetitive, complementary, third-party content for brands actively participating in social media. To make friends, you have to be friendly—that's true for B2C and B2B alike. Friendly friends discuss mutual interests that fascinate and benefit one another. They don't talk about themselves the whole time—that's rude and unappealing.

At aimClear, we teach clients that it's ideal to have a rich, informative, and consistently flowing social feed comprised of an estimated 80 percent nonbranded content; this leaves 20 percent left over for promotional material. (We've split up that 80 percent into two subcategories: 50 percent for third-party content and 30 percent for real-time journalism, both nonbranded.) Of course, we're met with pushback on occasion, often from larger, more regulated brands. The percentage breakdowns will vary on a company-to-company basis, but remember—this is social media, and the goal is to make friends (how? by being friendly). Friends don't talk about themselves 24/7. Take that mentality to the table when discussing sources of content for sharing.

As you've learned throughout this book, modern-day community managers have dynamic job descriptions that span reputation monitoring, orchestrating of feed content, publication management, and handling of intracommunity bloodshed and brand crises. It's not feasible to spend hours each day hunting down topical articles, videos, and infographics worth tweeting about and posting to Facebook or Google+.

This task can be even more cumbersome for community managers working at an agency—CMs who may not speak the language of their client's niche or know where to find a steady stream of titillating business buzz. Fortunately, there are fabulous tools to be leveraged for streamlining the aggregation of top-shelf content that can then be magnanimously distributed among a company's social community. To in-house and agency community managers: Content aggregators are friends! These sites are meccas of articles, images, videos, and other forms of content searchable by category and pre-vetted for social popularity and a general propensity to go viral. Rejoice!

Engaged community managers can get lost for centuries cruising around all the fresh posts and photos, or they can spend five minutes in the morning with a cup of coffee, skimming the goods and bookmarking a handful of links to sprinkle throughout the day with thoughtful editorial. Don't forget! Many social media dashboards feature advanced scheduling functionality: Create posts in the morning, schedule them to fire across multiple social media channels, monitor for @mentions and other chatter, and focus on another task at hand. Just don't forget to slightly tailor the messages so they speak the vernacular native to each social channel.

Now let's look at three of our shop's favorite content aggregators that make locating quality content to share fun, easy, and cheetah-fast. (Reminder: There are oodles of content aggregators beyond these three. Once you're finished perusing this section, thumb back to "The Galactic Guide to Social Media Channels" section in Chapter 3, "Hit the Ground Running!," for more inspiration, and of course, we encourage some investigating on your own.)

First things first. Look to classic keyword research and social demographic research for keen insight on how your target audience talks about your company's goods and services, and what their own interests and hobbies are. Focus on the short-tail keywords and map them to one or all of the aggregators we discuss next.

Alltop

Whenever aimClear members speak at conferences on the importance of content aggregation, we're astounded to learn that some marketers and community managers *still* don't know about Alltop (www.alltop.com). This is one mother of a content aggregator! Alltop operates on preset categories, so don't worry about being too inventive while navigating and surfing for gold. Ten main categories break down into dozens upon dozens of subcategories, and each subcategory is a portal for a heaping pile of topical blog feeds with links to the five most recent articles.

Libraries, for example, is a subcategory under Interests. Check out Figure 5.1. Mmmm. Dig in!

Figure 5.1 Libraries category in Alltop

BuzzFeed

Want to post something fresh, popular, and trending with the community? Skip on over to BuzzFeed (www.buzzfeed.com), one of a few homes for "the hottest, most social content on the Web."

Links on BuzzFeed are often predisposed to social virility (a considerable amount of the content on BuzzFeed comes from Reddit and other similar viral aggregators) or are OMG-famous already. Spend a few minutes plugging in keywords from social demographic research to hone in on tasty, topical content target audiences will love (see Figure 5.2). It doesn't matter whether you're the CM for a welding company, a funeral home, or a debt collection agency—everyone loves adorable cat/puppy/sloth/red panda/random furry animal photos. *Everyone.*

Figure 5.2 Take a break from the industry-centric norm and share a pic of a cute animal with the community!

Pinterest

Pinterest (www.pinterest.com) is a social bookmarking darling that many non-arts-and-crafts brands think just isn't for them. It actually has a variety of uses beyond powerful content aggregation.

For starters, stick in some interests or keywords related to your social community or business (Figure 5.3). See if there's anything there to scope out. Odds are, there's a gem or two, at least.

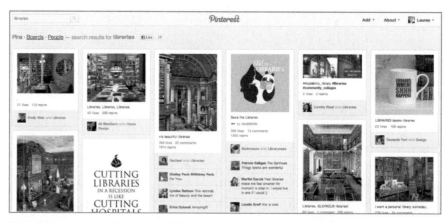

Figure 5.3 Simple industry keywords reveal fabulous content on Pinterest for the CM to share!

Factor in social endorsements. Look for content with an intersection of quality, relevance, repins, likes, and comments.

Pinterest is also a useful tool for data-driven friend making and cunning competitive intelligence. For example, if you find a cool piece of relevant content pinned by some unfamiliar user, head on over to PinReach (www.pinreach.com) to learn a little more about him or her. Enter the pinner's profile URL to identify their far-reaching pins, popular pins, and more. Perhaps this is an authority user the CM should begin wooing.

If a little Pinterest reconnaissance is on the agenda, insert your competitor's website in the tail end of this URL: http://pinterest.com/source/*COMPETITORWEBSITE* .com. Behold! Now you can see everything anyone in the world has pinned from that competitor's site. Study and take note. Are these corporate rivals doing something your company is not? Are they creating or rebroadcasting hot content your CM has missed? Use their activity and engagement for inspiration. Devise a counterattack and strike!

Looking for a more tailored pot of content? Flip back to Chapter 4, "Content, Reputation, and Hardcore Listening Hacks," for a complete guide to creating a Google dashboard for ultimately customized content aggregation. Instruct the CM to cruise through the dashboard each morning while he/she sips a steamy latte and pick some choice stuff to post.

Strategic Personalization and Real-Time Journalism

When aimClear performs social audits for clients, one of the first things we look at is how *real* their social feed appears to be. How would we grade their performance? A feed comprised wholly of branded content gets an F, and we'd give them a Z if that grade existed. A feed populated with third-party, noncompetitive, complementary resources and a bit of branded links here and there deserves nothing higher than a C+, possibly a B−. Why?

The community can get that kind of content *anywhere*, even from a 100 percent automated robot feed (tsk, tsk). Spewing links to content, branded or not, isn't reason enough for community members to follow, like, befriend, or recommend your brand to their inner circles. There must be something special about the CM and her brand—some personal touch that makes that online presence unique, enjoyable, and endearing. There has to be added value.

Rewind to the section in Chapter 2, "Timeless Tenets of Non-Gratuitous Social Behavior," about conversation-seeding engagement tactics. Any or all of those techniques for starting some social chatter fall under this 30 percent chunk of the company social feed. Thanking the community, posing questions, creating awards, posting reviews, churning out boots-on-the-ground journalism of cultural events or industry conferences, tweeting "Hi, @JimBob, how's your day?" and so on…. These forms of communication are about the CM giving something to the community and asking for nothing (aside from friendly engagement) in return. Selfless contributions really turn heads among the right kind of community members! Don't skimp on this percentage of content. If you do, the community will notice and possibly tune you out.

Branded, Self-Promotional Content

It's worth highlighting again (and again and again): Social media efforts aren't just about friendship bracelets and sunshine and pussycats. Social media marketing is about *marketing*: making money or, at the very least, achieving thoughtfully established KPIs. Integrated in the CM's sharing of relevant, fascinating, third-party content and quality conversations with fans and customers, it's completely legit to sprinkle in links to branded goods (product pages, press releases, new blog posts, etc.). The key is to do it when it feels natural, welcome, or when the content pushed out accomplishes one of the tasks we discussed previously (such as answering a question or solving a problem).

Just don't overdo it! Most community members are smart enough to know when they're being tricked, manipulated, or spoon-fed spammy self-promotional content one 140-character bite at a time. Blaring blatantly self-promotional material at a community will get your company nowhere. It might even cost you some street cred. Companies that really rock don't hock their product 24/7. Want to rock? Ditch the "try my product" shtick, and keep branded sharing within reason.

Great Conversations and Desirable Users Defined

When it comes to social media friends, focused quality, influence, loyalty, and relevance outweigh quantity.

The world is filled with irrelevant communities comprised of friends and followers having little to do with the community's supposed theme. Reciprocally, there are fantastic smaller communities that have deadeye focus. They're wound so tightly, made up of incredibly valuable user segments, and rife for themed content producers. Give any savvy CM a few thousand seriously focused Facebook, Twitter, and LinkedIn followers, and it's easy to incent and incite engagement. The best way to create a community is to *cause* it. Quality of friends matters more than quantity.

There are a few different ways to think about community focus. The first is to make general friends—a more random sampling of the public with little targeting. This can make sense if you're, say, Amazon.com. Amazon sells many products to many people. As you read this, Amazon does not really need to worry about your focus because getting you to subscribe via a Facebook like or Twitter follow could pay in the long run. You are a human. You have a computer. You bought this book, so you probably have a credit card. Perhaps that's enough targeting. Later on, maybe you'll need a coffee grinder. If you're the local hardware store in a smaller 80,000-person city, general subscription strategies might work. It's a small city so marketing won't cost much. Everybody needs a hardware store sometimes. General friend making is only for truly general companies like general stores and toilet paper manufacturers. Everybody poops. Everybody needs toilet paper.

General friend making is not usually efficient for companies that sell niche products because it can take a massive sampling to generate enough focused customers from a general pool. Say a content marketer selling period-authentic furniture sets up a table outside the Mall of America and offers $50 to absolutely *anyone* willing to log in to Facebook on the spot and like the marketer's furniture page. Next week, when that marketer publishes an awesome blog post about quarter-sawn mission on her brand's Facebook page, how many of those random likers will care? What percentage of those walking outside a mall care about this theme? Maybe a few, but on the street those types of fixated interests are kind of random. To the outside world, a large collection of people looks like a community. To the furniture content marketer, who knows what the cat dragged in? We're not likely to do furniture marketing here, at scale, with a community culled from general mall traffic.

The best tactic for community building is to carefully define the audiences we seek, market to those users, and give them good reason to connect with us by follow or like. Building focused community can be hard. Here are four great methods to find great users:

- Get your current customers to follow or like in social.
- Market content in the social community relevant and interesting to users.
- Run themed promotions online and in the physical world with a friending component.
- Participate in themed conversations so others become aware of you, as well as meet, like, and follow you.

Getting current customers to follow or like just got easier in Facebook. FB now allows select advertisers to target a list of email addresses with FB Ads. Wow! The feature, as of this writing, is available to advanced operators via Power Editor, FB's desktop ads management tool.

The best reason to move existing customers over to social is so marketers have access to customers' friends, the second degree of separation. It should be noted that moving private customers over to public social media also might expose them to competitors hoping to poach your treasured customers. Sometimes it's worth it. Other methods for moving friends to social include sending emails to your customer list by offering friends-only deals online in social.

Also, moving customers to social is not only about friending and following. Businesses have learned to ask for reviews, video submissions, and comments with flyers on the table or with hotel bed stand brochures. Figure 5.4 shows a flyer on a table at Sweet Basil Café in Cannon Beach, Oregon, asking for a Yelp review. This can be an effective way to leverage the energy and patronage of existing customers. Keep in mind that it's not just about putting any old card on a table. Be cool and tasteful in how you ask people to friend and follow. Make sure to include URLs to the social profile and not just a lone social media icon. Include a call to action that spells out that you're asking a review, follow, or whatever. If it's possible to offer value back, then do. We've seen restaurants that offered a tear-off coupon from the table tent, which also reminded the user to follow or review, all the way to coupon redemption.

Figure 5.4 Restaurant flyer asking for Yelp reviews

Joining Mainstream Conversations

It stands to reason that in order to participate in conversations that matter to business, we've got to find them first. One of the easiest (and coolest) ways to locate relevant conversations is to check out comment threads in major publications.

Mashable's presence on Facebook reveals that their fans engage in public about particular topics. Head over to Mashable's Facebook page. Choose any blog post. Click where FB indicates that people "like" that post. These days, most major publications somehow mash up Facebook with their website. Figure 5.5 shows a Mashable thread about iPhone cases that are also chargers. If I work for a company that sells cool iPhone accessories, the users who are leaving comments probably matter.

Figure 5.5 Mashable comments thread about iPhone cases/chargers

Facebook reveals users who have publicly commented and liked the page post. Take note of topic-specific Facebook users as target friends. It's natural as pie to jump into these types of conversations and a fantastic crucible in which to make friends. This approach works for many mainstream publications that feature extremely specific articles.

Leverage this methodology to identify and locate a variety of users who are interested in focused topics. It's a great way to engage with your ideal social targets!

Mapping Relevant Search Keywords to Conversations

For all the human richness in social media, still the only way we have to describe people's interests are with keywords. For example, the only way anyone has ever figured out how to describe that a married 42-year-old man likes roof gardening and growing tomatoes is to say exactly that! The "married" dude likes "roof gardening" and "growing tomatoes." As technologically advanced as social media programmers are, words are still the only tools we have to describe likes and interests, just like search.

The online marketing industry and most companies have as many as 15 years of history dealing with keywords. Search marketing is all about keywords that might denote a potential customer's intent. Businesses usually know the keywords that matter and lead to sales. It only makes sense to target conversations based on keywords included in the dialog.

Here is an example. If our company sells to those who Google "Birding binoculars" (search keyword), it makes sense to search Twitter for conversations about birding, as shown in Figure 5.6. It turns out there is a universe of influencers, social content, and conversations surrounding birding. It could be said that we mapped our important keyword to social.

Figure 5.6 Use search keywords to find users who care about your topic in social.

Chances are pretty good that you already know the keywords most important to your business. Two classic tools marketers use to determine desirable keywords are web analytics, such as Google Analytics, and search PPC reports, such as Google

AdWords. Just check out which keywords result in visitors engaging on your website and conversion.

Psychographic Research Using Facebook

Psychographic variables are any attributes connecting users' personalities, values, attitudes, interests, and lifestyles. Some intellectuals also refer to them as IAO (interests, activities, and opinions) variables. Psychographic variables complement and contrast classic demographic variables (such as gender and age), behavioral attributes (such as loyalty and usage habits), and firmographic variables (such as industry, seniority, and functional areas). Psychographics are deeper and should not be confused with classic demographics. For example, the age of a user is not just defined by years. Perspective is also gleaned by psychographic attributes like mind-sets and cultural criteria.

Social communities usually have paid advertising tools that, when wielded by smart marketers, reveal the makeup of the community. The Facebook Ads creation tool (`www.facebook.com/advertising`) is the easiest to use and has the largest sampling of users. Even if you never run a single Facebook ad, the process of choosing an audience using the paid ad tool discloses tons of information about the makeup of FB.

Figure 5.7 shows more than 20,000 FB users in America who are women, 24–38 years old, who like watching their kids play sports. That tells us a lot about who's in Facebook and what they're interested in. Shrewd community managers use FB Ads to undertake social research. It's so powerful that, in countries where FB has a high percentage of the population in its user base, researchers use Facebook to undertake population studies that border on anthropological in nature.

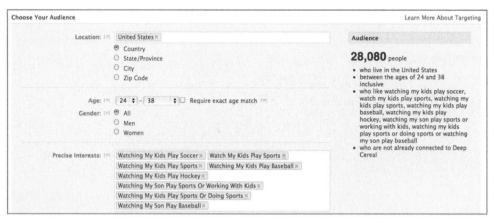

Figure 5.7 Use the Facebook Ads creation tool to discover the makeup of the community.

Figure 5.8 illustrates the concept of the whole user, targeted by psychographics. Think of these variables as traits that express interests, occupations, roles in life, predilections, and other personal characteristics. It's like demographic research and persona modeling to the *n*th degree. I decided to use myself as an example. Keep the following types of Facebook interest/product associations in mind as you peruse the following infographic, and use them as jumping boards for your own psychographic targeting explorations.

- I (Marty) am susceptible to buying Ben Taylor songs because I have loved his dad's (James Taylor) music since I was a boy.

- Marketers have a great shot at selling me exclusive foodie experiences because my social graph indicates I'm interested in James Beard Award–winning restaurants.

- I'm a terrific target for Chanukah candles in November because I love the old City of Jerusalem.

- Hotels, airport transportation, and Broadway shows may interest me because of my Javits Convention Center proclivity. It's worth testing.

- You might be able to get me to visit an orthodontist because I sometimes suck my thumb when I sleep.

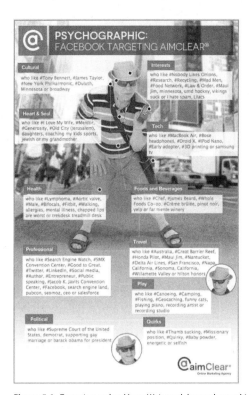

Figure 5.8 Targeting author Marty Weintraub by psychographics

Psychographics can be inventoried in multiple channels. Figure 5.9 shows aggregated YouTube, Facebook, and LinkedIn targeting to identify pilots and flight attendants. We pulled the data from YouTube's search box, Facebook Ads, and LinkedIn

Ads. We've identified these occupations by specific job titles, Airbus simulator videos, and flight attendant training classes.

We use this data for two main reasons: to understand the makeup of YouTube, Facebook, and LinkedIn, and, of course, to serve users paid advertisements.

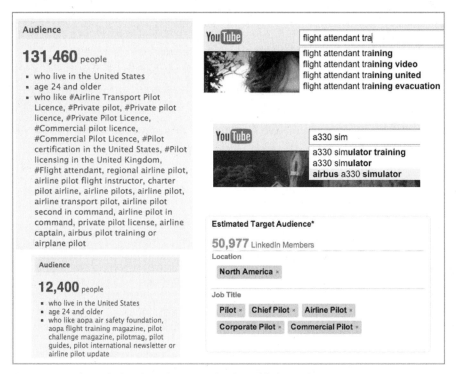

Figure 5.9 YouTube, Facebook, and LinkedIn targeting for pilots and flight attendants

As an industry, we have finally arrived in the holistic-user-targeting future! Psychographic variable research is now the gold standard by which to hold marketers accountable. Now and forever, best-in-class execution means paid and organic campaigns that deliver seriously sliced-and-tagged traffic by empirical attributes holistically across social and search. Haven't heard of psychographics? Well, you will.

The multichannel psychographic process requires intuition, guile, and determination. Understanding nodes of the whole customer means that marketers have fascinating strategic and tactical tools on hand.

Targeting Whole B2C and B2B Customers with Footprints

When it comes to taking stock of personality traits that define what it means to be an individual, there are a number of qualities to consider. Head on over to www.aimclear .com/cm/chapter5 to download a questionnaire for your own use in organizing the

psychographic research process. Let's start with the infographic in Figure 5.8, which categorizes me (Marty) by

Interests From television shows I obsess about to concern for a more sustainable environment, interests are a wide open topic. It's interesting to note that interests can be things a person does *not* like. Interests mean a lot of things. In Facebook, many personal characteristics are expressed as interests. All of the categories that follow could be thought of as interest subcategories.

Culture The aspects of my life about music, the ways of my home city, and other fine arts.

Heart and Soul These are the qualities that speak to what truly matters to me. If an interest is so deep that it moves a person, then it could be considered heart and soul.

Tech What's my software and hardware footprint? Where do I come from as a technical human being?

Health Health is a huge deal and a concern for most people at some level. From YouTube videos about cancer to Tweets about being in the hospital, users can be indexed by health issues.

Foods Yum! It makes me hungry just to think about eating a cannoli in Boston's North End! Can you sell another dessert? How about a hotel room in Boston's financial district along with a packaged food tour?

Professional Many of us spend a lot more waking time at work than at home with our families. Our occupation is a huge part of many a human's identity. Jobs are not just for B2B, by the way. Ski instructors buy parkas and lip balm. Daycare providers need extra toilet paper, learning toys, and disinfectant.

Travel Where does your audience like to go? Is it along the north shore of Lake Superior or Sydney, Australia? Travel can reveal range and belies other interests.

Play From intramural soccer to blackjack, how people play marks them as targets. A person who skydives may be more likely to buy life insurance or purchase risky products and take part in activities like motorcycles and white water rafting.

Politics Yes, politics are easily discovered and harbingers of many things. A 54-year-old pro-life married lady, living south of Savannah, Georgia, might be approached by a talk show host to discuss a polarizing new medication or by a community leader to join in a community outreach opportunity. A single, gay, liberal 24-year-old northern man may be interested in alternative theater, trips to Bali, and condoms.

Quirks From mild to wild, this interest bucket is super interesting. A person who snores may respond to decongestant ads, a better mattress, and marriage counseling. College students interested in smoking pot have proven easy marks to sell pizza delivery.

The downloadable document includes questions in the following areas:

Place of Employment Where do people work? This is a huge part of a person's identity.

Brand Affinities What brands, both ours and our competitors, do our customers follow?

Product Usages Do customers use Photoshop for interests related to sharing photos and Salesforce to define "sales"-related occupations?

Government, Military, and Regulatory History/Affiliations How can these attributes influence other interests?

Civic Organization Membership From PTA to MADD, these types of memberships can mean a lot.

Labor Union Memberships We won't get into politics here, but membership in some labor unions says a lot about a person.

Thought Leaders and Celebrities Followed Who do our targets follow? If the answer is Martha Stewart, such an interest may portend cooking and/or other homemaking interests.

Media Preferences What media channels and personalities do our customers follow?

Investments and Money Interests Although there is no way to target someone's income level in social media, certain things are markers. For instance, someone interested in various types of investments, publications, insurance issues, and so forth can yield targeting perspective.

Charities and Causes Followed What charities and causes matter to our customers?

Occupations As mentioned earlier, job titles are huge.

News Interests Any hot-button issues like gay marriage, save the whales, or the Queen's coronation?

Personal Habits These fall under the quirks category.

Physical Demographic Where do our customers live?

Economic Status Look for indicators. If a user works part-time at Jack in the Box or is a temporary worker, that means something different than being a CTO or Senior Manager. Occupations are great economic indicators.

The downloadable document expresses these human subdivisions in the form of a questionnaire. At aimClear, our account reps interview clients on intake, which usually results in a good understanding of who the customers are. Enjoy, and happy persona modeling.

Using Search to Connect Physical Constructs to Online

Once a community manager has theorized and determined which aspects of a person qualify that person as a great human to have in-community, there needs to be a process to find similar people to engage with and/or to serve ads. Search is the CM's best friend.

For instance, say the target market is all about young women who buy cosmetics. The intake questionnaire indicates that our customers frequent e-commerce sites that sell makeup and other things. I'm a guy and have not worn makeup since the early 1980s, which we can call my glam rock days. Still, I need to figure out which e-commerce websites have fan bases that are all about cosmetics. So, I'll head on over to Google for some help. Figure 5.10 shows search engine results pages (SERPs) that lead to Maybelline, which I've heard of (even being a guy). However, I was not aware of Makeuptalk.com and Lancôme. These companies have communities we can target for person-to-person engagement, as well as to serve them ads.

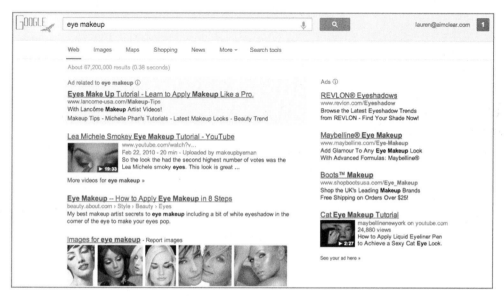

Figure 5.10 SERPs reveal communities that individuals may cluster around.

Keep in mind that knowing the who and where about your customers is easy if you're in the business of being a marketer. Of course, you know most or all of the places that users who fit the criteria hang out. However, for the professional community manager moving from industry to industry, sometimes it takes a little assistance from Google or Bing to find the places where customers may congregate for a topic.

Limitations of "In-Community" Search Tools

The important data points for finding great conversations to jump into are searching comment threads and sorting the results chronologically. We're looking for current conversations on topics and themes, as defined by our keywords and concepts that tend to convert. For the most part, social media communities do not have great internal search engines for the use of discovering current conversations. Facebook is terrible in this respect; Figure 5.11 shows the areas of FB that are searchable.

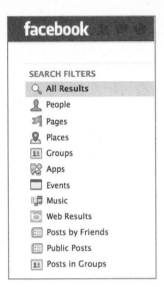

Figure 5.11 Areas of Facebook that are searchable

Sure, searching Pages, Places, Groups, Apps, Events, Music, Web Results, Posts by Friends, Public Posts, and Posts in Groups is fine, but they don't give CMs crucial information. Also, conspicuously missing from Facebook SERPs are videos and notes. There are poor tools, as of this writing, for searching videos and none for searching notes in FB. That's a major bummer since FB videos are awesome places to find conversations. Comments are not searchable either. Facebook is not alone. YouTube does not have comment search either and recently removed its beta comments search that used to live in TestTube, YouTube's experiments area.

Although social media sites may say in public that such limitations are all about user privacy, what they're probably about is making sure that community managers need to buy ads to reach themed users. The ability for a community manager to do so would reduce the need to buy ads because finding users would be much easier.

LinkedIn is an exception. Searching Updates yields mentions of any keywords, in chronological order, even for users who are not on your contacts list. Figure 5.12 shows SERPs for microbiology. This capability in LinkedIn amounts to an awesome tool because it's so easy to find users talking about keywords and concepts that matter to a business. Those users are great targets for engagement and friendship. By the way, all you have to do in order to request friendship from these folks is join a group they also belong to, which authorizes you to make the request.

The first questions a CM should ask, upon embarking on conversational missions in any new social community, are about search capabilities. Can you find conversations? Can you sort them by time?

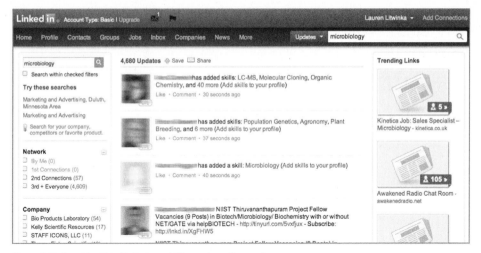

Figure 5.12 Searching LinkedIn Updates yields mentions of keywords.

Mining Deep "Site:" Operator Search

The good news is that, while social sites don't always provide good tools to search data (even public pages), search engines do. One of the most effective hacks to find current, themed conversations is Google itself. Bing is also very useful. Look no further than the classic advanced search operator that SEO practitioners have used for more than a decade. We use it to search single sites for keywords rather than the entire Internet.

For years, the "site:" search operator has provided a quick method to distill mainstream SERPs down to results from a single website or class of websites. The operator works for major international search engines including Google, Bing, Yandex, Baidu, and others. Concatenate keywords to filter SERPs layered by both site and keyword, as shown in Figure 5.13. When focused on identifying conversations in social, the "site:" search operator becomes a powerful tool indeed.

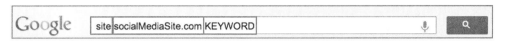

Figure 5.13 Google's "site:" search operator

The Google search displayed in Figure 5.14 allowed our community manager to discover a conversation that took place on the New York Times Facebook page about wine.

Figure 5.14 Use the "site:" operator to find conversations, even within Facebook.

Just think of how powerful this technique can be in the hands of a gregarious community manager, poised to conduct thoughtful person-to-person outreach. She could easily jump into the themed public thread shown in Figure 5.15 to participate in conversations with other users she already knows are both interested in specific topics and willing to publicly engage.

Figure 5.15 Find and participate in conversations with users who are interested in specific topics and are willing to publicly engage.

Not only can a savvy community manager mine individuals' interests and participate in the thread, there's a strong likelihood that he can DM (direct message) the Facebook user(s), dependent on each user's privacy settings. Since Facebook is famous for defaulting new users to porous privacy settings, which include allowing nonfriends to DM, the odds are good. There are more ways to mine friend-leads. Follow the golden Facebook "like this" path, as shown in Figure 5.16, to find an entire list of Facebook users interested in the topic, whether or not they participated in the thread.

For community managers committed to proactive outreach and finding topically relevant and engaged users, the "site:" search operator can be a conversational goldmine. It allows the CM to literally make lists of users to get to know.

The technique is much more powerful than just Facebook. Check out the "site:" operator footprint shown in Figure 5.17, designed to locate YouTube comment threads surrounding Syrah-focused wine tasting.

Figure 5.16 Follow Facebook's "like this" path to discover a list of Facebook users interested in a given topic.

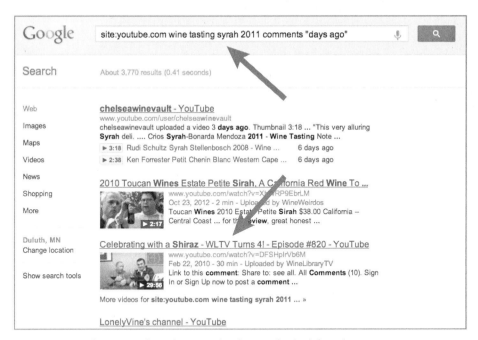

Figure 5.17 A YouTube "site:" search reveals comment threads surrounding Syrah-focused wine tasting.

The SERPs uncover a number of options for community manager comment-thread-diving. "Ancient Peaks Renegade Paso Wine" includes a worthy thread and a ton of related videos, several of which have great conversations to join and users to meet (Figure 5.18).

Figure 5.18 YouTube comment threads and related videos offer the CM more options for engagement.

The "site:" search operator works splendidly in nearly any language a search engine handles. But keep in mind that not every search engine indexes each publicly discoverable corner of all social sites. For reasons ranging from political (Baidu and Facebook) to business (Twitter firehose and Google), it's just not all there in every search engine. The "site:" search operator is a useful utility for figuring out what parts of what social community are indexed by each engine. Try the "site:" operator in Baidu for Facebook or Twitter to discover the effect the Chinese government's suffocating requirements have had on Baidu.

Niche Topical Communities

Social sites that don't provide good search tools are only part of the problem when it comes to finding themed conversations. Some of the most important conversations to participate in, or at least monitor, take place behind closed login doors in nonpublic areas of websites that search engines don't index.

Case Study: AngiesList.com

Plenty of community sites don't allow search engines to search them at all, including B2B, B2C, and hybrids. Take Angie's List, for example (Figure 5.19).

Angie's List is a paid membership site where consumers review contractors ranging from air duct cleaning and mold removal to piano moving, shoe repair, and vascular surgery. When someone needs a plumber, roofer, dentist, electrician, auto mechanic, physician, dermatologist, landscaper (or anyone from its 500+ categories), they can pay to search Angie's List online, by phone, or via fax. After joining and logging in, they get ratings and reviews of local professionals who've done work for other members in the area, plus reviews sharing the type of work they've done, prices, professionalism, and timeliness.

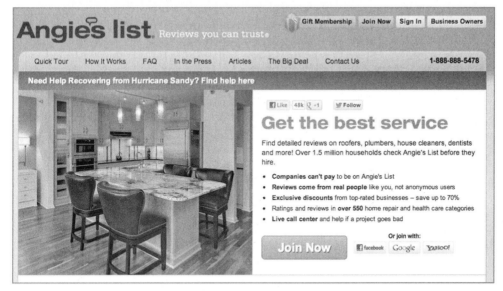

Figure 5.19 Angie's List is an example of a community site that doesn't allow search engines to index all of its pages.

Anyone who joins can review any service or health provider, which will then become part of their rating on Angie's List. This can be a nightmare or a blessing for a contractor. Companies and health professionals cannot pay to be put on the list, and they're not allowed to post grades about themselves.

Obviously this is a site that local contractors need to keep up with. There is a complaint-resolution department at Angie's List with a good reputation, and resolved issues are noted on the site as such. Obviously, bad reviews can be disastrous, especially if a contractor does not know about it. If you're the community manger for a business that can be reviewed in a private community, you better join and keep your eye on things. What you don't know can hurt you.

Case Study: Dentaltown

Many industrial sectors have B2B-specific micro-communities. Usually, parts of the website are public and others are members only. Oftentimes they're not that big and are commensurate with the size of the industries they serve. If such a site exists for your trade's niche, you probably know it already.

Dentaltown is a private website created exclusively for dental healthcare professionals. Nonhealthcare professionals who fake it to get in will be removed by admins upon review. Compared to Angie's List, Dentaltown is much smaller due to the simple fact that there are fewer healthcare professionals than consumers interested in fixing their houses or finding doctors. However, getting a bad rap in Dentaltown among colleagues who may be consumers of your dental-focused products, or worse yet, who will stop referring business to you, is a bad thing.

Much of Dentaltown is public facing, meaning that search engines index the pages and the "site:" operator works. However, only short snippets of message board posts are public facing, meaning you can *find* keywords on the message using the "site:" operator but you can't read the complete board posting. Figure 5.20 shows what might be a nasty comment about Choice Health Plan. That's good. We found it. However, we can't read the entire post unless we hold a Dentaltown account. That, in itself, is a great reason to join the community and monitor it. Also, if the mention of Choice Health Plan was not in the public-facing snippet, we may have missed it entirely because the "site:" operator only tells us about what the search engine has indexed.

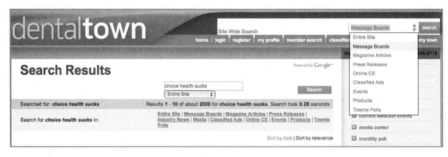

Figure 5.20 A snippet of a negative comment thread in Dentaltown, a private website for dental professionals

The bottom line is to always understand niche topical communities where chatter about your company can impact others' perception. Another important reason is to understand competitors and the industry as a whole space. New products are introduced, consumers are happy or revolt, and community members discuss the most important issues of the day.

Mozenda

Logging into multiple niche communities over and over again to conduct searches can be cumbersome, especially when there are numerous sites to keep track of. We use a tool called Mozenda (Figure 5.21), which is an object-based data extraction tool. That means Mozenda can go most places on the Web and scrape pages into a database or email the data to you. Mozenda can even be used to create an RSS feed with the data. One of Mozenda's coolest features is the ability to log in as you search a site, generate the data, log out, and rinse and repeat on a schedule. Mozenda is a secret weapon when it comes to finding themed conversations in nonpublic places.

It's important to check the terms of service for a site you want to scrape, because most have some language that basically says no machines are allowed to automate reading the site's content. It's against Google's terms of service. Dentaltown is a little mushy in their rules, as they do allow users to make a copy for personal use. Mozenda can handle its extraction duties by invisible methods that mask the user agent and stagger requests to feign human behavior. In other words, you can usually get away with using it.

Figure 5.21 Mozenda is an object-based data extraction tool that can help find conversations in nonpublic places.

We always point these facts out to our clients. Some say, "Hell yeah! Get me the data!" Others are more conservative and would prefer that we don't use Mozenda. To my mind, if we can hire a room full of people to search, copy, and paste from web browsers from sites we are authorized to consume, we'll use Mozenda with our clients' permission. To us, black hat is when you get data that you're not entitled to. That's not what's happening here. We're getting data we are entitled to by more efficient methods. That's gray hat, baby!

Groups, Directories, and Other Human Congregation Points

We've been discussing best practices for locating themed users who we can engage with for friendship, to participate in communities that marketers build, and ultimately for sales. There are myriad directory websites out there that do the job for us. If they understand social media directories, community managers can save a lot of time finding focused users to meet and greet. Head on over to `www.aimclear.com/cm/chapter5` for a downloadable list of directories.

The "Wefollow" Directory Model

For identifying target friends on Twitter, one directory we like is wefollow (`http://wefollow.com`). Start with suggestions in the search box at the top. Let's say we're looking for friends who are interested in landscaping, as depicted in Figure 5.22. It's easy to see the relative distribution of users in relation to keyword permutations.

Figure 5.22 A search in wefollow .com helps us find Twitter users interested in landscaping.

Wefollow SERPs consist of Twitter users who self-identify (self-tag) with individual keywords. The default SERPs are sorted by most influential, according to the wefollow algorithm (Figure 5.23). There's also the option to sort by most followers.

Figure 5.23 Wefollow.com SERPs are sorted by most influential, according to an internal algorithm.

Drill into individual users for more detail, wefollow rankings, and other self-tagged keywords (Figure 5.24). This is a great way to stem segments and brainstorm.

Keep directories in mind when seeking users with interests congruent to your businesses. Then, you know what to do. Follow them, lurk, and engage in endearing ways.

Figure 5.24 Drilling into individual users in wefollow can reveal other potential keywords.

Google Search and Chrome: The CM's Secret Weapons

The "site:" operator works in most international search engines. Also, many foreign search engines have the same sorts of limitations in terms of identifying timely themed conversations as American mainstream communities do. Another problem is that most American community managers don't speak Chinese or Russian. So, even if I could search Alibaba or VKontakte, I'd have absolutely no idea what I was looking at. Enter Google's Chrome browser, which, in conjunction with the "site:" search operator, works in nearly every search engine and language, and the world is your oyster.

International, Multilingual, and Translation Hacks

Google's Chrome browser includes a deadeye translation tool. It's not perfect, but the results are impressive. Check out this Baidu "site:" query where we search B2B social media powerhouse www.alibaba.com for activity on the Chinese character meaning "configuration" (Figure 5.25).

Figure 5.25 A Baidu "site:" query shows results for the Chinese character meaning configuration in alibaba.com.

Since I don't speak fluent Chinese, I'll use Chrome's utility to translate (Figure 5.26).

Figure 5.26 Google Chrome's translation tool allows CMs to view conversation threads in other languages.

Awesome. Now we've got a starting point in Alibaba to scope out activity on the concept of configuration, as shown in Figure 5.27.

Figure 5.27 Translated SERPs using Google Chrome's translation tool

The search for "wine grower" in Russian shown in Figure 5.28 returns a sweet "site:" SERP in Yandex. Using Chrome's translate function, have a look in English. It's not hard to uncover a winery sporting a cool conversation to jump into.

Figure 5.28 The SERPs reveal a winery conversation to participate in.

There are friends here to make, for sure. After all, wine is a universal language (Figure 5.29)!

Take this technique for a spin. Check out www.renren.com in Yandex to see what indexes, or try www.LinkedIn.com/answers in Australian Google. After all, there might not be an SEO use to optimize public-facing areas of social media participation if the target engine does not index it. Try Russian or Italian keywords and take note of what indexes in Bing for Orkut or Xing.

Figure 5.29 A Facebook conversation about wine in Russian

The "site:" search operator is a super useful tool to dissemble what parts of social media sites are indexed by search engines around the world. You'll soon discover that most foreign ideations of Google handle most communities the same way. The "site:" operator is also a powerful tool for identifying public conversations under way in various social communities. Leverage it to find users to thoughtfully engage and to send direct messages to, as their privacy settings allow.

Evaluating Buzz Detection (Listening) Tools

The reason we've included the social side of reputation monitoring in this chapter is because listening is a huge part of finding themed conversations. Many tools are available to listen with, which could be thought of as buzz detection. The best-known tools include Google Alerts, Radian6, Sysomos Heartbeat, Trackur, Scout Labs, and numerous others. (In the interest of full disclosure, we have been a Sysomos client for more than two years.) Visit `www.aimclear.com/cm/chapter5` and download our white paper, which compares feature sets from various reputation monitoring tools, lists their features, and explains what's what. It is a given that reputation monitoring tools also listen to search engines.

As companies like Salesforce and Oracle continue to build social media services for large companies, Twitter has partnered with one of them in a strategic alliance. Radian6, the social media monitoring service purchased by Salesforce in March 2011 for $326 million, recently announced that it has inked a strategic alliance with Twitter giving Radian6 customers "complete access" to Twitter's full bore output (called firehose). What's important here is to note the trend of social communities making special deals with certain vendors. Firehose deals are not new for Twitter, including a former deal with Google. The takeaway is this: When choosing a monitoring tool, ask if the manufacturer has any relationships with channels that make the tool better. As opposed to breaking out how to operate all these different tools here in the book, this subchapter is all about key features we seek when evaluating tools. Great buzz monitoring tools are expensive, and for a reason. Expect to pay between $500 and $1,000 per month, dependent on how many keywords you monitor. Google Alerts, which are not great, are free, and also for a reason. Google Alerts only report what Google indexes, which is only a portion of the online universe. If you only use Google Alerts, you're missing a lot.

Basic Features

Here are the basic features you should seek in a good buzz-detection tool. You can get decent tools for free, starting with www.socialmention.com. Start with these features as a baseline:

- A good list of public channels covered. You want your listening tools to cover as much of the known online universe as possible. That means you better be listening to anything that happens out in the open (does not require login) in social, news, images, and video. Read the fine print. Does your reputation monitoring tool cover blogs, social networks, Twitter, YouTube, wikis, message boards, video sharing sites, and news sources? If not, change your solution.
- A breakout of the channels in which users are mentioning your brand.
- Email alerts or RSS feeds you can use to send alerts from a personal dashboard using Outlook. When something happens in any channel, you want to know about it fast. A good listening tool provides a do-it-yourself interface to set up keywords you monitor. Some have a dashboard that your clients can log into.

Advanced Features

More expensive tools have deeper features. Here are the features to look for in higher-end monitoring tools. To our mind, that means Sysomos Heartbeat and Radian6.

Key Influencer Identification It's important to quickly identify the people leading conversations and shaping opinion in order to engage with them to build relationships. Whereas less expensive solutions alert community managers to the individual who mentioned the keywords, advanced buzz-monitoring tools find other users based on patterns of influence and divided by channels.

Geographic and Demographic Data Get your hands on data clarifying social media participants and the conversations they're having, including their age, gender, and profession. Sysomos does a very good job at this.

Automated Sentiment Automated sentiment means using algorithms to identify words that may indicate how users feel about your brand, for instance, if there is a mention of your brand in the same tweet as the words "sucks" or "f--k." Keep in mind that automated sentiment is not and will never be perfect. However, it is always improving and regardless of its imperfect nature is much better than nothing and gives the CM a nice place to start when diving into this data. Look for advanced tools with automated sentiment. Usually automated sentiment is expressed as positive, neutral, or negative.

Share of Voice Share of voice is all the rage. Our clients ask us for it. Unfortunately they usually don't know exactly what it means until we explain. Usually when someone is referring to share of voice, they are asking about overall volume of chatter for a certain keyword concept compared to others. For instance, compare

- Brand A, Keyword 1
- Brand B, Keyword 1

Advanced tools report share of voice at the aggregated channel level (Facebook, YouTube, Twitter, forums, news, etc., together) and at the individual channel level. The holy grail of buzz monitoring is competitive share of voice in a grid with sentiment.

Dominate with Paid
Organic Amplification

The only social that is truly free is within communities of those who already like your Facebook page, follow your LinkedIn profile, and otherwise subscribe by any model. In this chapter, you'll learn how social communities limit what others, outside your community of friends, can see. Then, we'll undertake a systematic study of ways to pay communities to reenable the missing organic features and dominate the distribution system.

Chapter Contents

Friend-of-Friend Visibility

Social media is a distribution system. One of the most important features of socializing users in online communities is friend-of-friend visibility (FoFv). FoFv works like this:

- User A interacts with a brand.
- User A's friends (the brand's second degree of separation) sees User A interact with the brand.
- The second degree (FoF) tends to interact the same way with the brand.

The reason this often holds true is because the second degree sees user A's interaction with the brand as a *recommendation* of a sort, a social endorsement. Social endorsements work like magic for apps, likes, videos, pictures, and pretty much anything. In social media, as in life, the astronomical growth of sites like Facebook, Twitter, and LinkedIn has a lot to do with how well those sites captured the FoFv phenomenon to leverage the power of social endorsement to grow engagement. FoFv is a fantastic thing for brands and is very valuable. As social sites evolved, FoFv was free, also known as organic. How cool is that?

The bad news is that FoFv is not entirely free anymore. Social communities are restricting FoFv more and more unless brands pay. FoFv is an obvious place for social sites to monetize because it's one of the most valuable features for businesses. In fact, Facebook has nearly removed many organic FoFv features, even among users who have all liked the same brand. Thankfully, it's possible to reenable FoFv by paying. It looks nearly the same as when it was free and, for many community managers, works better because fewer brands are willing to pay for what used to be free. Think of it as paid organic.

Marketers have been tracking this change for more than a year. The precipitous drop became more acute since the advent of the timeline, the ticker, and the arrival of a billion users. The good news: You can buy the feel of organic dominance. Yes, really. Understanding how paid organic works in each social channel is the key to dominance. Most CMs are not masters of paid organic, so careful attention to this chapter will give you an advantage. Earlier in this book we discussed the concept of being a hybrid marketer. Knowing the difference between organic and paid organic community management versus regular old paid ads is critical.

Social Ads vs. FoFv Ads

Paid organic FoFv amplification ads are subtly different from their older sibling, straight social ads. A typical social ad in any channel does not leverage FoFv and simply drives a user from that channel to another place, in or outside of the same channel. Think of a regular Facebook Ad. You target the ad to whomever you want in FB, and send them to a destination URL either inside or outside of Facebook.

Regular LinkedIn Ads are the same way. First comes targeting, then creative, and then the destination URL that routes the clicks wherever you want, inside or outside of LinkedIn. YouTube Promoted Videos are straight-up social ads, targeted contextually, and they drive users to watch a video you're promoting. There is no social endorsement. That ad is just that: a paid advertisement.

Regular social ads can be thought of as a kind of indirect paid amplification because organic activity can still result. A YouTube video ad, though it does not make use of any social endorsement, can still be a powerful tool to ignite social activity. For instance, we might target those searching for basketball techniques in YouTube to watch a point-guard training video (Figure 6.1). The viewer might share the video with her team in Facebook or Twitter, or paste it in an email. The regular social ad in this scenario can cause FoFv but did not leverage FoFv in the first place. The user needed to intentionally share the ad for the point-guard training video to propagate socially.

Figure 6.1 Regular social ads such as this YouTube ad can be considered indirect paid amplification.

DIY Facebook Ads and Sponsored Stories

As of this writing, Facebook is by far the most advanced paid organic platform. These types of FB ads, called sponsored stories, are seriously effective. There are also a number of highly efficient regular social ad formats that drive users to engage with a brand's content. Together they form the most effective one-two social marketing punch of any channel. Coupled with a billion highly targetable users all over the world, Facebook has led the march to the next generation of social marketing. No other platform comes close to FB's sophistication.

That is a double-edged sword for FB because they've yet to provide a simple-enough user interface metaphor for the average community manager to easily master. It takes constant work at aimClear for our team, used to dealing with these concepts every day, to stay abreast of FB's random, nearly daily undocumented changes.

It's outside the scope of this book to provide a step-by-step tutorial for constructing each type of ad we describe in this chapter. By the time you are reading this, the physical user interface (UI) methodology will have changed multiple times. However, little has changed about what these units do, over the lifetime of Facebook, once each type of social ad and FoFv ad was introduced. As you read this, there may be more types of ads, but the current ones will likely be very much the same. Here's a breakdown of what each ad unit does.

Facebook Ads

Let's clear up a common misunderstanding. Technically, all the ad types (units) in FB are a flavor of FB Ads. Sponsored stories are the subset of FB Ad units that leverage FoFv. Most marketers are familiar with FB Ads that are *not* sponsored stories, so let's deal with those ads first, then lay out the most important types of ads to master. They're tricky to even say. A page-post-like story is different than a page post ad. You have to say it slowly and think. After working with these ad units for years, our coworkers still find themselves occasionally saying something different than they mean. Fielding an integrated FB Ads campaign firing on all cylinders takes concentration and precision.

There are basically two major types of Facebook Ads that are not sponsored stories:

- Those that drive users to external URLs (non-FB pages)
- Those that drive users back into promoted FB content

Figure 6.2 is a classic Facebook Ad. This ad sends those who click to whatever destination URL the marketer designates. As a rule, it's the most expensive type of FB Ad, because FB charges more for marketers to send users outside of FB than to stay within. Charging more for this type of ad is brilliant, really, because then marketers have more of an incentive to keep their quarry inside FB. This ad appears on the right-hand sidebar and in various other locations, for example, when a user is looking at pictures. The KPI for this type of non-FoFv ad is traffic to the destination URL. It rarely results in likes. Use it for direct-response lead generation, sales, signups, and other commerce. Community managers won't use this much. It's more for the folks who run pay-per-click ads and their common KPIs.

Figure 6.2 A classic Facebook Ad that sends clicks to a destination URL specified by the advertiser

Figure 6.3 is the other major variety of non–sponsored story FB Ads. Called a page post ad, this unit is targeted to FB users, appears in the right-hand sidebar, and is more complicated than it looks. It promotes a specific post on a brand page's wall. If the wall post is a link from an external site, then every part of the unit, except for the upper-left logo and brand name, sends users outside of FB. The logo and brand name drives users to the brand page itself, where users do one of the following:

- Go to the brand page and do nothing
- Go to the brand page, like, and leave
- Go to the brand page, like, and head to the external site that is posted on the wall
- Go to the brand page and visit the external site without liking
- Take other actions, such as sharing, commenting, etc.

Figure 6.3 Example of a Facebook page post ad

Because users targeted have the option to click inside of FB, clicks tend to cost less. This ad results in likes that are expensive and cheap traffic to external sites. It's the most underused type of FB Ad and is extremely powerful. Use the page post ad to drastically increase the reach of your brand's wall posts. We train our clients to think of this type of ad as a traffic driver that gets focused seed likes for the community. While the likes are expensive at face value, they're not expensive when averaged in with what you'll generate with sponsored stories.

What's cool about these ads is that there are many flavors. If the wall post is a video, then the page post ad could have a play button. Image wall posts behave in interesting ways. There are also ads that promote apps and other types of content, such as events. If you can post something as a brand in FB, you can probably promote it with an ad unit pointing directly to it in FB.

Page Like Sponsored Story

The page like sponsored story is an amazing FoFv animal that results in relatively inexpensive likes and other actions. Once placed by a community manager, the brand's friends (those who have liked) become evangelists for the brand without them even knowing. Here's how it works:

- User A likes a brand.
- User A's friends (the brand's second degree of separation) see that User A (and any other common friends) liked the brand.
- The second degree (FoF) tends to interact the same way with the brand and likes it too.

The page like sponsored story (Figure 6.4) is particularly powerful when you dial in psychographic targeting, meaning that only friends of friends who have certain interests see the social endorsement.

Figure 6.4 Example of a page like sponsored story

As we'll discuss in a bit, page like stories used with page post ads pack a wicked promotional punch and are the epicenter of a Facebook paid organic content release.

Page Post Like Sponsored Story

This ad unit is fascinating, and in our opinion most valuable for engagement in-Facebook branding and sending external traffic—not page likes. When a Facebook user likes one of a brand's content posts, that's different than a page like because the effect does not last. Upon liking a page *post* the following happens:

- User A likes a page post.
- Some of User A's friends see it in their newsfeed.
- Some of User A's friends like it and further the distribution of the content.
- The content occasionally goes viral, but most usually peters out, because FB has limited FoFv for brands that don't pay.

If you're the highest bidder for the targeting, your page post like stories can show up in users' newsfeeds. Whereas the right column click-through ratio (CTR) tends to be around 1/3 of 1 percent (.03 percent), newsfeed posts click through at around a 3–5 percent CTR. Again, users have the option of going to the brand's wall or directly to the external asset (if that's what's on the wall). Page post like ads do not tend to result in wall likes; rather, they drive traffic externally or to the wall's post. The price is reasonable and, because CTR is around 100 times greater, results in more volume in smaller targeting groups.

Have a look at the page post like story in Figure 6.5. There is little to distinguish it from an organic page post, except for the very small, gray "Sponsored" in the lower-left corner. We believe that users don't see it and those who do don't seem to care. This is absolutely FB selling organic where it was free before.

Figure 6.5 Example of a page post like sponsored story

To review, the three ad units we've discussed so far are

Page Post Ads   These promote individual wall posts. If the brand places an external link on its wall, the majority of traffic will click out, externally, to that page. The page post ad can be targeted to all of FB, or filtered by demo and psychographics, including the brand's fans. Page post ads generate expensive, albeit focused, likes, prodigal (and inexpensive) traffic to the external destination URL, and other actions such as comments and post likes. Page post ads are a staple in the community manager's playbook.

Page Like Stories   These are FoFv ads that amplify page likes to friends of friends. These ads generate lots of likes at a reasonable cost, and not much traffic to external assets. They are relatively inexpensive because they send users deeper into FB, which is what FB rewards with low costs. Page like stories are also fundamental to community managers, underused, and seriously effective. The most brilliant of FB's ads, page like stories unwittingly enroll FB users to endorse brands, practically without the user even understanding that they've been exploited. These are especially amazing when targeted for friends-of-friend visibility with interests congruent to the brand.

Page Post Like Stories   While these ads generate traffic to external assets as well as post likes, they don't usually generate page likes, a turnoff for some advertisers. They're great because, if you're the highest bidder, there is a good chance that your ads will be displayed in targeted users' newsfeeds. Since the newsfeed has such a high CTR, page post like stories can be used to squeeze more engagement out of a smaller psychographic segment.

Twitter Ads

Twitter ads are just becoming widely adopted. They're rudimentary, yet effective. Twitter ads are super-duper easy to think about and are divided into two basic categories:

- Lower-cost DIY ads, which can be run from an individual's Twitter account
- Ridiculously expensive ads placed directly by a Twitter account representative who generates a placement order

Twitter ads are only sort-of-kind-of ads. Twitter does not give us details as to whether or not the algorithm taps friends of friends. There is no transparency and no DIY targeting, except for geographic. It's efficient to spend money on an ad platform that has such a limited vision of who's being targeted and how. Still, Twitter ads work to drive traffic to external destination URLs and to gain focused followers. In fact, Promoted Accounts are, hands down, the best and most authentic way to buy followers because followers gained are focused and usually not spammy.

We'll have a look at each type of ad, what they're good for, and how community managers can use them to pimp external content and build community. Let's start with Twitter's DIY ads. Once Twitter grants your account access to ads, click the Twitter Ads option as shown in Figure 6.6.

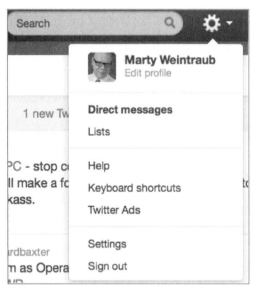

Figure 6.6 Twitter Ads will appear as an option once Twitter grants you access.

DIY: Promoted Tweets

Twitter's Help Center says, "Twitter Promoted Products empower advertisers to reach a wide audience with an amplified voice." That's an awesome description.

Usually nonfollowers don't see your tweets organically. Paying Twitter for Promoted Tweets shows selected tweets to nonfollowers. When you promote your tweets, Twitter will display your most engaging tweets (according to Twitter) to your followers and "those with interests similar to your followers." The goal is to get clicks on the link or links that are in the tweet being promoted. These CPC (cost per click) clicks are reasonably priced, with a CTR that resembles search. Promoted Tweets should be considered in any marketing mix, where driving reasonably priced PPC traffic is valuable. For the community manager, use Promoted Tweets to drive traffic to content, not as a primary method to gain followers. You'll get some, but that's not so much the point.

It is unknown whether the algorithm favors FoFv when displaying Promoted Tweets to relevant nonfollowers, but you might assume that it does. Promoted Tweets are paid organic amplification, because users who are *not* following you, who Twitter believes would be interested (algorithmically), do see your tweets. We expect Twitter to roll out keyword targeting to further filter targeting.

Specify a daily budget. Twitter will automatically end your Promoted Tweets once the daily budget limit is reached. Twitter also suggests a maximum bid that attempts to get the most engagements for you within your budget. Estimated results are based on a historical analysis of how your followers have engaged with your tweets in the past.

To improve the performance of Promoted Tweets, be sure to tweet relevant and engaging content. Twitter mechanically analyzes your tweets to find as many as five of your most engaging recent tweets, shown in the right column in Figure 6.7. There's also an essential feature that removes the ones that you don't want Twitter to promote. Since Twitter decides which nonfollowing users will see your Promoted Tweets, only choose ones that have relevant keywords as relates to the external link you're promoting. **One important note: Replies and retweets are not considered for promotion.**

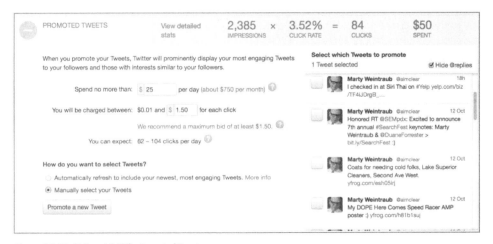

Figure 6.7 The Twitter Ads UI for Promoted Tweets

DIY: Promoted Accounts

A great community manager always wants to win followers with content and engagement. Still, there are times when it makes sense to spend money promoting a Twitter account to a targeted group of potential followers, especially when a company first starts using Twitter.

Promoted Accounts are about getting followers. Twitter uses data, by criteria unrevealed to advertisers, to feature your account to users who don't follow you yet. It works. When community managers purchase Promoted Accounts, Twitter will display that account prominently in the Who to Follow section to "users that are most likely to be interested in your account."

The CM will only pay for new followers gained. Measure the success of Promoted Accounts by cost per follower. Take time to check that followers gained are actually people. This is the most up-and-up way to buy followers to increase community size.

Choose a daily budget. Twitter automatically stops promoting your account once this limit is reached. Twitter recommends a maximum bid that it believes will get the most follows within your budget. On the right in Figure 6.8 is a preview of how your Promoted Account will look to a user. Metrics provided are follow rate as a percentage of follows/impressions, follows (how many), and spend.

Figure 6.8 The Twitter Ads UI for Promoted Accounts

FoFv is factored into algorithmic placement of the ad unit. There is a social endorsement component to promoted follows that is compelling to users who see it. Figure 6.9 shows a Promoted Account for Kenshoo, a PPC bid-management platform. Note that our good friend Joe, who follows Kenshoo, is being pimped without his permission by Twitter's ad, to add extra motivation for us to follow Kenshoo. Kenshoo's community manager has a powerful tool in this ad. In fact, we'll follow Kenshoo. We trust our friend Joe. If he follows Kenshoo, maybe we should too.

Figure 6.9 Promoted Accounts include a built-in social endorsement.

Promoted Trends

Big-dollar advertisers use Promoted Trends to amplify conversations and drive interest toward your brand by seizing a user's focus on Twitter. Promoted Trends display on Twitter for mobile users (iPhone, Android, and Tweetdeck, among them) and are served to all Twitter web users while promoted.

Users who click on a Promoted Trend are routed Twitter search results for that subject, along with a relevant Promoted Tweet from the advertiser at the top of the page. Most of the rest of the tweets on the search results page are from real users. It's possible for a Promoted Trend to get gigantic exposure and to be used to jump-start and amplify a dialogue on Twitter. Sponsoring trends adds really cool options to the CM's toolkit, including the ability to hijack actual news trends. During one of the 2012 presidential debates, candidate Mitt Romney discussed eliminating funding for Public Broadcasting. PBS even bought ad space on Twitter and exclaimed in a Tweet: "PBS is trusted, valued and essential. See why at http://www.valuepbs.org. (please retweet!)"

Are Sponsored Trends, not available in the DIY UI and much more expensive, worth it? Sometimes the answer is yes and sometimes no. At their worst, they can be a wasteful expenditure of precious media dollars. The gold at the end of the success rainbow is that Twitter drives other channels, including television news. Twitter has sparked revolt and made stars out of previously obscure users. Politicians have been taken down and out of office and communities have been mobilized for flood relief. It's a lot cheaper than a Super Bowl commercial.

Political Ads

Political Ads are Twitter campaigns bought by political marketers. Political Ads function in the same way as campaigns run by other advertisers on Twitter. The difference is the purple icon, which denotes political ads. Figure 6.10 shows a Political Ad in the Web UI. Users see text about who paid for the ad when they hover over it.

Figure 6.10 A Political Ad as shown in the Twitter Web UI, displaying who paid for the unit

YouTube

Videos are all the rage, and YouTube dominates the video landscape. Many community managers will be asked by stakeholders to promote YouTube videos. Like Facebook and Twitter Ads, video ads can be used for promoting your videos to YouTube users and driving traffic to external destination URLs. We've asked aimClear blogger Manny Rivas, an internationally respected YouTube marketer and clinician, to contribute to this section to explain the various types of ads that can be placed in YouTube.

Whether you are looking to use video ads for branding, generating leads, direct response, or you just want to drive views to a new video, YouTube Ads are just the ticket.

There are two places where you can manage YouTube ads: Google AdWords and Google AdWords for Video. Some ad units can be created in both locations and others are platform specific. The table in Figure 6.11 shows all the video ad units Google offers and where they can be found.

	AdWords	AdWords for Video
TrueView InStream		X
TrueView InSlate		X
TrueView InSearch	X	X
Call-to-Action Overlay	n/a*	n/a*
TrueView InDisplay	X	X
InVideo Static Image	X	
Expandable Video V1	X	
Click to Play	X	
InStream	X	

*CTA Overlay ads are created and managed in the YouTube Channel Video Manager

Figure 6.11 Video ad units offered by Google

TrueView InStream

The TrueView InStream ad unit shows before short- or long-form videos in YouTube and the Google Display Network (GDN). Five seconds into the ad, viewers have the option to skip the ad by clicking a button in the lower-right corner of the screen (Figure 6.12). If the video is longer than 30 seconds, the advertiser is charged when the viewer reaches the 30-second mark. If the video is shorter than 30 seconds, the advertiser is charged when the video ends. This unit is best for

- Branding KPIs
- Video message testing KPIs

This ad format can be very cost-effective when exposure and branding views are a core objective. If done right, TrueView InStream ads can provide some of the highest view-through rates out of all TrueView ad formats. Be sure the first five seconds of your video ad are "sticky." In other words, this portion of the video should entice the viewer enough to keep watching. If you intend on using a bumper, wait until you've gotten the viewer's attention before you roll it. If direct response is the objective, be sure to build in a call to action.

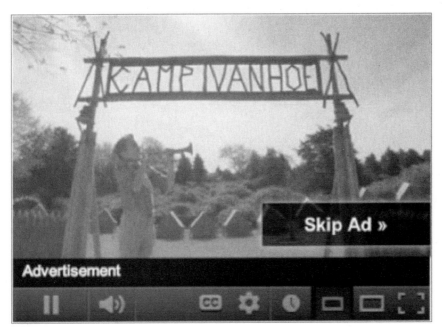

Figure 6.12 Example of a TrueView InStream ad unit, which gives viewers the option to skip after five seconds

TrueView InSlate

The TrueView InSlate ad unit shows before long-form videos on YouTube or the GDN. The viewer can watch one of three video ads from different advertisers, or watch the selected video with four commercial breaks, as shown in Figure 6.13. Advertisers are charged when their ad is selected. This unit is best for

- Branding KPIs
- Ad message testing KPI
- Video message testing KPIs

The thumbnail and ad copy are very important with InSlate ad units. Make the ad creative pop and experiment with copy that speaks to the short length of the video. Choosing video placements closely related to the topic of the ad will have a positive influence on your click-through rate.

Figure 6.13 TrueView InSlate ads offer the watcher ad-viewing options prior to long-form videos.

TrueView InSearch

The TrueView InSearch ad unit (Figure 6.14) displays in YouTube search results. Much like a search ad, advertisers target specific keywords for their ads to show against in search results. The advertiser is charged when the viewer begins watching the ad. It's best for

- Direct response KPIs
- Lead generation KPIs
- Ad message testing KPIs
- Social engagement KPIs
- Profit maximization KPIs

Figure 6.14 TrueView InSearch ad units are shown on YouTube search results pages.

Just as with traditional search ads, InSearch ads can be targeted by level of intent. InSearch ads can be effective in transitioning a potential customer from the research and consideration stage to taking action, especially for products that are easy to showcase and detail with video. Couple the video with a call-to-action overlay ad that directs viewers to the conversion-focused landing page. Brand channels should direct InSearch ads to the channel page and feature a CTA banner at the top of the page that drives viewers to the website.

TrueView InDisplay

TrueView InDisplay ads are displayed next to related video watch pages on YouTube and GDN partner sites. The advertiser is charged when the user watches the ad. It's best for

- Direct response KPIs
- Lead generation KPIs
- Ad message testing KPIs
- Social engagement KPIs

The AdWords for Video UI will require the description lines to be filled out, even though, as Figure 6.15 shows, only the headline will be displayed on the YouTube watch page. This increases the importance of drawing the viewer in with the 25-character headline.

This Is My Ad
by movieclipsTRAILERS
2,144,210 views

Figure 6.15 TrueView InDisplay ads are shown next to related video watch pages.

As with TrueView InSearch ads, couple the video with a call-to-action overlay ad that directs viewers to the conversion-focused landing page. Brand channels should direct InDisplay ads to the channel page and feature a CTA banner at the top of the page that drives viewers to the website.

CTA Overlay Ad

Call-to-Action Overlay ads, as shown in Figure 6.16, are made available to InSearch and InDisplay TrueView video ads. The CTA ad is created and managed in the video edit screen of the YouTube UI. It's best for

- Direct response KPIs
- Lead generation KPIs

Figure 6.16 Call-to-Action Overlay ad

LinkedIn Ads

LinkedIn Ads are expensive but worth it if used properly. Like other channels, there are some ad units that drive users to external destination URLs and others that keep users inside LinkedIn. LinkedIn has always been rather weak at generating organic, let alone paid, FoFv. The ads are mostly social ads with a boring palette (Figure 6.17). Dear LinkedIn: These features would be extremely powerful in motivating users to behave the same way as their friends. Study Facebook and do better.

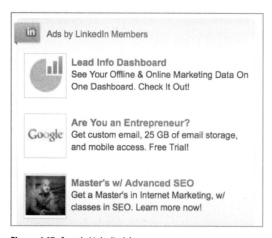

Figure 6.17 Sample LinkedIn Ads

Still, LinkedIn Ads that send users within LinkedIn can be considered paid organic amplification, because users routed to your personal profile might ask to connect, join a group, follow a company, or otherwise engage (Figure 6.18). Hopefully

LinkedIn will provide more fixed internal routing options in the future, such as sending users to Answers, Group Pages, and so forth. There is a workaround. Internal routing can be hacked by entering the full URL of the internal LinkedIn destination into the Your Web Page option.

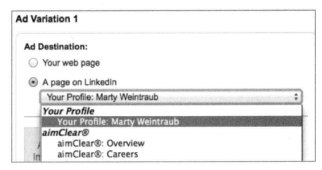

Figure 6.18 LinkedIn Ads that send users to an internal page can be considered paid organic amplification.

LinkedIn DIY Ads target users in an impressive grid. Figure 6.19 shows Skills targeting, which can be effective. LinkedIn Ads can be geo-targeted as well, though options are limited. There's no zip code, DMA, or miles/radius targeting, and the UI is cumbersome.

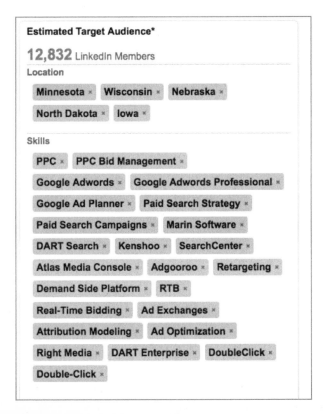

Figure 6.19 LinkedIn Skills targeting

The workaround for finding missing geographic specificity is due to target Groups that have city names in the title, such as "Duluth Economic Development." LinkedIn Ads allow for a small image, headline, and body copy. They display several different ways in different areas of LinkedIn.

There's no way to buy LinkedIn Ads except via the GDN (some text ads), directly, and whatever you can get out of the LinkedIn Ads DIY UI. LinkedIn would do more businesses if there were an exchange, which is probably in the works. In the DIY UI, LinkedIn gives an option to publish on the LinkedIn Network. This option, which targets LinkedIn users when they're on third-party affiliate sites, gives community managers more volume in small psychographic spaces.

Even with these caveats, the targeting options are awesome. Figure 6.20 shows a targeting matrix of corporate job titles at specific companies. Job titles can also be targeted by job function and/or seniority, such as "Health Care Services/VP." LinkedIn users can also be targeted by school, group, gender, and age.

Figure 6.20 A LinkedIn targeting matrix of job titles at specific companies

LinkedIn should be taken seriously for B2B and B2C. Remember that occupations matter a lot to most users in every channel. Ski instructors buy lip balm and parkas. Senior design specification engineers buy touch-screen components and excellent beer.

The modern community manager is the PR department's best friend. Nearly every media role, from morning show host to city desk editor, is targetable. Serve these media roles ads along public relations KPIs. Market to media in a grid with specific publications such as *The Washington Post*, *Wired*, *Rolling Stone*, *Boston Globe*, and *TechCrunch*. LinkedIn is the modern PR firm's secret weapon.

Other Channels

Let's not forget traditional search PPC ads. It often makes sense to market social assets with search. Don't forget when deploying Google AdWords search PPC ads to leave a site link or two for social KPIs. If someone searches for a brand, it might make some sense to include a branded link to the corporate video or Facebook Page, for example.

We've had good results with StumbleUpon paid Stumbles. They're cool because StumbleUpon users don't know the impressions are paid and the advertiser gets killer sentiment feedback along with cheap clicks. Reddit sells traffic by targeting. The traffic is quirkily awesome for some applications, especially for promoting applications. Reddit is geekmaster heaven. Our best advice is to hang out on every channel you target. That's the point, really.

> **Note:** Community managers should master the PPC model in each community they participate in on behalf of the mission and KPIs. Be the hybrid. Dominate the social future. The dominance of the mashup is undeniable.

As the social Internet matures, paid channels and new targeting methods will emerge. What's important for community managers now is to make a commitment to study and/or master emergent social targeting opportunities.

Put It All Together! Anatomy of a Multichannel Content Release

Think of a content release as a hub-and-spoke system. The content you want to promote on your blog, home site, or social pages is published, radiating out from the center. Content is the center of everything, and it is distributed to the channels (Figure 6.21). The circle is the universe of paid and organic channels. Content radiates outward from the center from one system to and between the next.

Figure 6.21 If you think of content as a hub-and-spoke system, content is at the center of everything.

OK, let's look at a common scenario. Your team just published a massively cool blog post. What comes next? Hopefully you work in a system where the community manager advises the content team, or you do it all. If not, the community manager's involvement starts here. Let the content release begin.

What are we after?

- Focused likes, follows, etc., at a reasonable average cost
- Measurable community psychographics in Facebook
- Awesome paid organic traffic to our site
- KPI conversion attributable, at least in part, to social
- Ongoing list marketing that pays, for users who followed, liked, and subscribed by social
- Reasonable ongoing costs to maintain the community

Content is the center, and should be on a site you own. It's time to radiate out to social to promote that content. You've been busy in social channels, sharing, supporting, hanging out, asking questions, and citing complementary and noncompetitive content from your sharing dashboard. You and your avatar are respected on Twitter and Facebook. Now let's get busy, hybrid CMs.

We're using Facebook, Twitter, and YouTube for this mock release, because they are commonly used channels these days. LinkedIn, forums, and any channel you play in, on behalf of your brand, can be scripted in such a release. The script we follow in the release is the editorial calendar. Many CMs do it on the fly. At aimClear, we have teams of paid organic mashup CMs, and social ads production teams to service the account rep if we need to move a lot of earth. Let's rock this puppy.

Start Organic

- Your content is the lifeblood of your brand. It should always represent the brand's identity and seek to evoke a connection with its audience(s). Additionally, it should be optimized for search and be tailored to share on whatever social channels you have. This will look different for every brand and is contingent on a strategic communication plan. Be sure the tweets and wall posts are packaged and optimized to become ads with keywords, social intent, headlines, and proper images.
- Always be aware of any format restrictions for the channels the content will be released in. Tweets have to be 140 characters. Facebook images should basically be square.
- Post a single link on the Facebook wall, tweet it, and take what traffic is there among followers.
  - Facebook says some 16 percent of users will see your content, on average, if you post to the brand page 5–7 times per week. This can be substantial. For

every 100,000 fans, 16,000 will see the post. Of that, 640 focused users (4 percent CTR in newsfeed assumed) will come to your external site.

- Figure 6.22 shows 3.52 percent CTR for a high bid in Twitter Ads (Promoted Tweets), and 2,385 impressions for this author's 8,735 followers. What we really care about here is the 3.52 percent CTR because it's an indicator of how our organic Tweets perform. You can totally test potential virility of content and words using paid tweets to vet organic.

| ⊖ | PROMOTED TWEETS | View detailed stats | 2,385 IMPRESSIONS | × | 3.52% CLICK RATE | = | 84 CLICKS | $50 SPENT |

Figure 6.22 The CTR of Promoted Tweets can indicate how organic tweets perform.

- Don't be put off if you're small. Communities of 10,000 Facebook fans still send 64 users. If you're marketing a high-ticket item or a local business, the eyeballs of 64 users twice a month might results in piles of restaurant reservations, or remind users that time to book that special cruise is running out, for example. Twitter scales downward beautifully, too.

Time for Paid Organic Amplification

- We know if we do nothing, not enough users in any channels will see it. We started organically with the followers we have and who have seen the results. We then decide whether to promote the content with money or not.
  - One note on vetting potential with organic-only releases. When content resonates organically, that's great. Move ahead and invest in amplifying it. If it didn't resonate, make sure there was a big enough sampling to make the call. It's true that initial organic buzz for content portends really great content that should be scaled. However, we've seen so many cases where truly great content was not revealed organically. Skillful community managers placing paid organic social ads set them on fire.
- Run well-targeted Facebook page post ads to desirable psychographic segments. Now you're getting exposure to your audience, including those in your community who are in the target segments. The page post ad results in traffic to the external asset bookmarked on the wall and visits to the Facebook brand page. You get pricey likes and cheap traffic. It's all good.
- Run targeted Facebook page like sponsored stories. Friends of friends in the target's psychographics see a social endorsement of likes. Wade through FB's UI and be sure you're in a CPC bid model and bid high. It's interesting to note that the minute a new user likes from the page post ad, that user is now eligible for the page like story. The very minute the new user likes, the user is exploited as a reference, personally evangelizing the brand! Wow. That is *so* cool.

- Run Promoted Tweets. Choose one or two focused tweets that have good results organically, and promote them with paid. The Twitter Ads algorithm chooses targets and distributes impressions. The result is additional traffic. Twitter Ads can be excellent for distributing content at a cheap cost-per-click. Certainly Twitter Ads cost less than search and Facebook Ads.

- Run YouTube TrueView InSearch ads. Target specific keywords for ads to show up against in search results. Market to search intent. This will drive traffic to the content for a reasonable CPC.

- Optional: As things heat up, run a Facebook page post like story. This won't get you likes, but it will generate FoFv in second-degree newsfeeds. The CTR to your external page will be good, with other actions occurring, including shares and comments. Use this ad unit to amplify further. We like to use it when something heats up in terms of engagement.

- Rotate running and pausing all forms of Facebook Ad types (page post ad, page like story, and page post like story). Users burn out on too much of this. Make up a rotation based on how many impressions are being served a week. Start and pause on a flexible schedule of ad types. If your targeting includes multiple buckets, then you can include pausing target groups in the start-pause pattern.

- Measure the results. Chapter 8, "Measuring Success! State-of-the-Art Social Metrics," is all about analytics and measuring.

Advanced Cross-Channel Paid and Retargeting Mashups

This section is advanced. For you intense CM/PPC hybrid jocks, check out this mashup scenario. If you prefer, go ahead and skip to the next chapter.

- Drive high-intent targeted social traffic from any channel to a landing page to attain KPIs.

- Set Google remarketing and Demand-Side Platform (DSP) retargeting code on the landing page. Now you've cookied a list of users at the psychographic targeting level. (Remember the specificity of multichannel psychographic targeting. It rocks for attaining KPIs.)

- Follow that list of users with retargeting/remarketing ads 3–4 times per day (impression cap) everywhere they go in the targetable universe (including Facebook Exchange, or FBX) for about three days. Grind additional conversion percentage for the KPI. Be unobtrusive and don't abuse your users.

This protocol is but one of gazillions of retargeting mashups. Set retargeting cookies in the public customer support funnel of your site. Follow users around for reviews. There are so many ways traffic can originate and perpetuate between social channels. Coupled with FoFv social endorsement ads, things can become amazingly creative. Let's look at an example:

- Using LinkedIn and Facebook Ads, target all the molecular biologists who work for Fortune 500 companies in America, the UK, Australia, and Canada.

- Drive them to a YouTube video on your blog's landing page.

- The KPI is watching the first 38 seconds of the video.

- When engagement occurs (for great marketers), post the YouTube thread link on your brand's Facebook wall.

- Buy targeted page post ads and page post like sponsored stories to drive traffic to the YouTube thread and Facebook likes.

You get the message. The trick is to be clear about what each channel's paid amplification provides. Look, if you're not doing paid organic amplification, it's possible that you're blogging to nobody. Even if your blog is a giant publisher, you're only doing part of what you can do and are left to be strictly organic.

Adding to Editorial Calendar

In Chapter 4, "Content, Reputation, and Hardcore Listening Hacks," we discussed editorial calendars—leveraging a comprehensive production schedule and winning by a higher level of content organization. Editorial calendars are also fantastic for mapping out the timeline and mechanics of content releases. The real mojo is when CMs add paid organic amplification to the ongoing process of choosing topics, researching, writing, approving, and publishing in social channels. The more we see of this era of social propagation, the more it becomes clear that organizational prowess is what wins. Layering a tuned content release process with a badass content creation program is what wins time after time.

In Chapter 4, we discussed editorial calendars as a means to organize your publishing plan across touchpoints. Let's look at pointers for layering paid amplification over your editorial calendar.

Add paid organic amplification to the editorial calendar. Say what channels you're going to play in, both organic and paid. Boil the tactical execution list down to abbreviations on the editorial calendar. Here are some examples to start with. You'll get the idea quickly:

- Facebook Wall Post: FBWP
- Facebook Page Post Ad: FBPPA
- Facebook Page Like Story: FBPLS
- Tweet: Tweet
- Twitter Promoted Account: Twerp

- LinkedIn Brand Page Post: LIWP
- LinkedIn Personal Profile Post: LIP
- LinkedIn Page Ads: LIPads
- LinkedIn External Ads: LIEads
- YouTube TrueView InStream: TvIs

All right then! Now you're well on your way to mastering the social distribution system. Now we're thinking about content releases in terms of what occurs organically and what occurs by paid organic distribution mashup. Good work!

You understand how social communities limit what others, outside your community of friends, can see. You've implemented systematic paid organic tactics to reenable the missing organic features. You, brave community manager, *dominate* the social distribution system!

Community Crisis Management

Sometimes, the same community CMs cultivate, care for, and connect with on behalf of their brands can turn against that brand or each other. In this chapter, we'll dissect social media crisis management from the top down. That includes establishing a crisis protocol, implementing house rules for branded social spaces, using best practices for kicking people out of your community, and maintaining a cool head and a steady blood pressure. We hope you'll walk away armed with the right tools and knowledge to face any social media conflict, tiff, or red-level disaster.

7

Having a Crisis Plan in Advance

Community member meltdowns and brand PR nightmares are unpredictable, but arguably inevitable. Social snafus will happen to every company at some point, on some scale. The saying is true: You can't please everyone. A customer is bound to have a poor brand experience and take to Twitter complaining to friends, or even @YourCompany. People have opinions and values. Not all will align with the CM's or the CEO's, for that matter. Folks get heated. Now more than ever, those grievances are being aired all across the World Wide Web, occasionally peppered with downright libelous claims and sometimes in language you wouldn't dare show Mother.

Community managers can't forecast the keystrokes of an angry Facebook fan or the reaction to a new corporate YouTube video, but that doesn't mean they can't be prepared for the worst. Companies that have a clear and comprehensive crisis plan established in advance are doing themselves an invaluable favor. It makes for much smoother sailing around the wild seas of cyberspace, and a generally happier, healthier, saner community manager.

Of course, it's not just about maintaining the CM's peace of mind. Many players hold a stake in the reputation and well-being of a brand and its social community. We like to call them *stakeholders*. From the C-suite to core employees, PR players to legal team and beyond—all of these parties greatly benefit from an advanced social media crisis plan. It helps ensure, among many other things, that optimal responses will be seamlessly shared across all social channels.

Keep in mind that we're not just talking about conflicts or crises that arise *on* social media and solving them with social media. We're talking about good old-fashioned PR disasters that happen offline as well. Poor in-store experiences, on-site accidents, you know...stuff that happens "IRL" (in real life).

So let's push up our sleeves and dig in, shall we? There's a box of knee and elbow pads behind you.

Defining Social and Legal "Safety" and "Doomsday" Keywords

All of life is a system of stimuli and responses. If you're walking down the sidewalk and see someone you recognize waiting for the bus, you might stop and say, "Hi! How are you?" If you walk by and see that same person lying bloody and moaning, you might react a little differently, to say the least. The real world as well as the world online are composed of situations, triggers, and corresponding reactions. For social media community managers, those triggers come in the form of keywords—some positive, some negative, some brand-centric, and some competitive. Core responsibilities of today's cutting-edge CM include listening to and understanding online conversations involving those keywords, and responding with cat-like agility, speed, grace, and confidence.

The listening and understanding factors of this equation are greatly served by a fine-tuned reputation-monitoring dashboard with alerts set to fire on an assortment of "safety" and "doomsday" keywords that vary in level of intensity. Think back to the RSS dashboard you built in Chapter 4, "Content, Reputation, and Hardcore Listening Hacks." The same principle applies here; it's simply a different set of keywords to monitor for. Can you dig it?

Consider a consumer goods manufacturer that sells ooey-gooey cookies, baked, packed, and shipped from its own confectionary plant. Alerts might be placed on keywords related to the cookie industry, permutations of brand names and products, and keywords that indicate cookie chatter in general. Doomsday words for this brand might include "rats," "food poisoning," "recall," and the like, mashed up with some reference to the cookie company and its products.

When it's time to develop a crisis plan, have a sit-down with everyone involved in the company's PR and overall reputation. This might include lawyers. If you're an agency, don't forget to include the client. Together, flesh out a complete list of doomsday words, including legal jargon and social slang. Leave no stone unturned and no keyword untapped. Plug these into your reputation-monitoring dashboard, and then organize by buckets of severity.

The purpose of bucketing keywords is to ensure that the right alerts are sent to the right people. A different set of monitoring concerns comes into play when doomsday words trigger. It's essential to have these alerts forwarded to decision makers, stakeholders, the boss-man, and other top dogs as soon as possible so that the proper action can be devised and executed in a timely manner. Set the big guys up to receive alerts on doomsday words as your company and client see fit.

Conversely, not *everyone* in the company needs to get an email at 2:36 in the morning when @CookieLover tweets she just housed an entire box of @YourBrandHere macaroons and thinks she might puke. Maybe it's just the on-call CM who receives around-the-clock pings for any and all alerts. If she's worth her salt, she'll know when it's time to raise the alarm and who needs to be brought into the loop.

Doomsday Keyword Master List

It's free goodie time! Here we have a list of doomsday keyword ideas and permutations. Plug, play, and enjoy!

- [Brand] "Accident"
- [Brand] "Awful"
- [Brand] "Bad"
- [Brand] "Broke"
- [Brand] "Business Practices"

- [Brand] "Busted"
- [Brand] "Collapse"
- [Brand] "Conditions"
- [Brand] "Contaminated"
- [Brand] "Death"

- [Brand] "Disaster"
- [Brand] "Exploded"
- [Brand] "Explosion"
- [Brand] "Fail"
- [Brand] "Failed"
- [Brand] "FDA"
- [Brand] "Federal Law"
- [Brand] "Fined"
- [Brand] "Fired"
- [Brand] "Horrible"
- [Brand] "Infected"
- [Brand] "Injured"
- [Brand] "Inspection"
- [Brand] "Investigation"
- [Brand] "Killed"
- [Brand] "Layoff"
- [Brand] "Lies"

- [Brand] "Lost Jobs"
- [Brand] "Malfunction"
- [Brand] "Messed Up"
- [Brand] "OSHA"
- [Brand] "Privacy"
- [Brand] "Probe"
- [Brand] "Recall"
- [Brand] "Ripoff"
- [Brand] "Safety"
- [Brand] "Scam"
- [Brand] "Screwed Up"
- [Brand] "Shutdown"
- [Brand] "Sucks"
- [Brand] "Terrible"
- [Brand] "Violated"
- [Brand] "Violation"

Establishing a Code of Conduct

Another part of social media crisis preparation is knowing what's fair and what's foul when it comes to community behavior, along with having a solid plan of attack should a crisis occur. One of the best ways to defend against unruly user-generated content (UGC) on a branded social profile is to set the record straight before the first crusty comment is slung. In other words, build a code of conduct your community should expect to abide by, or face the consequences.

Call another company brainstorm with everyone who should be present, along with PR, legal, client, and C-suite if required. Create, compile, and publish an approved code of conduct for all your social community to see. A prime location for this might be in a dedicated tab on your brand's Facebook, YouTube, or Google+ page (less so for Twitter; even the crudest @mentions don't actually appear *in* the company's profile/stream). Also consider including an overview of social rules with links to more in-depth explanations on your company website. The choice is yours. Regarding FB, Tide is one company that has the right idea. Check out Figure 7.1 to see how they showcase their house rules on Facebook.

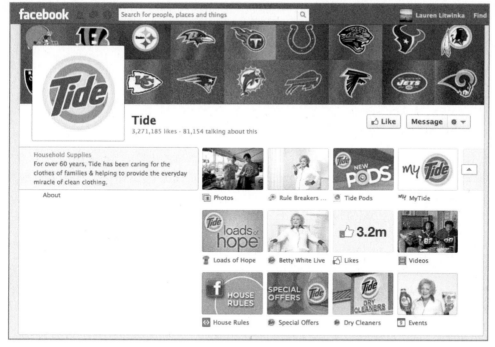

Figure 7.1 Tide leverages individual Facebook tabs for contests, special offers, videos, and yes, house rules.

When drafting company house rules, consider including all or some of the following:

- Words of welcome and appreciation
- Clarification of what the branded social page represents
- Expectations of community member conduct
- Invitations for participation; ideas for things to share
- Specific forms of unacceptable behavior (cussing, harassment, and so forth)
- Repercussions for unacceptable behavior
- Any other disclaimers

There's no cookie-cutter template here. Pick and choose the elements that will comprise the brand's code of conduct as they apply. Make them reflect the company in form and content, and be mindful of how well they speak to the target community.

On that note, it's worth feeling comfortable with conversational language here. Assume that 99.9 percent of your fan base won't read the house rules if they resemble a humdrum Terms of Service stuffed with legal language. Be colloquial, to an extent.

Make the content digestible and approachable. Consider using humor. Avoid a warden-esque approach (no one's broken the law yet). One word of caution: Don't let being friendly cause you to lose focus. The goal is to state the company's position firmly and clearly: What's okay, what's not? Distinguish between what the brand regards as an expression of opinion and downright disrespect.

Now, it's time to prep for what to do if someone breaks the law.

Crafting a Crisis Protocol and Hierarchy of Contingent Responsibilities

It is paramount that you set a code of conduct in a concrete crisis protocol. The CM should know exactly what to do when an aspect of the code is broken and feel that they know how to react properly. As you have learned, not everyone has to receive every email alert for every keyword. The same holds true for house rule violations and complaints from the community. It's more than a little ridiculous to speed-dial the company attorney and summon the PR enclave when a Facebook fan gets feisty or a rogue tweet flashes: "@YourBrand sux!" However, it's imperative to have a crystal-clear understanding of where that threshold lies. The social media community manager must know the answers to these crucial questions, even before a crisis occurs: "What do I have the authority to handle on my own? What kind of situation requires input from someone above me?"

The process of creating a crisis protocol can, in fact, begin with a larger series of questions. Once the answers are agreed on internally, they can be compiled into a detailed crisis protocol and circulated to the appropriate team members for study and reference. Let's cruise through some of those fundamental questions:

- Who's at the helm? This is your chain of command. Is it a single community manager or a team with a rotating schedule? Know who they are. Make sure *they* know who they are. This is your company's first response fleet, the person or people who have a finger on the pulse of your brand's social community, social assets, social mentions—everything.

  - Is the community manager on call 24/7, nights, weekends, even holidays? Or do they tune out at the close of a workday and resume in the a.m.? When a nasty comment is posted on the company FB page at 9:45 on a Friday evening, does the CM react or let it be until Monday morning?

  - If we expect the CM to be on call 24/7, is he/she equipped with the proper technology to always be connected? A smartphone? Wi-Fi at home? Does the company compensate for these items?

- Who gives the seal of approval? This is your escalation protocol. When things get messy, immediate action does not always mean immediate engagement with the assailant. Still, it's ideal to act as soon as possible, once the CM and appropriate company members have their ducks in a row. Before moving forward, it's important to have buy-in, but from whom? Make sure the CM knows whose seal of approval is required for the form of engagement in question *before* reaching out on behalf of the brand. Consider the following, in the face of a negative event:

- Who do we alert? Consider creating a document akin to a "School Snow Day" phone tree. Know who needs to know first, and how high up the chain the news should travel.

- Who gives the green light? The CEO? Head of PR? Department/team/project leader? Client? Have a clear, unified understanding of whose approval is needed before moving forward.

- Does the company have cohesive, concise key messages in the face of certain types of conflicts or crises, preapproved by the green-light givers? What are the messages? Who knows them? Who has the authority to share them? Are they written and archived somewhere for easy retrieval?

- What's the method of outreach? This is your consumer response protocol. Online, offline, public, private, by email, by phone? Iron out the method of outreach before the CM is expected to jump in.

  - When do we take things offline? Do we try to resolve publicly, or hop into email ASAP?

  - Do we stay offline? Or return to the scene of the complaint with a statement of resolution to update the community?

  - Do we have a dedicated customer service email address ready to share when a community member freaks out? Who checks it? How often? Is it publicly available along with other company contact info, or only shared on an as-needed basis?

Distinguishing a Crisis from a Conflict

Trolls, spammers, and dissatisfied customers, oh my! With all the forms of negativity that may trickle into a company's social space, it can be difficult to tell the difference between a true social media crisis and a mere conflict. Let's take a look at some identifying elements of a crisis so we can better understand what it's *not*.

True social media-fueled crises can be identified by

- Instability and uncertainty (chaos!)
- New issues inciting a change in opinion of the masses
- Potential to affect a large portion of target audience

Time to dig into each of these a bit deeper; we'll also illustrate some sample scenarios. We'll use these identifying elements to help recognize sticky social media conflicts vs. serious social media crises.

Instability and Uncertainty

As the social spokesperson for a brand, it's the responsibility of the community manager to be up to speed on pretty much everything brand-related at all times, especially when things get a little nutty. When an issue pops up and explodes on the social media scene, the CM has to be prepared to react. If she feels well informed and confident responding to community members' complaints, this generally means it isn't a crisis. If the CM doesn't know more than the community about an issue causing concern, that's a red flag.

Time for a sample scenario: Snack Food Company X unknowingly distributes a shipment of snacks that contains a tainted ingredient, and five consumers get food poisoning. The Net gets wind, and news stories, blog posts, YouTube video rants, angry tweets, and Facebook Wall posts amass in droves, all while Snack Food Company X is just getting first reports of the events. Is this a crisis or a conflict?

If you guessed crisis, you're right. Even if this mishap did not cause physical harm, when brand conversations about an event not yet fully understood permeate at a rate faster than the company is able to manage, it's a crisis. Lacking all the answers, Snack Food Company X is under the gun to get the facts, craft brand messages, address the masses, dispel inaccuracies, convey the truth, and undertake serious damage control, all in a hail of social media arrows that fly 24/7.

New Issues Inciting Change in Opinion of the Masses

It's not always fun to dig up the past, particularly when the past is messy. Less fun is when the past is dug up for you. Resurgence of an unfortunate company incident, or reiterations of a negative perspective of a brand, can be bummers and buzz-kills. But do they suggest a crisis?

Not necessarily. Brand bashing is no picnic, but if the mentality is nothing new, and mass opinion is more or less "unchanged" (one way or the other), the situation can be taken care of. Recommendations for these issues include thick skins and supportive PR as needed to dilute negativity. When more and more voices join a fresh argument or complaint against a brand, it suggests a crisis on the horizon.

Sample scenario time! Taco Bell. It's fast food, folks, not gourmet cuisine. The discussion surrounding this chain's questionable meat is nothing new. That said, it's still alive and kicking (the argument, not the meat). Negative tweets, blog posts, and Facebook statuses attack the percentage of *real meat* in Taco Bell's concoctions on a daily, even hourly basis (Figure 7.2). That's a lot of bad press. Is this a crisis, or a conflict?

Conflict. Actually, more of an obstacle than a conflict, but not a crisis (unless the world up and decides to kick the king of Doritos Locos Tacos to the curb for want of better beef). Taco Bell is one of a few household names in the fast-food biz. It's only natural that brand conversations, whether positive, negative, or indifferent, pour in with some frequency. As that frequency remains at baseline, it's controllable, predictable, and not lethal.

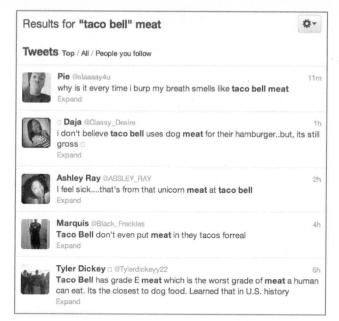

Figure 7.2 Around-the-clock tweets about the caliber of Taco Bell meat

Potential to Affect a Large Portion of Target Audience

When a single consumer has a poor brand experience and flaunts a sob story on a company Facebook Page or similar social space, it's not a crisis for the community manager on the other end. The magnitude of those affected by a given event is a dependable metric by which to distinguish a crisis from a conflict. Is the majority, or an increasingly large portion of the online community and target audience, up in arms over what's going on? Assess this while preparing to move forward.

Bear in mind that intra-community uprisings aren't always caused by a bunch of people feeling wronged. One person with one uniquely terrible brand experience can garner a sympathetic mob. On that note, more useful questions to ask include, "Does this single story have the potential to go viral? Could the virility cause lasting brand damage?" If the answers are yes, a crisis could unfold.

Saddle up for one final sample scenario. Hotel Chain Z has more than 50 hotels along the East Coast. A customer had a poor experience with one hotel in particular and ranted incessantly on Twitter. The customer happens to have decent sway in social media. Despite the hotel's attempts to reach out in an effort to resolve the issue, the customer continues to tweet negative sentiments about Hotel Chain Z. Crisis? Conflict?

Conflict, with definite potential. Depending on how *bad* the experience was (did a deranged hotel employee try to kill him, or was his bed lumpy?), a situation like this has the potential to evolve into something more serious if not dealt with swiftly and successfully. Otherwise, it's a conflict. Issues that occur on a local scale are solvable in a way that crises are not.

High-Level Assessment Questions

As community managers march into the digital trenches, we encourage them to consider these questions when a social storm is a-brewin':

- Do I know more than the community?
- Am I capable of responding to the nature of the complaints?
- Is this a resurgence of old news?
- Are new, expanding groups of people upset?
- Has there been a major shift in brand opinion?
- Is this happening on a local or global scale?
- Does the conflict have the potential to go viral?

We'll wrap up with some final words of advice: Relax! Keep cool. Most of the time, what social CMs will be dealing with won't be a true social media crisis. Quickly assess whether it is or not. If not, toss that creepy term out the window—it will only cause added stress and anxiety as the CM is trying to do her job, which is, remember, to provide value through content and conversation, and to mediate, curate, and monitor any and all conversations surrounding the brand, in good times and bad.

Social Community Triage: Do's and Don'ts

Okay! Now we know how to tell the difference between a social media conflict and a crisis. But no matter the situation, it has to be dealt with properly. Crisis or conflict, the community manager needs to know how to act (and when to just walk away). Let's look at what to do when complaints, conflicts, or crises crop up on a brand's social profile and it's up to the CM to deal with them.

Discerning the Intent

Negative brand sentiment, like ice cream, comes in many different flavors. Before the community manager acts, addresses, or eliminates negative posts on the brand's social page, she should (read: really, really, really should) discern the intent of the post. Is it a legitimate complaint from a frustrated customer? Is it a poor review as a result of a poor experience? Is it spewed nonsense from a repeat troll offender?

Maybe the company's policy is to remove everything negative. Or, maybe it leaves legit negative reviews up for the sake of transparency. Refer back to the "Establishing a Code of Conduct" section. Without a clear-cut code of conduct, social media is the Wild West. But with house rules on your side, the questionable gray areas become less fuzzy. Regardless, best practice is to have a real understanding of what motivated the post before taking action.

The customer is always right, or so the saying goes. We'd argue that's not always the case. There is a noteworthy range of people out there, in case you haven't noticed. Scope out the spectrum illustrated in Figure 7.3 for our take. Hypothetically speaking, a customer might feel personally slighted, cheated, and swindled when truly no monkey business occurred, then go on a ranting rampage and make it his/her sole mission to destroy the brand's social reputation by way of irrational accusatory comments. Discerning intent (and frequency of contributions from said commenter) is a helpful step to understanding whether the customer is or isn't "right."

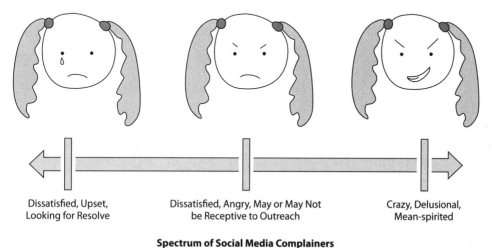

Dissatisfied, Upset, Looking for Resolve

Dissatisfied, Angry, May or May Not be Receptive to Outreach

Crazy, Delusional, Mean-spirited

Spectrum of Social Media Complainers

Figure 7.3 The faces of those who complain against brands on social media

As we charge forth to explore these do's and don'ts, let's use the sample situation of a Facebook promotional contest gone wrong.

Imagine this: A small crew of sore losers, collectively code-named Fan X, crops up after they lost a photo-sharing Facebook contest hosted by Brand Z. Fan X leaves a barrage of comments on the brand's Wall, claiming the contest was rigged, that Brand Z conducts shady business, swearing to never buy from Brand Z again. After assessing the situation, Brand Z decides to craft and post a succinct statement on Facebook that addresses the issue at hand. What should Brand Z's community manager do? Also, what should the CM *not* do?

Addressing the Masses: Do's

Follow these pointers for optimal addressing of the community at large.

- Do document everything! When a social media conflict (or crisis) is underway, it's crucial to document *everything* in a timely manner. Best practice is to take screen captures of community activity as it happens, with timestamps, and save them all in a folder or document. Add links to the individual post, if so desired, for warp-speed navigation back to the original post. This can be achieved by clicking on the timestamp of any given tweet or Facebook post, for example. Having all of the evidence on file should assist the CM nicely when compiling a report to show the client or debrief the in-house team.

- Do craft a comprehensive response. If this is the route of choice, be sure to keep the focus, highlight the facts, dispel misconceptions, and explain the brand's standpoint. This response could be one or two sentences or a brief paragraph. Concise is the name of the game. (Depending on the situation, the CM may actually decide *not* to respond/stoke the fires. We'll get more into that in our tips for lowering blood pressure.)

- Do ask for input from the in-house team. Two (or more) heads are better than one. Bring team members in on the think tank as a response is being written. Consult with upper-ups as needed. Get the seal of approval before posting!

- Do post the response in an easy-to-find location. The specific location is a matter of personal or company preference. Replying in the runaway comment thread has a perk, because everyone involved will get a notification of the company's comment. But here, it can also become easily buried and lost. On Facebook, there's a case to be made for posting the brand response as a fresh status update or note. Then again, the CM may not want to put it on display for those who didn't even know a conflict was underway. So again, it's a matter of preference. You can always host the company statement on the company/client website or blog and link to it in a response thread on Facebook or in a tweet.

Addressing the Masses: Don'ts

Avoid these don'ts of community outreach during a conflict, or beware!

- Don't overapologize. The only thing worse than being attacked by negative comments is giving power to the commenters by begging for forgiveness. There's no need to fuel antagonists by groveling. Remember, responding to complaints doesn't always mean appeasing the complainer (especially if *they're* in the wrong). That said, don't be a stoic jerk, either. Find a harmony between recognition, understanding, and authority in the official response.

- Don't repeatedly repost the brand's statement. Once the community manager posts the formal response, she did her job. Don't feel pressured to hunt down the mailing address of everyone involved to send them a postcard featuring the same sentiment. Repetitious posting is just as gross as groveling. Consider sharing a shortened URL that points to the message as needed.

- Don't take it personally. That's easier said than done. Many community managers really connect with their community, and when there's animosity, it may feel like serious heartache. Angry users can sling insults at an icon or a logo without much hesitation, forgetting there's a human being on the other side of the monitor. Still, it's imperative to maintain a level head when dealing with negative Nellies. In the immortal words of the Godfather, "It's not personal; it's business." Complainers are more often upset with the brand experience, not the community manager.

Removing Comments and Banning Fans

The time has come to roll up our sleeves and dig deep into one of the most debated facets of online community management: removing comments and banning fans. Grab your gardening gloves, sharpen those shears, and read on for the low-down on pruning social fans and followers! But wait! Before we start talking about weeding user-generated content and uprooting fans forever, let's set the record straight. It's community manager mantra time. Ready?

Repeat After Me: Not All Negativity Is Bad

That's right. Under most circumstances, we're firm believers in *not* removing comments simply because they don't paint the best company portrait. Facebook Pages and other company social profiles are created to give brands online presences in a bounteous social community. If these profiles represent brands, by extension they represent the products, services, or causes provided by those brands. We've said it before, but if consumerism has taught us anything over the last century, it's that not every brand experience is a positive one.

Remember, that's normal. It's unrealistic to assume you can satisfy every customer, every time, and vanquish natural human sentiments such as disappointment or frustration from the commercial universe. Consumer complaints have been around since the dawn of consumerism. Negative reviews and accounts of poor brand experiences are not the worst thing to have on your Facebook wall. Why?

- They bring a poor consumer experience to the company's attention. Now that the CM knows about it, it can be addressed.
- They (hopefully) indicate the customer wants resolution. After all, he or she took the time to contact the brand via social media to vent.
- They provide an opportunity for the company to turn a complainer into an evangelist, or at the very least, solve the problem.
- They make the brand seem human. Negative reviews can emphasize the legitimacy of positive ones.
- They serve as honest feedback to a community of existing and potential customers that deserve it.
- They can encourage satisfied customers to come to the CM's aid, defending the brand with positive experiences of their own.

In summation, don't remove comments simply because they are negative. Please. You run the risk of aggravating community members even more than they already may be.

Okay. Now it's on to the juicy stuff.

Refer back to our complainer spectrum. Negative comments can come from letdown customers. They can also come from total nutbags. Sometimes they're aimed at the brand, other times at fellow community members. It's important to be able to distinguish a legit complaint from straight-up harassment. Once the nature of the complaint is discerned, it's time to decide what to do about it.

Establishing house rules for the social space will truly help with the following sections. Once the rules are in place, understanding whether a comment or fan should be removed is way more obvious. The fan either crossed the line or didn't.

When Is Removing Comments Okay?

What makes a Facebook, YouTube, or similar social channel comment delete-worthy? The definitive threshold should be established on a brand-by-brand basis, taking into account the nature and demographics of the community. Comments containing mild profanity or racy verbiage might be totally okay for Energy Drink Brand X, but not so much for Family Owned Restaurant Z.

There are some general warning signs it might be time to trim the thread, like if the comment(s) contain(s)

- Baseless accusations, as in "You cheated me! You rigged that contest! Your company is corrupt! You are conspiring against me!"

- Libelous content, as in "Your product killed my sister!" (despite the fact that sister is alive, and she's also leaving angry comments on your page).

- Profanity, as in "You motherf@#$%^&* bi@&$#@ little &*#$*&# I swear *@&$(#!."

- Hate speech, as in "You're all a bunch of [insulting term relating to race, creed, orientation, etc.]."

- Reverse hate speech, as in, "You fouled up my order because I'm [sexual orientation], didn't you!? I didn't win because I'm [ethnicity], right??!!"

- Harassment, as in any of the above on a recurring basis. This goes for harassment against the community manager as well as fellow community members.

Once again, do yourself a favor. Establish and implement a company code of conduct *before* issues arise. You'll have a black and white understanding of what constitutes a comment worthy of deletion.

When Is Banning a Community Member Legit?

Banning or blocking community members, whether they're Facebook fans, Twitter followers, or whoever, can make for a stickier situation than simply removing comments. As such, it's something to be thought about carefully, prior to taking action. It's a real statement to block someone from participating in a brand's social space, but sometimes it's necessary to ensure a safe and welcoming environment for the rest of the community.

One clear warning sign to be watchful for when considering blockage is when a community member refuses to acknowledge CM outreach, in tandem with repeated posting of libelous allegations; hateful, racist, prejudiced comments; or other forms of harassment. If the complainer continues to sling invaluable, insulting, harmful content at the company profile and the people who gather there, he or she most likely falls on the far right of our spectrum: the crazy, delusional, mean-spirited side. It's the CM's right and responsibility to kick him or her out if she sees fit.

Time for another round of do's and don'ts, this series revolving around—you guessed it—removing comments and banning fans. CMs who decide to delete a comment or ban a fan should consider these do's and don'ts when moving forward:

- Do cover your bases! Document everything, screen-cap all questionable engagement as it happens.

- Do have faith in the support from loyal community members. They may rally around you and shut the assailant down on behalf of the company.

- Don't remove comments simply because they're negative. Community managers have to have a thick skin against legit negativity and be ready to act.

- Don't back down from those social house rules. If someone's breaking them, step in and take control.

The Community Manager's Conflict Playbook

All right, soldiers. Still with us? So far in this chapter we've dug through a hefty helping of best practices and techniques for preparing for and understanding what constitutes a social media–fueled crisis. Now it's time to look at how to use those tactics to put out different kinds of fires that may arise during the professional life of today's social media CM. In this section, we'll address various less-than-ideal scenarios and propose solutions in a step-by-step outline. By now, the damage control tactics we'll employ for each sample issue should look familiar. We hope viewing them in this action plan, start-to-finish layout is useful. Ready? Steady? Charge!

Sample Issue #1: Bad Online Experience

Promotional coupon codes are a great way to incentivize online sales, but they can leave a pocket for possible technical difficulties. Customer X comes to a website in hopes of applying an advertised coupon code for a discount upon checkout. There's an error, and it doesn't work. Irate, Customer X clicks over to the company Facebook Page and posts a nasty rant/complaint. What's a CM to do?

Resolving: Bad Online Experience

As with many of our sample scenarios, there are (at least) two different approaches to resolving this situation. First, let's dissect the "Quick and Quiet" method.

- Document. The CM should take screen captures of Customer X's Wall post(s), as well as engagement surrounding said post; they will be invaluable later on to back up the CM's side of the story, especially if she works for an agency and hopes to debrief the client during or after the fact. Save the images in a dedicated folder, or compile them in a Word document with any additional verbiage and links needed for clarification.

- Remove the post, if possible. If Customer X "tagged" the brand's Facebook Page in a post on his or her own page, or if it's a tweet, the CM is more or less out of luck. (Again, we recommend not getting too trigger-happy when it comes to deleting legit customer complaints.)

- Inform the immediate/affected internal team or client. Shoot a quick email to anyone who needs to know what's up so they're not in the dark. The company crisis protocol should serve the CM well here. The last thing anyone needs right now is to feel pressured to "guess" about internal matters.

- Verify the complaint and solve the issue. Attempt to re-create the customer's problem. In this case, check out the company site and try applying the coupon code. Is a similar glitch encountered? Get in touch with the in-house developer, webmaster, or whoever else can help solve the issue. If the glitch does not occur, and it's believed the customer made a mistake or is insane, consider reaching out to Customer X in the same social channel where she/he ranted. Ask the customer to please try again or contact a dedicated customer support email address for further assistance.

- Contact Customer X privately, if possible. If he or she is a returning customer, perhaps there's a customer email address on file. If @CustomerX is following the company, the CM can send a direct message. Facebook Page admins can now privately message fans. Apologize for the inconvenience, thank Customer X for bringing the issue to the company's attention, explain that it's been solved, and consider offering an extra incentive to come on back, such as an additional discount.

- Compile a case study and circulate. The good news is these sticky issues can be a valuable learning experience for the brand's internal team and/or the client. Assemble screen caps and any follow-up engagement with Customer X or other brand fans into a cohesive case study. Circulate it among the team members so everyone is up to speed and in the loop.

The second approach is similar to the "Quick and Quiet" method, with a few notable differences. We call this the "Public and Pleasing" approach. It's advised for folks uncomfortable with removing UGC simply because it's negative in nature. Refer to the previous section for clarification of any of the steps we've already run through.

- Document.
- Inform the immediate/affected internal team or client.
- Acknowledge publicly. Jump in the Facebook thread, tweet-stream, etc., and inform Customer X you're working on the problem. Apologize for the inconvenience (without groveling).
- Verify the complaint; solve the issue.
- Update the community. Jump back in the thread when everything's fixed so the community, especially Customer X, knows what's up.
- Compile a case study and circulate.

Sample Issue #2: Bad Offline Experience

Customer Y calls one of your brick-and-mortar locations to set up an on-site service. Something goes wrong and the employee on the other end of the line accidentally botches the scheduling. When Customer Y comes in, he/she can't be seen and has just wasted his/her lunch hour. Frustrated and irritable, Customer Y posts a rant on your company Facebook Wall. What's a CM to do?

Resolving: Bad Offline Experience

Put on your helmet and elbow pads. Let's do this.
- Document.
- Inform the immediate/affected internal team or client.
- Cross-reference. Get in touch with the on-site location in question. Verify Customer Y's story with the customer service department to understand what happened (and who was really at fault). Arrive at a sensible solution and possible compensation, for example, an appointment at his/her convenience or a discount on the service being performed.
- Acknowledge publicly.

- Offer offline follow-up. Ask Customer Y to shoot an email to the company's dedicated customer service address so there can be a private follow-up. Offer the company's solution or compensation. Hope for the best. (Remember our spectrum. Some people might be so angry, they won't want to engage.)
- Compile a case study and circulate.

Sample Issue #3: Promotion Gone Wrong

This issue looks familiar! Now let's tackle it from start to finish. A company hosts a prize-based photo contest via a third-party app on Facebook. When the winner is announced, some losers freak out, claiming favoritism, harassing winners, questioning the legitimacy of the judging process, claiming the hosting brand is corrupt, complaining they didn't win for absurd reasons (racism, prejudice), all on the company's Facebook Wall. What's a CM to do?

Resolving: Promotion Gone Wrong

Never a dull moment. Here's the roadmap to safety:
- Document.
- Inform the immediate/affected internal team or client.
- Craft an official brand statement. A scenario like this affects more than just one disgruntled customer, and as such, might require a public message aimed at the whole community. Compose a thoughtful, succinct brand statement that addresses the issue, dispels any misinformation, and explains your brand position. (Be professional! Don't get emotional about things. "It's not personal; it's business!")
- Publish the brand statement. Be sure to put it in a place where it will be seen by the folks involved.
- Monitor for 24 hours. Don't respond to *every* comment your brand statement garners, but be aware of them.
- Prune comments and community as needed. Unfortunately, some folks might continue to rant, placing them dangerously close to the troll category. If they cross the line, throw 'em out. It's your space, after all.
- Walk away! Don't overapologize and don't continuously regurgitate the brand statement for every new complainer who joins the mob. The CM did her job by posting the response and mediating the masses. It's up to each community member to accept it or not.
- Compile a case study and circulate!

Sample Issue #4: Talkin' Smack About Your Brand

YouTube Fan Z leaves nasty comments every time the CM posts a new video on the company profile. Some are just rude and unconstructive. Some flat-out attack the brand. Some are straight-up libel! What's a CM to do?

Resolving: Talkin' Smack About Your Brand

- Sticks and stones will break your bones, but smack-talkin' will never hurt you! Document.
- Inform the immediate/affected internal team or client.
- Gauge intent. Determine if the complainer has or had a legitimate complaint, and if it's manifesting in these nasty comments, or if he/she is just a troll.
- Respond appropriately. If it's a legit complaint, handle it like a regular poor brand experience. If it's baseless, remove comments at will. If it persists, block the user (and/or call the lawyer if it really gets out of hand!).
- Compile a case study and circulate!

Sample Issue #5: Brand Product Kills Someone

Company R manufactures snack food, and gets a shipment of tainted Ingredient J. Consumer Q eats the product, gets food poisoning, and dies. Negative brand mentions are cropping up on Facebook, not to mention various news sources—online, print, and televised. Yipes! What's a CM to do?

Resolving: Brand Product Kills Someone

Red alert. Follow these steps, and hold on tight.

- Alert all appropriate stakeholders immediately and activate crisis plan.
- Document.
- Monitor. Implement 24/7 reputation monitoring of brand, misspellings, and product names. Doomsday alert! Dispel damaging misinformation, listen for tone—hostile or sympathetic—and gauge association of brand to tragedy.
- Damage control. Work with the company's PR team (in-house or agency) to do damage control on a professional, comprehensive level.
- Compile a case study and circulate.
- Partner with PR to help identify what next steps may be useful in restoring the brand's reputation.

Damage Control: Turning Lemons into Lemonade

Sometimes, a social media conflict arises not from a band of angry community members but from an accidental slip of the community manager's finger. In Chapter 2, "Timeless Tenets of Non-Gratuitous Social Behavior," we explored various social media dashboards and their ability to incorporate multiple accounts across multiple social channels. What a convenience! However, this functionality also increases the likelihood for a most unfortunate event: misfiring posts from the wrong account.

It's common for a community manager to rig up a social media dashboard to include all of the accounts for which she's responsible, including, perhaps, her own personal Twitter or Facebook account. Toggling back and forth between profile identities is easy enough, but it's just as easy to occasionally overlook. A silly little something the CM meant to tweet from her personal Twitter account could accidentally wind up in the corporate tweet-stream; such was the case when the @RedCross community manager accidentally tweeted the gem in Figure 7.4.

American Red Cross
@RedCross

Ryan found two more 4 bottle packs of Dogfish Head's Midas Touch beer.... when we drink we do it right #gettngslizzerd

HootSuite · 2/15/11 11:24 PM

Figure 7.4 The community manager for the Red Cross accidentally tweets a sideways post under the wrong profile!

Whoa, baby. Though this tweet doesn't involve profanity or horribly disgusting or insulting content, it's most certainly not Red Cross caliber. (We have to admit, though, "#gettngslizzerd" is kind of funny, under much different circumstances.) In the blink of an eye and the push of a button, the Red Cross's nearly 800,000 Twitter followers bore witness to this boo-boo, which, apparently, wasn't deleted from the official feed for about an hour. Conflict? Oh, yes. Crisis? Possibility of brand damage, for sure. Let's say conflict with serious potential, unless the proper damage control is taken, post haste.

We don't know what went on behind the scenes at the Red Cross social headquarters, but soon enough, both @RedCross (Figure 7.5) and @riaglo the CM (Figure 7.6) were back online, posting what we can only assume were carefully crafted responses to the booze bungle.

We've deleted the rogue tweet but rest assured the Red Cross is sober and we've confiscated the keys.

about 11 hours ago via ÜberTwitter
Retweeted by 86 people

RedCross
American Red Cross

Figure 7.5 The Red Cross responds to the misfired tweet.

@riaglo
Gloria Huang

Rogue tweet frm @RedCross due to my inability to use hootsuite... I wasn't actually #gettingslizzard but just excited! #nowembarassing

4 hours ago via HootSuite ☆ Favorite ↻ Retweet ↩ Reply

Figure 7.6 The Red Cross CM, Gloria Huang, acknowledges the misfired tweet.

Well done. Gloria acknowledged her mistake, explained the truth of the situation, and incorporated additional hashtags for a friendly vibe. The Red Cross crafted a memorable tweet that balanced apology with information and even humor, and was very well received by the entire Social Web. They even got on the radar of the brewery in question, Dogfish Head. Figure 7.7 shows the beer company's response to the tweet debacle, which even included a call for donations for, yep, the Red Cross.

> RT @Michael_Hayek: #craftbeer @dogfishbeer fans, donate 2 @redcross 2day. Tweet with #gettngslizzerd. Donate here http://tinyurl.com/5s72obb
>
> 2 hours ago via TweetDeck ☆ Favorite ⭜ Retweet ↰ Reply

Figure 7.7 @DogFishBeer calls for donations to the Red Cross after a misfired tweet.

Could this social media faux pas have turned out any sweeter? Is this always the outcome for similar situations? Not a chance. But it just goes to show how far a cool head in the face of sticky social situations can go!

Additional Strategies for Lowering Your Blood Pressure

We hope all of the tips, tactics, and teachings from this chapter can be used to lower the blood pressure of the social media community manager. A fixed, fleshed-out crisis plan *before* a crisis occurs, and a clear, unified understanding of house rules and crisis protocol—heck, even being able to distinguish between a crisis and a mere, manageable conflict—are supremely beneficial to the community manager and her company when they are delving into social media. Here are some extra goodies for you to take home and savor.

Be in Charge! It's Your Community

After the house rules are put in place, it's up to the community manager to, well, manage the community. When a rule is broken, she must act swiftly and professionally. A certain level of instinct comes into play as well. If the actions of a community member aren't directly violating the code of conduct, perhaps because the type of action wasn't considered when the rules were created, the CM must be prepared to use her best judgment in deciding when and how to proceed. Don't let people push you around, and don't allow the space to be overrun. Take control!

Fight Fire with Water, Not Fire

When antagonists rise up, the knee-jerk reaction may be to get defensive in return. Community managers are human, after all. Adding fuel to the fire of an impending social media uprising won't benefit anyone involved. Take a deep breath, collect yourself, and proceed with a professional, helpful demeanor. If the critic is truly insufferable, kill 'em with kindness, as they say!

Take It Offline, ASAP!

At the end of the day, best practice for tackling social media conflicts or crises is to take the conversation offline, immediately. Move to DMs. Offer a dedicated customer service email address where the dialogue can continue away from the masses. Maintain control of the situation by minimizing the number of people involved. Social media bystanders could turn into bullies. Don't give them the chance! Work with the affected community members privately and quickly.

When in Doubt, Don't React

The time between noticing a complaint or potential social media conflict and feeling prepared to adequately respond isn't always as short as one might like. Folks need to be informed, responses need to be crafted, and everyone needs to agree. Don't jump the gun by reaching out to a letdown community member right away. Get your ducks in a row before proceeding. The person will wait (they have to!). Just don't let too much time pass (days), or it will appear no one's listening on behalf of the brand.

Measuring Success!
State-of-the-Art
Social Metrics

So many solutions out there attempt to lend ordered metrics to the social media chaos. Appendix B offers a sizable catalog of options. This chapter highlights a select few analytics tools that we usually reach for. They aren't the flashiest or most expensive tools out there; however, each is free or affordable for most and provides the most important metrics.

We'll start with Facebook, LinkedIn, YouTube, and Twitter, which offer both organic and paid analytics to measure success. Then, we'll discuss some tools at different price points and share what we like about each one as well as how to use it day to day.

Chapter Contents

Mainstream Channel-Native Analytics

In this chapter, the words *analytics*, *metrics*, *stats*, and *measurements* essentially mean the same thing. Metrics are determined in planning and are accounted for in business objectives or are integrally linked through KPIs. Metrics are helpful in planning what you'll be measuring in strategy development.

Major social media channels have their own built-in analytics. Facebook, LinkedIn, and Twitter provide more data if community managers pay. Free or paid, the first place to start in measuring your channel results is in these native tools. Each channel's native analytics have features that justify dozens of pages in a book like this. We'll provide an overview of what they are, what you can see, and what each channel's metrics are useful for.

Facebook

Facebook offers the most robust suite of native tools in the social media channel industry by far. The organic analytics package, Facebook Insights, gives marketers a sweet look at the data. Insights also provides key statistics about paid organic amplification. Facebook Ads reports offer tons of vital information with which to measure the success of FB Ads and Sponsored stories. Between Insights and Facebook Ads reports, community managers can see most of what they need to see.

Organic

 Head over to aimclear.com/cm/chapter8 and grab the document that shows reports we recommend in Insights. When you're an administrator of any Facebook page, you've got access to Insights by clicking the Show button. Figure 8.1 shows the Insights Overview page.

Figure 8.1 Facebook Insights overview page

Insights is divided into four major sections:

- Overview, which provides at-a-glance access to the major data points, including Total Likes, Friends Of Friends, People Talking About This, Weekly Total Reach, Check-ins, and Total Subscribes.

- Likes, which shows how many new likes the page has received.

- Reach, which is the major metric here, because it gives you the total number of Facebook users who saw your content for the week. Reach is equivalent to an impression and can be either paid or organic.

- Talking About This, which provides a cool breakout of demographics that pertain to the likes you're accumulating.

Figure 8.2 shows the Overview page below the fold. This report lists posts in chronological order. Engaged Users represents the number of unique users who have clicked on your post. Figures are for the first 28 days of a post's life. Click on any engaged user number and you'll get the breakout of various types of clicks. Click Reach and Facebook reports the ratio of organic, paid (if running FB Ads for the post), and viral reach. Paid reach is also available at the post level in Facebook Ads reporting, which we'll explore in the next section

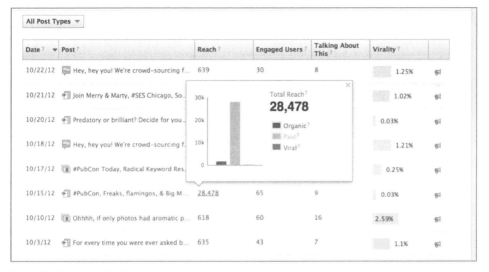

Figure 8.2 Facebook Insights Overview page below the fold

Figure 8.3 shows the People Who Like Your Page screen that appears when you click Likes on the Insights Overview page. There's a cool breakout of demographics that pertain to the likes you're accumulating. Dig in to learn even more about the age and location of your fans. There's also a graph that illustrates likes and unlikes accumulated over the time period.

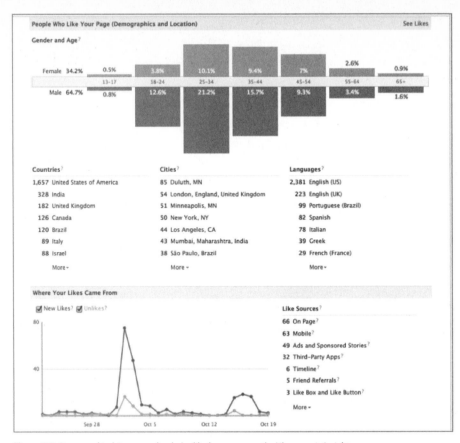

Figure 8.3 Demographic data on people who've liked your page on the Likes page in Insights

Figure 8.4 shows the How People Are Talking About Your Page screen that appears when you click Talking About This on the Insights Overview page. It's helpful to measure exactly what content users are talking about. Use this data to inform your content strategy.

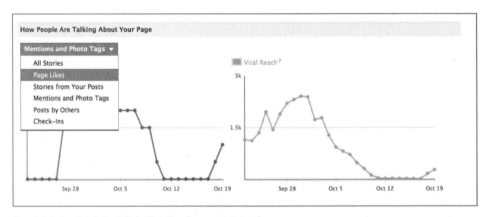

Figure 8.4 How People Are Talking About Your Page screen in Insights

Insights data can easily be exported, at the page or post level, by date range and spreadsheet format. Some marketers export this data for integration in other systems to aggregate multichannel analytic data. Some of the analytics tools discussed later in this chapter also aggregate Insights data directly. Insights itself, in the Facebook UI, is not always the best environment to view Insights data. You'll learn more about that in a bit. Figure 8.5 shows the Insights native export tool.

Export Insights Data

Export data directly to Excel (.xls) or comma-separated text format (.csv). Choose either Page level data or Page post level data. You may select any date range, with a maximum of 500 posts at a time.

Select Data Type:
- ◉ Page level data
- ○ Post level data

Select File Format:
- ◉ Excel (.xls)
- ○ Comma-separated values (.csv)

Select Data Range:
Start Time: 9/21/2012
End Time: 10/21/2012

Insights data is not available before July 19, 2011.

Download   Cancel

Figure 8.5 Facebook Insights can be exported at the page or post level for a given timeframe.

Paid

Facebook organic is an amazing thing. Great results for badass content can occur naturally from friends sharing or media spend. CMs can blow up the Internet and change the world. Still, we've made it clear in this book that Facebook does not distribute content as much unless you pay. That means you need to use page post ads for each post you want to promote. Facebook Ads reporting gives you some of the same metrics as Insights (organic) does, and a lot more. Figure 8.6 shows Facebook Ads metrics for a page post ad promoting an image.

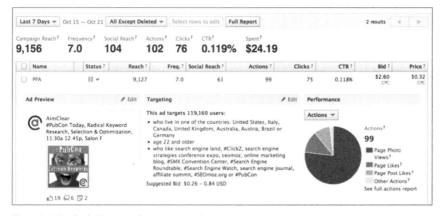

Figure 8.6 Facebook Ads metrics for a page post ad

Campaign Reach shows the total number of unique users who were exposed to your ad; this means unique impressions. Frequency represents how many times those unique users saw an ad. To see total impressions, multiply Reach by Frequency or click the Full Report button at the top of the screen to see a more detailed report. Social Reach is a groovy stat; it specifies how many people saw your sponsored story or ads with social endorsement from the user's friend. If you see an ad or story in FB that says one of your friends likes the promoted object, you've been "reached" socially.

Click Actions to see each of the ways FB users can interact with the promoted content. Actions include page photo views, page likes, page post likes, and comments, among others. The result of the page post ad can be considered a few different ways. We measure cost per action and make sure that the distribution of actions in the pie chart is what we want to see.

Use the Reports tab on the left-hand side in FB Ads to generate all sorts of useful reports. The Advertising Performance Report includes statistics like impressions, clicks, click-through rate (CTR), and media spend. Responder Demographics provides basic demographic information for FB Ads. Actions By Impression Time, Inline Interactions, and News Feed offer additional thin slices of the ads' performance. Figure 8.7 shows the FB Ads user interface for creating reports.

Figure 8.7 Use the Reports tab to generate a variety of reports on Facebook Ads.

LinkedIn

LinkedIn offers precious little in the way of analytics. The paid features provide an astonishingly light set of metrics feature. The free version gives almost nothing. Still, any data at all is a good thing, right?

Organic

The Who's Viewed Your Profile screen reveals who has been looking at your profile recently and how many times you have shown up in search results. Well, sort of. As far as who's viewed your profile, many LinkedIn users opt out of being visible to other users in their preferences. Also, less data is available for free LinkedIn accounts and more is available for premium. It's useful to keep track of who's been stalking your profile. Sometimes it's a new lead you've been courting or a new person to target for interaction and friendship.

We haven't found a serious use for understanding how many times our profile has shown up in search results. It's a general indicator of the strength of an account in terms of SEO. In most social communities, including LinkedIn, the more connections, friends, or followers gained in the community, the higher the ranking inside the community and in some search engines. This phenomenon occurs because, the more connections made, the more internal link energy is focused on outward-facing profile attributes.

Your ranking boost/friends ratio is contingent on how powerful your friends are. Theoretically, the more powerful your friends and the overall "juice" flowing through your public-facing profiles, the more times your profile should show up in search. Use the how-many-times-have-you-shown-up metric as a general indicator of the growing organic search strength of your profile.

Depending on various factors, you may see these two stats for today, the last three days, or the last seven days. LinkedIn decides and there is no way to toggle time. Pretty lame, huh? Figure 8.8 shows the metrics that are available on the LinkedIn Home tab.

Figure 8.8 LinkedIn metrics available on the LinkedIn Home tab

Figure 8.9 shows detail behind the search stats. It's pretty cool to see how search is trending and what keywords are driving search.

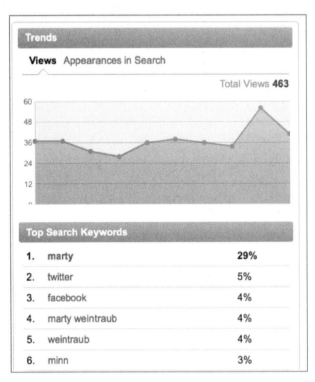

Figure 8.9 Details provided on search stats in LinkedIn

Company page administrators can access Follower and Page Insights (metrics) from the Status Update link or in the Edit drop-down menu on the company's page. Follower statistics are updated every day and give page administrators actionable insights about followers and updates and show whether the content is resonating as measured by engagement.

LinkedIn has various inline metrics that can be used to judge success in various activities. One of our favorites lives within LinkedIn Answers, a forum-style area where users share questions and answers. It's a cool deal to get a "best answer" designation, or better yet, to get multiple best answers. Figure 8.10 shows what the designation looks like for a very successful Answers contributor. A smart community manager pays attention to metrics that measure individual users' street cred, including their own.

Watch for inline metrics. You'll find them at the user level in many social sites and they often show fantastic information that can be used to choose friends. Apply them to yourself and set goals to be more authoritative.

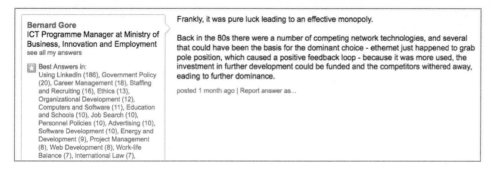

Figure 8.10 Best Answers designation for a successful LinkedIn Answers contributor

Paid

Light-years behind Facebook and YouTube, LinkedIn Ads are super basic. You get nothing but the simple facts. Figure 8.11 shows pretty much the sum total of available data points. LinkedIn Ads metrics are much more notable for what they don't do rather than what they do. Conspicuously absent are

- Any tie-in whatsoever to LinkedIn organic

- Any indication of what actions users took after clicking to an internal LinkedIn page

- Conversion to a follow or connection (Friend)

Campaign	Clicks	Impressions	CTR	Leads	Avg. CPC	Total Spent ▾
Total for All Campaigns	406	567,175	0.072%	4	2.50 USD	1,013.06 USD

Figure 8.11 Metrics provided on LinkedIn ad performance

The Leads column is toggled when the ad click results in a user submitting a lead request using LinkedIn's internal lead-generation form system. That's a nice start, but it falls far short of the type of conversion tracking marketers need.

To track LinkedIn Ads with more granularity, use Google Analytics after tagging your ads properly. Another classic hack is to segment your campaigns more. If the CM is marketing with LinkedIn ads to teaching assistants and teaching team leaders, create two separate campaigns and tag them differently. Measure the results in Google Analytics. This hack works in any ads platform, so keep deeper tagged campaign subdivision at the ready in all your paid social marketing travels.

Twitter

Twitter just keeps getting cooler and cooler. Organic tweets scoop content, news, and, every once in a while, even change the world. The Promoted Tweets product sends wonderfully focused traffic to external sites at a low cost, and Promoted Profiles gets tons of inexpensive and focused followers. However, when it comes to native metrics, Twitter is Neanderthal.

From the early days, Twitter has provided a robust API and has been all about providing access for third parties to build Twitter analytic utilities. As a result, still today, the best way to find Twitter stats is from platforms like HootSuite and Sysomos Heartbeat. You'll find a complete list of analytics platforms for Twitter in Appendix B, "The Big List of Community Management Tools and Analytics."

Organic

On the organic side, native Twitter metrics are a great big snooze, although it's important data. Figure 8.12 shows the standard breakdown of total tweets tweeted, followers, and how many you're following. Drill into any of those three vital metrics for a list. One great thing about Twitter is that everything except direct messages (followers only) pretty much takes place in public. That goes for who follows whom.

Figure 8.12 Native Twitter metrics include the number of tweets, the number you're following, and the number of followers.

Paid

Figure 8.13 shows the Promoted Accounts cumulative follower growth chart. You won't be able to access this chart unless you've signed up for Twitter ads. The gradated blue lines plot both paid and organic follower activity. It's kind of strange that the only place you can see organic follower growth trends within Twitter is in the paid ads analytics. The stats are typical. Maybe by the time you are reading this Twitter will add other basics like cost per follow, both paid and blended (paid and organic), and cost per click (CPC). Can't we have an average cost per click here?

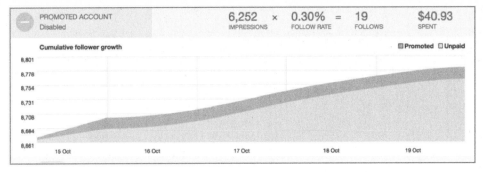

Figure 8.13 Twitter Promoted Account cumulative follower growth chart

Figure 8.14 shows metrics for Promoted Tweets. Granular data for which tweets generated clicks are served up. Again, it's baffling to us why there is no average CPC stat and any level of granularity.

PROMOTED TWEETS Disabled	1,844 IMPRESSIONS	×	0.98% CLICK RATE	=	18 CLICKS	$13.82 SPENT
Select which Tweets to promote 1 Tweet selected ☑ Hide @replies	All Tweets	All Promoted Tweets	Only currently promoted			
☑ Marty Weintraub @aimclear 22 Oct <3 RT @dohertyjf: @aimclear @distilled :-). We're pretty crazy about @aimclear as well!	1,022	0.29%			3	$2.30
☐ Marty Weintraub @aimclear 22 Oct	822	1.82%			15	$11.52

Figure 8.14 Stats available for Promoted Tweets

Google Analytics

At the root of all social traffic to your website is that visitors are just that—visitors. For all the fancy social analytics tools out there, classic web analytics still play a vital role.

Classic Google Analytics

Both paid and organic posts can be segmented and separated out to measure traffic, engagement, loyalty, source, conversion, and anything else classic analytics do. You care about new versus returning visitors; time on site; page view per visit; and whether they're using mobile, iPad, Droid, desktop, and so on. Once a user has clicked to your site from a social site or social-powered web application, it's no longer totally about social. Web analytics are your best bet to measure. Figure 8.15 shows a Google Analytics dashboard.

Figure 8.15 Google Analytics dashboard

Google Analytics Real Time for Content Releases

Little is more illuminating to a community manager than watching content blam all around the Internet in real time. Publish that blog post, send the tweets out, post on the brand's Facebook wall, sit, and watch the traffic roll in. It's so exciting to see that German visitor take the content bait while the CM observes what pages and actions the visitor undertakes. We've learned so much from watching content propagate in real time.

There are several tools out there ranging from free to inexpensive. Figure 8.16 shows Google Analytics' real-time dashboard, which is in long-term beta release. However, it doesn't hold a candle to third-party real-time analytics tools like Woopra, which we will review a little later in this chapter.

For current traffic, the dashboard shows top referring sites, social sources (segmented), and top keywords that resulted in the traffic. Since Google does not reveal all keywords that drive traffic to the site anymore (encrypted search), the keyword segmentation is declining in value. Still, it's useful to see any keywords still visible. It's exhilarating to watch the pinpoint appear on the map, denoting a new visitor. The scrolling page views per minute bar graph lends perspective.

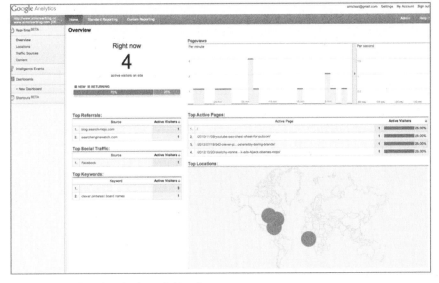

Figure 8.16 Google Analytics' real-time dashboard

Google Analytics and Social Analytics

Google Analytics has sewn-in social-specific metrics. Most of the features are essentially preset custom segments such as traffic, engagement, and flow, but only for visitors from mainstream social sites. They're not that much more valuable than classic web analytics.

A notable exception is a small set of graphs surrounding Google+ and a handful of participating social communities (Figure 8.17). Of course, Google owns Google+, so of course Google+ is the biggie here. Facebook, LinkedIn, and Twitter are not represented in the social data hub that drives these graphs. Still, the data can be quite useful.

Who is Using the Social Data Hub?

The list of partners integrated with the social data hub includes:

AllVoices	**Diigo**	**Google Groups**	**Reddit**	**yaplog!**
Badoo	**Disqus**	**Hatena**	**Screen Rant**	
Blogger	**Echo**	**Livefyre**	**SodaHead**	
Delicious	**Gigya**	**Meetup**	**TypePad**	
Digg	**Google+**	**Read It Later**	**VKontakte**	

Figure 8.17 Social communities that participate in Google's social data hub

Access Google Analytics' social analytics by clicking Social on the left side of the main UI. Figure 8.18 shows the Google Analytics social activity stream. Here CMs can see the URLs users shared, how and in what channel they shared them (via a "reshare" on Google+, for example), and what each user said. If you're busy in Google+, like you're supposed to be, this view is really neat.

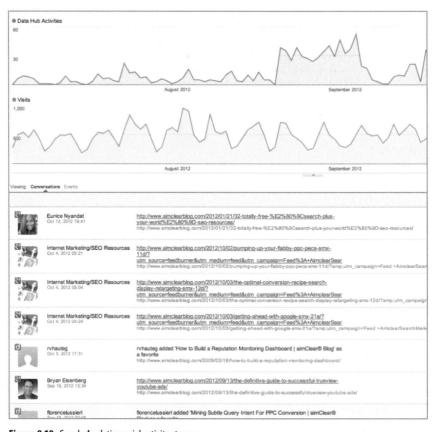

Figure 8.18 Google Analytics social activity stream

Flow reports in Google Analytics illustrate the paths visitors take through your website, including particular content like events and goals. Check out how visitors enter, engage, and leave your site. These reports are also useful for troubleshooting your site by identifying any page from which visitors choose to exit or loop back to previous content in unintended ways.

Google Analytics' social flow is the same, except that it segments out traffic from social channels. Take a minute and study Figure 8.19. It's a Google Analytics social flow chart and clearly shows how visitors from Facebook and Twitter tend, on average, to travel through the aimClear Blog. The boring brands and Pinterest blog posts draw a lot of social traffic but pass little of it through to other areas of the site.

The Pinterest post is one and done. However, users who visit from Facebook to view our homepage tend to visit the services and about pages. Traffic to the psychographic modeling post also tends to visit the homepage.

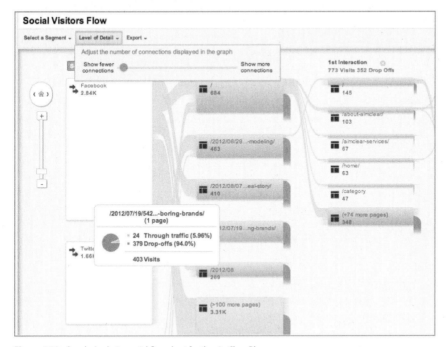

Figure 8.19 Google Analytics social flow chart for the aimClear Blog

This data is actionable and powerful coupled with conversion tracking, say for a user who submits a form. Check out social visitors flow for a bird's-eye view of how inbound community members behave.

Free (and Handy) Utilities

Head on over to aimclear.com/cm/chapter8 and download our über list of free social analytics utilities that rock. One of the most amazing things about the social analytics space is how many robust utilities exist that are free. That's always been the case in online marketing quarters. In keeping with tradition, some "freemium" tools provide limited, though still cool, functionality with an upgrade path for deeper metrics.

Also, unless there is web scraping going on, available data points are the same as the community's tools themselves. In other words, a third-party tool that reports Facebook organic stats has the exact same data points as are available native in Insights. The same goes for Twitter. Third-party tools manage the data differently and use it for different purposes. For instance, EdgeRank Checker works with Facebook organic API data and parses it out by hours of the day. Native Insights does not offer

269

■

FREE (AND HANDY) UTILITIES

hourly feedback. EdgeRank Checker takes the same data in real time, logs it a different way, and offers value to the community manager by generating different actionable data. The CM now knows that posting pictures at 10 a.m. on Mondays tends to generate more activity. Here are a few of our favorite tools, if you are stranded with no budget whatsoever.

Social Mention

Figure 8.20 shows SocialMention.com search engine results page (SERP). Social Mention is a search engine that scans for buzz in blogs, microblogs, bookmarks, comments, events, images, news, video, audio, Q&A, and other networks.

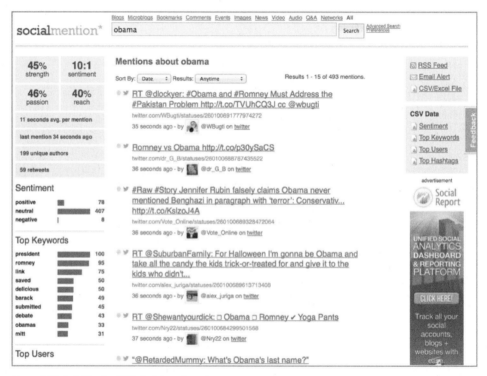

Figure 8.20 Social Mention SERPs for "obama"

There's a decent automated sentiment module, and CMs can drill into individual channels. What's super cool is that you can generate RSS feeds and pipe them into your personal dashboard.

Figure 8.21 shows Social Mention's advanced search screen. You can use negative keywords to filter out noise when you are creating feeds for alerts.

socialmention*

Find results that have...

all these words:

this exact wording or phrase:

But don't show items that have...

any of these unwanted words:

More Options...

Results from source: Blogs

Results from location:

Results from: Anytime

Results per page: 10 results

Language: any language

Sort results by: Date

Don't show results from these users
(comma separated):

Advanced Search

Figure 8.21 SocialMention advanced search options

Klout

Figure 8.22 shows the much-maligned Klout score. There's been a lot of disagreement about whether Klout matters, including articles in major newspapers and plenty of debates among online marketers. We say it's better to have Klout than to not have it. And, who cares about Klout?

KKLOUT

Hi Marty!

62

1-day   -0.09 ⬇   7-day   +0.34 ⬆   30-day   -0.28 ⬇

Figure 8.22 Klout score for Marty Weintraub

Klout is one company's idea of what authority and influence means based on the activity of your social media channels. If you only have 100 people that follow your nonprofit organization, and one of them gives $20 million to the organization, Klout won't pick up your Twitter account's true authority. That said, it's a cute little preset authority-measuring toy.

Inexpensive Winners

There's an amazing universe of tools that don't cost an arm and a leg. Some go on to become classics and last. Others, like PostRank (sold to Google) have been purchased by huge companies. In this section let's explore some tools that we keep around aim-Clear as standard hacks.

EdgeRank Checker

EdgeRank Checker (mentioned earlier) is good fun. The biggest breakthrough about EdgeRank Checker is that the marketers had the audacity to name it that.

Still, EdgeRank Checker is one of the more attractive repurposed organic Facebook metrics re-bakers that spin data into visualizations and graph output to lend alternative insights to the standard report formats Facebook already offers via Insights. The Recommendations section offers some nice visualizations that are actionable, such as time of day or media types that work. The method for moving through date ranges is intuitive. We like the granularity because Facebook does not offer some of the zoomed-in views via Insights. It's probably worth using EdgeRank Checker just for that.

EdgeRank Checker also analyzes industry-wide anonymous aggregate data to provide a wide spectrum of recommendations. By studying what works across the board, users can optimize post frequency, best times of the day to post, how content works, and other data points within their industry. Figure 8.23 is an example report.

BEST / WORST METRICS		KEY METRICS (AVERAGES PER POST)	
IMPRESSIONS HOUR	IMPRESSIONS DAY	LIKES	8.14
9AM / 12PM	**THU / FRI**	COMMENTS	0.57
2,628 / 1,265 impressions	2,628 / 890 impressions	IMPRESSIONS	1,672.14
LIKES HOUR	ENGAGEMENT DAY	SHARES	0.43 (3 shares / 7 posts)
9AM / 1PM	**THU / FRI**	CLICKS	6.67
26 / 3 likes	1.36% / 0.05% eng. per fan	AFFINITY	62.57%
COMMENTS HOUR	POST TYPE	VIRALITY	0.69%
9AM / 12PM	**LINK / STATUS**	UNIQUE IMPRESSIONS	2,090.57
2 / 0 comments	0.60% / 0.30% eng. per fan	UNIQUE STORYTELLERS	8.57

Figure 8.23 EdgeRank Checker provides stats that allow the CM to optimize what and when they post.

HootSuite

HootSuite is seriously a hoot. We've met founder Ryan Holmes, and he's really a visionary dude. HootSuite serves the same purpose as TweetDeck (Facebook, LinkedIn, Foursquare, and Twitter functionality) and adds the following:

- YouTube, by way of an app.

- Google+, which is rare and radical. Google has been very protective of what tools can administer Google+.

- Multiple tabs with multiple windows (see Figure 8.24).

- Control of how often each feed refreshes.

- Robust, channel-by-channel scheduling.

- Analytics by the channel.

- Google Analytics integration.

- YouTube-branded reports, ranging from free to expensive, that aggregate data from combinations of channels:

    - Powerful preset reports

    - Totally custom reports

Figure 8.24 HootSuite at a glance

The free version is very powerful. The paid version, at a whopping $9.99 per month, is radical. It starts to cost more as CMs save more data and other add-ons. The reports are wonderful (Figure 8.25). HootSuite is a must-have at the free level. We're particularly fond of the retweet trending report, as shown in Figure 8.26.

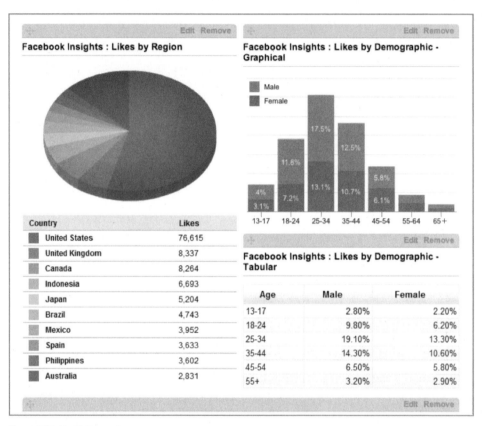

Figure 8.25 HootSuite reports

Woopra

More analytics mavens are becoming aware of Woopra, a relatively inexpensive software package available on the Web and as a desktop application. Let's preface this section with a warning: Their customer service is weak. Use them at your own risk. However, in our opinion it's worth the trouble. Just don't rely on it as your only analytics source.

Woopra is an analytics package close to Google Analytics in concept, though not nearly as deep. That said, the presets are awesome, and it's way more powerful than it looks. Woopra is best known for its gorgeous daily dashboard (Figure 8.27) and extremely useful real-time analytics features. What's less known are Woopra's killer KPI reporting capabilities using custom segmentation features Woopra calls filters.

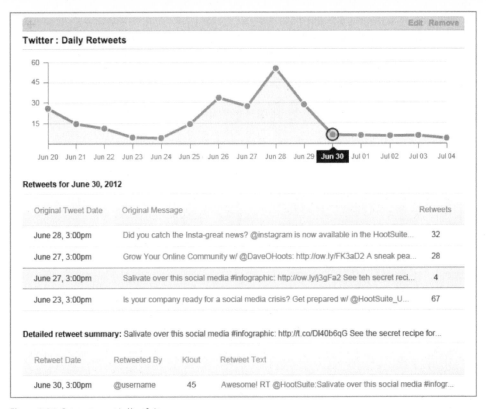

Figure 8.26 Retweet report in HootSuite

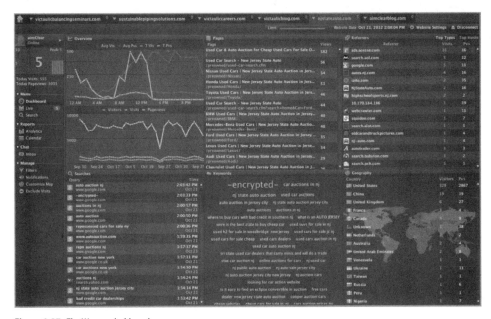

Figure 8.27 The Woopra dashboard

We love Woopra's calendar feature, shown in Figure 8.28. In tandem with filters, CMs can build a radically cool KPI calendar. Use it to show the progression of conversions from Facebook, traffic from Twitter, and any other filter you create. The upper-left corner shows KPI performance for month-to-date. Moving across the top row, you see conversion for the average Monday, Tuesday, Wednesday, and so on. Then, KPI success is tracked by the day for the rest of the month. This report kicks ass.

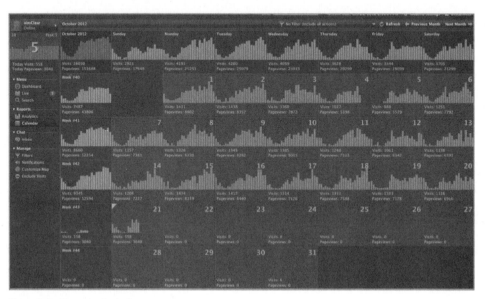

Figure 8.28 Woopra's calendar feature

Raven Tools

At aimclear.com/cm/chapter8 we've created sample Raven Tools reports that are not available as examples on Raven's website. aimClear uses Raven Tools with some clients. Like HootSuite, Raven white-labels (brands as you) sweet reports that aggregate native metrics from Twitter, YouTube, Facebook (organic), Google Analytics, and other sources. It's the same concept as HootSuite but with a stronger agency management metaphor and accompanying client center (Figure 8.29). The idea with social metrics is to aggregate channels to gain blended insights.

Other Inexpensive Tools

There are other tools we like a lot. Sprout Social is one of them, as is the concept behind Dennis Yu's BlitzMetrics. Twitalyzer includes such functionality as "watchword" tracking; Google Analytics integration; powerful data trending tools; timelines for tracking hashtag use; topics, images, and locations, network, and sentiment analysis.

Figure 8.29 Raven Tools UI showing Facebook and YouTube metrics

Enterprise Management Tools

Radian6, Salesforce, Adobe Products, IBM Coremetrics, Acquisio, Marin, Conductor, and a number of other tools fill various parts of the content management, social profile management, social PPC, and blended analytics universe. Some are very expensive and deserve to be so. Others cost a lot and are kind of dumb, in our opinion.

 It's outside the scope of this book to delve into each platform, because, like Sysomos Media Analysis Platform (MAP) and Heartbeat, each deserves a chapter unto itself. There's a generation of tools that are developing at a dizzying pace. Start by researching the ones mentioned here and head over to aimclear.com/cm/chapter8 to grab the list of enterprise social analytics tools.

Evaluating Tools: A Checklist for Deciding What You Need

 So, what's a community manager to make of all of this? We've created a flowchart to help CMs decide what tools they need for the types of measuring they intend to do. It's posted at aimclear.com/cm/chapter8 for your use and pleasure.

Measuring Who's in Your Facebook Community

Businesses worry about not going after the right or big enough metrics. "Where is the ROI?" they ask. Some CMOs even admit (typically in private) to feeling lost. Is the best tactic to seek lots of friends and followers? Do we even have to be in social? If engagement is really an important success metric, what type of engagement metric should we be going for? How do we measure engagement in meaningful ways that can be associated with revenue? What can we communicate to the C-Suite as reasonable KPIs? How do we justify expenditures? In this section, we'll discuss the classic question, "Are our Facebook likes valuable?"

The beginning of any intentional community building effort is a dogged determination to place focused fans in-community by intentionally targeted psychographics. Community building can't be willy-nilly. Random fans won't be nearly as useful for content marketing. The objective is to place a confirmed percentage of our target psychographic segments in-community. This task, though seemingly simple, is daunting for many and a lot of hard work for most. Here's how you measure it.

When it comes to earning likes in Facebook, it's essential that marketers continually study who is actually in the community by density analysis. We always want to know the user count and percentage of key demos we own by subscription. This is important because, ostensibly, the idea of getting users to like or follow is so we can market to them with ongoing content. If the users who like our page have interests that jibe with our corporate mission, things will be a lot easier later. Unfocused likes most often have less value.

For instance, if there are 351,740 people in the United States interested in #Muscle car, we want to know

- What percentage of the 351,740 is in our community? Say, out of the 32,506 users who like our page, there are 14,252 confirmed users who like #Muscle car. That means our community owns (by like-subscription) about 4 percent of the #Muscle car Facebook segment.

- What percentage of our overall community does the target segment comprise? Of our 32,506 users, 14,252 like #Muscle cars. That means that about 43 percent of our community consists of our target segment.

- What percentage of our friends' friends (second degree) are in the target segments? If we test to see how many friends of our 14,252 #Muscle car friends also like #Muscle cars, we might see that 56,708 are also interested. That's about 16 percent of the 351,740.

Studying the makeup of a first-degree (friends) organic Facebook community (those who like your brand page) is easy. Essentially, you're performing psychographic research on your own fans, as if you were going to place Facebook Ads. Don't be confused. We're all familiar with using the Google AdWords keyword tool to profile keywords for SEO. Just because you use the AdWords keyword tool, that doesn't mean you're going to place search PPC ads. You do the same sort of thing with Facebook Ads. Even if you don't place any ads, it's valuable to turn the Facebook create-an-ad tool inward, studying only your own community, as shown in Figure 8.30.

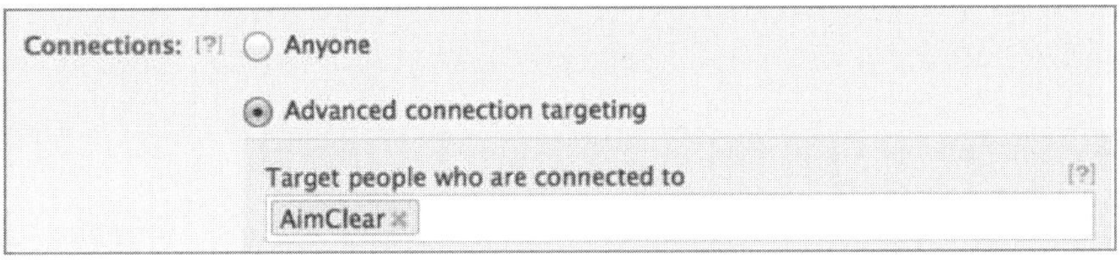

Figure 8.30 Turn the Facebook Ads UI inward to study your own community.

Now, filter your own fans by classic Facebook Ads targeting (Figure 8.31).

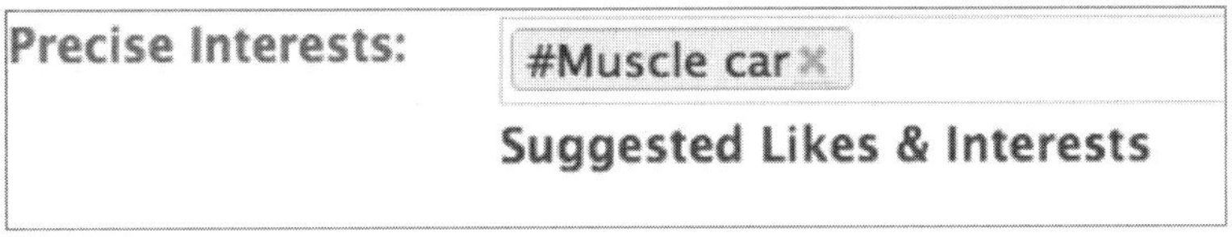

Figure 8.31 Filter fans by precise interests.

Studying friends of friends (second degree) in the target segment is easy, too. Just use Facebook ads to target Facebook users whose friends are connected to your page. Again, dial in the #Muscle Car Precise Interest or whatever your target is.

It's fundamental that marketers continually evaluate the focus of likes received. Use the Facebook create-an-ad tool to measure user count and percentage of key demographics you own. This is critical because, supposedly, the goal of getting users to like or follow is so you can interact with compatible friends for marketing purposes. If the users who like your page have interests that mesh with your objectives, future interactions can be themed in ways to benefit all parties. From message testing to content marketing, these peeps will groove. Otherwise, you're getting likes for the sake of likes.

Social Media Community Manager Job Description

There are a number of personal qualities, skill sets, and backgrounds that make for a super CM. This appendix offers a granular look at crucial skills, essential duties, and a job description for the CM role and provides verbiage you can use for job descriptions, blog posts, tweets, and other outreach. The content of this appendix is available as a download, in classic job description format, along with questions to ask candidates during interviews. In the download, available at www.sybex.com/go/ communitymanager, *we also provide text snippets to use in shorter print classified ads and tweets.*

Creating a CM Job Description

Do you tweet and use Facebook all day, every day? Is building social community so ingrained you just can't stop? Do you take pride in customer service excellence and fancy yourself an entrepreneur? Do you understand the difference between a brochure website and a publication, and do you know why feeds are important?

We're seeking a highly motivated individual with experience and fanatical passion for blogging, microblogging, and community participation leadership. This position is full-time salaried with benefits and includes attendance at mainstream and niche conferences.

We want you!

Over the past few years, the relatively close-knit blog universe has exploded in a massive confluence of social expression and corporate reaction. A cottage industry of owner-operators, trawling social media on behalf of themselves and others, has cropped up in lofts, dorms, agencies, and iPhones. These are the new social media community managers and corporate is clearly looking.

Often the key to integrating social media into the marketing mix is about *not* hiring immediately, but rather sharing CM duties across departments. That said, there comes a time in many a company's evolution that bringing in a full time, hands-on community manager makes sense. What type of person should you hire? Back in 2009, we put that question to our friend Lisa Barone, noted SEM industry blogger/social media addict/evangelist. Here's what she had to say:

Hire someone who is addicted to the conversation and will be around on the weekends to approve comments, continue discussions, and put out fires when needed. 9-to-5ers need not apply. Make sure they have a thick skin. When you're managing a community, attacks will come and someone will always have a problem with what you're doing. They need to know when to step up, when to say nothing, and how to steer conversations down constructive paths. Above all, make sure it's someone you trust with your brand. They're going to be your eyes and ears into what's happening. Don't hire someone with a rock star complex.

Want to know something cool? The foundational pillars of Lisa's description of ultimate social media community managers haven't changed. That said, over the past years, the role of community manager has definitely moved toward the front of many C-level executives' minds. No longer only the stuff of geeks and nerds, feeds and social communities have gone mainstream.

Now we'll put our human resources hats on and offer our job description for a community manager. Please feel free to use any part of it and adapt as you see fit.

Finding Qualified Candidates

One inescapable reality of the online marketing industry is that finding great employees is a challenge, even if you know precisely where to look. Mainstream and niche job sites, specialized SEM job boards, trade organizations, and word of mouth are common channels for recruiting. However, with demand growing, sometimes it's necessary to get creative in recruitment efforts.

Social Ads to Recruit Social Employees

One of the best ways to recruit great online marketing team members is to deploy Facebook and LinkedIn Ads. As we've discussed, both Facebook and LinkedIn Ads can be targeted to job titles in a grid with the company users work for. Think about it. Facebook lets you target by age, school, degree, and professional interests. LinkedIn lets you target many of the same attributes, as well as skills. LinkedIn skills targeting is deadeye for recruiting.

Here's an example that worked. PR folks make awesome community manager employees, and with the withering of the traditional PR industry, many staffers at all levels are looking for new gigs. The ad in Figure A.1 cost about a hundred bucks to run for a few days. It resulted in hiring aimClearian Ryan, who is a treasured employee at our shop. After he had been with us for about six months, we hired one of his former associates as a result of her relationship with Ryan. The Facebook ad was fantastically successful.

Figure A.1 aimClear's tightly targeted Facebook Ad resulted in the hiring of not one but two aimClear employees.

College Advertising and PR Clubs

One of our favorite places to find CM candidates is at the advertising club of the local college. Many colleges have ad and PR clubs that participate in the American Advertising Federation (AAF), National Student Advertising Competition (NSAC), and Public Relations Student Society of America (PRSSA). These clubs and NSAC are an incredible place to find new employees.

AAF is America's venerable national advertising trade association. Fifteen district operations represent different regions of the nation.

As for NSAC, each year a corporate sponsor provides an assignment or case study outlining the history of its product and current advertising situation. The case study role-plays a real-world marketing issue that must be solved. Students research the product and its competition, identify potential problem areas, and devise a completely integrated communications campaign for the client. Each student team then pitches its campaign to a panel of judges. Regional NSAC competitions are held each spring in the 15 districts throughout the United States. The winning team in each district and one wild card team then advances to compete on the national level at the AAF National Conference in June.

aimClear has five team members in Duluth who participated in NSAC. They were magnificently prepared to be in the big time. Heck, they role-played big-time prior. Identify the local student clubs that participate in these programs. Volunteer. Get to know the seniors.

Industry Communities

It sounds cliché, but social media itself is an awesome way to find social media candidates. Try participating in Twitter's hashtag #SocialChat and mention that you're looking. It's OK to post on the SMX, SES, or PubCon Facebook walls that you're looking for employees. There are LinkedIn groups devoted to hiring social media employees. An awesome reason to spend time making LinkedIn connections in the first place is because they sometimes end up applying for jobs.

We've found employees at mixer events surrounding major conferences and by reaching out to individuals we like via a contact form or direct mail. Back in 2009, I (Marty here) met my co-author Lauren at a party aimClear threw in New York City and was professionally smitten. A few weeks later, I flew back to the city to take her out to dinner at Tavern on the Green and to talk about her future. The rest is history.

It's true! (Lauren here) I was live-tweeting one of Marty's sessions about Facebook marketing at SES New York in March 2009. I reached out via Twitter to congratulate his great presentation and to introduce myself digitally (we wouldn't meet in person until SMX East, seven months later). After that, he followed me on Twitter and we stayed on each other's radars. Perhaps to evaluate my capabilities as a writer and community manager, he asked me to write a guest post for aimClear Blog that summer (brilliant tactic: flattering for the guest blogger, fresh content for the blog, and a chance for the employer to learn more about a potential hire). Then came the bash in the Big Apple, Tavern on the Green, and the move to Minnesota that December. What a whirlwind.

Qualifying Social Media Experience

You know by now that a day in the life of a social media CM isn't all sunshine, kittens, rainbows, and Facebook pokes. So, what professional experience should today's data-driven community manager possess? Here are some reasonable expectations:

- Has a bachelor's or associate's degree in advertising, marketing, graphics, web development, communications, English, IT, music, theater, anthropology, history, or a related field.
- Excels at research and possesses excellent writing skills and the ability to crank out editorial and technical writing.
- Has work experience or training in advertising, PR, online marketing, or a similar field.
- Is proficient with Microsoft Office products.
- Is dedicated to blogging and use of Facebook.
- Understands the power of feed marketing.
- Demonstrates creativity and documented immersion in social media.
- Is able to map out a marketing strategy and drive that strategy, proven by testing and metrics.
- Has experience sourcing and managing content development and publishing.
- Is able to jump from the creative side of marketing to the analytical side; is able to demonstrate why their ideas are analytically sound.
- Has management experience or readiness for promotion to management.
- Uses discretion to identify threats and opportunities in user-generated content.
- Understands the social media universe, including YouTube, StumbleUpon, Delicious, Digg, Reddit, Flickr, forums, Twitter, wikis, and blogs. The candidate should be a social media addict who maintains a personal mix of participatory expertise from among these channels.
- Possesses functional knowledge or some experience with HTML/CSS.
- Understands search engine optimization, including basic keyword research.
- Possesses excellent verbal and written communication skills.
- Is able to work individually on a project or in a team environment.
- Is eager to meet and exceed objectives and take on more responsibility.
- Demonstrates outstanding organizational skills and the ability to handle multiple projects simultaneously while meeting deadlines.
- Is able to communicate results to management in a fast-paced environment.

This is not a complete list, but it's a great place to start. Consider these characteristics when you're on the hunt for a worthy new addition to your social media marketing department, and keep your eyes, ears, and instincts sharp for additional genuine attributes.

Essential Duties and Responsibilities

Now that you have an idea of qualifying social media experience, let's explore core duties and responsibilities rock-star CMs should be prepared to tackle on any given day:

- Interact with our customers to align unselfish service of their needs with our corporate objectives.
- Be the eyes and ears of our brand as if their own reputation depended on it.
- Build and maintain our content distribution network by way of social media channels.
- Participate in minute-by-minute conversations that surround our content and brand; answer comments; be a mediator.
- Identify threats and opportunities in user-generated content related to our brand; report to appropriate parties.
- Interact with legal, search, client, and cross-corporate agencies.
- Create content for feeds and snippets in various social media sites.
- Schedule and organize multiple departments that generate content on a daily basis.
- Conduct keyword research, including cataloging and indexing target keyword phrases.
- Participate in social media, as himself/herself and white-hat avatars, on our behalf.
- Optimizing tags on our feeds and sharing sites such as YouTube/Flickr and search engines through copywriting, creative and keyword optimization, and buzz-pocket mining.
- Tag and title content with an understanding of how the words chosen impact natural search traffic and rankings via recurrent optimized content.
- Manage and track link-building campaigns, coordinated with all facets of our business.
- Create and update daily, weekly, and monthly reports.
- Analyze campaigns and translate anecdotal or qualitative data into recommendations and plans for revising the social media campaigns.

Salary-Setting Resources

Community manager salaries are diverse and dependent on the city the job is in, as well as the company. As a rule, you can make more working in-house as opposed to working for an agency, but for the most part, working in-house is not as cool (in our admittedly biased opinion!).

Several annual studies and websites are devoted to helping companies set, and employees get, the right salary. We like the resource shown in Figure A.2, also available at `http://socialfresh.com/community-manager-report-2012/`.

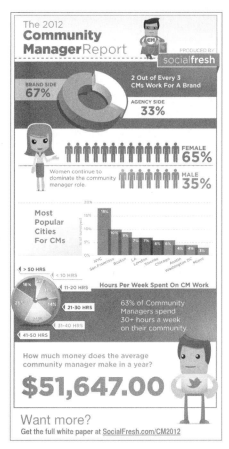

Figure A.2 Salary studies such as this one from SocialFresh can help determine appropriate salaries for community managers.

Remember that salary is relative. Those who work at aimClear and are successful can pretty much work wherever they want for the rest of their career. They also earn 30–40% more than the local marketplace and get generous bonuses. They go to lots of conferences and enjoy great food and wine at work nearly every day. Houses cost a lot less in Duluth than in many cities. Factor all that in, as either the boss or the candidate.

A number of government, collegiate, and commercial tools offer snapshots of wage and occupational averages. Some offer job descriptions. Each should be taken with a grain of salt and looked to for ideas. An average is just that—an average—and does not take into account your company's dynamics and value to a potential employee. Take a look at the following sites for additional resources:

- www.bls.gov/ncs
- www.bls.gov/ncs/ocs/compub.htm
- www.salary.com
- www.salaryexpert.com
- www.abbott-langer.com
- jobstar.org/tools/salary/index.htm
- www.calmis.ca.gov/file/occup$/oes$.htm

The Big List
of Community
Management Tools
and Analytics

*All right! It's playtime. This appendix houses
a list of awesome tools for today's data-driven
community manager—everything from content
aggregation to holistic automation to hardcore
analytics. It's far from complete—new tools are
hitting the streets every day. Best practice is to
keep your eyes open and a finger on the pulse
of the fine online publications that cover social
media news, including the launch of emergent
tools and platforms. We didn't play favorites.
Everything is alphabetically ordered.*

B

Ads Managers and Research Tools

Community managers wear many hats. Some even resemble that of an online advertiser. Neat! These platforms are ideal for working with large batches of ads, among other things:

- Acquisio
- Facebook Power Editor
- Google AdWords Editor
- TubeMogul

Blog Comment Management Tools

Enjoy these handy tools for collating and organizing all the comments your fabulous company blog posts are sure to accrue:

- Disqus
- IntenseDebate
- Livefyre

Content Aggregation and Curation

When it's time to share content that's *not* branded, these powerful content aggregators are helpful resources to mine content someone has already gathered and organized for you:

- Alltop
- Bo.lt
- BuzzFeed
- Crowdspoke
- Curation Station
- Fooooo
- Eqentia
- FeedMagnet
- Google Blog Search
- IceRocket
- Mass Relevance
- MyCube
- Regional news sites
- Trapit
- Unilyzer
- YourBuzz
- YourVersion
- ZoomSphere

Content Publication

These publication platforms can be the perfect cozy home for your company's branded content. There's also some groovy publication and promotion tools to be had in this section:

- Awareness
- Checkthis
- Edit Flow
- MyLikes

- Percolate
- Posterous
- SlideShare
- Tumblr.com
- Virtue
- WordPress

Facebook

So many of the tools on this list are awesome when mapped to the Facebook universe, but the babies in this section are Facebook-only:

- Adotomi
- Facebook Insights
- FBsearch.us
- GraphScience
- Hy.ly
- memelabs
- North Social
- Pagemodo
- ProfileBuddy
- Silentale
- TabJuice
- Wildfire

Image Libraries and Editing Tools

A picture says a thousand words! Here are some helpful tools for finding and optimizing the perfect image for your latest blog post or social ad:

- Aperture
- Flickr Creative Commons Search
- Fotolia
- Adobe Fireworks
- IrfanView
- iStockphoto
- Pixable
- Pixelmator
- Shutterstock
- Skitch
- stock.xchng

Monitoring and Reporting

One of the best ways to prove social ROI is to bring real data to the table. These monitoring tools are just the ticket, tackling everything from robust analytics to brand sentiment and demographic insight to organic conversation mining. Some are channel specific; others cover the social media galaxy:

- Addict-o-matic
- Alexa
- Amplicate
- Attentio
- AuthorityLabs
- awe.sm
- Beevolve
- bit.ly URL shortener (with analytics)
- BlogPulse
- Boardreader
- Brand Monitor
- Brandwatch
- CliMet

- Converseon
- CustomScoop
- Digimind
- Engag.io
- Engage121
- eThority
- Followerwonk
- GlobalWebIndex
- Google Alerts
- Google Analytics
- HowSociable
- Jive
- LocalResponse
- Lotame
- MediaFunnel
- MutualMind
- Netvibes
- NutshellMail
- Odimax
- PeopleBrowsr
- PostRank
- Quantcast
- Radian6
- Raven Tools
- SEMrush

- Sendible
- Sentiment Metrics
- Social Mention
- Social Radar
- Socialbakers
- SocialBro
- SocialPointer
- SpyFu
- Statmyweb
- StepRep
- Swix
- Sysomos Heartbeat
- Sysomos MAP
- ThinkUp
- Trackur
- truPulse
- TrustYou
- TwentyFeet
- Unmetric
- Viralheat
- Visible
- Webtrends
- YourBuzz
- YouTube Keyword Tool

Pinterest

Pinterest is not just for crafts, fashion, and food porn. These tools are sure to help you make the most of your company's Pinterest campaigns:

- Curalate
- PinReach
- PinAlerts
- Pinerly

- Pinfluencer
- Pinpuff
- Pinterest Bookmarklet
- Repinly

Scraping and Streamlining Feeds

Looking to automate some dirty work? Here are some of our favorite tools to get the job done:

- Mozenda
- RSS Icon plug-in for Firefox
- ScrapeBox

Social Dashboards

These are some of the coolest social dashboards around. Many are robust enough to handle multiple accounts across multiple social channels. Some even come complete with built-in task delegation, automation functionality, and analytics:

- Argyle Social
- ConversationBuddy
- CoTweet
- Cyfe
- HootSuite
- Oracle Involver
- Pluck
- PowerVoice
- Seesmic
- Sendible
- SocialFlow
- SocialTALK
- SocialVolt
- Spredfast
- Sprinklr
- Sprout Social
- Thismoment
- tracx
- TradeDesk
- TweetDeck
- uberVU
- Unified
- Zoniz

Scheduling and Holistic Automation

Shhh, we won't tell. Go ahead and leverage time-saving technology to schedule posts to fire across social media platforms at exactly the right time (note that several social media dashboards, such as TweetDeck and HootSuite, include native scheduling tools):

- BufferApp
- dlvr.it
- IFTTT

Site Research and Brand Name Verification

These pups fall under the umbrella of (reputation) monitoring. Use them to stay abreast of sites and usernames significant to your company for competitive intelligence and brand management, among other uses:

- Check Usernames
- Claim.io
- KnowEm
- SimilarSites
- SitesLike
- SimilarSiteSearch
- Wikipedia

Social Follower Directories and Managers

These directories and platforms are awesome for finding real social media friends (target audience members) and keeping track of ongoing engagement. This includes CRMs and CFMs:

- Bazaarvoice
- Contaxio
- Conversocial
- Engage121
- Facebook Groups
- GoChime
- Janrain
- LinkedIn Groups
- LiveWorld
- Nimble
- OneDesk
- Parature
- Radian6
- Rapportive
- Refollow
- Salesforce
- Shoutlet
- SocialTwist
- SpredFast
- Sprinklr
- Sprout Social
- Twellow
- Twibes
- Vitrue
- WeFollow

Social Influence

Who's the coolest kid on the block? Though the attributes that determine social influence are often debated, these tools are a good place to start to identify and connect with who's popular and who's, well, not so popular:

- Adly
- Appinions
- HooSaid
- Klout
- Kred
- PeerIndex
- SocMetrics
- Traackr

Social Sharing Widgets

Sharing is caring! These tools and widgets put sharing functionality across various social sites at yours and your customers' fingertips:

- AddThis
- ConversionBuddy
- Janrain
- ReachBuddy
- ShareThis

Twitter

From insights on followers to hashtags, these tools are specific to Twitter. And yeah, they're pretty twerrific:

- Chat Catcher
- Compete
- Crowd Factory
- DataSift
- Followerwonk
- Friend or Follow
- GroupTweet
- Listorious
- monitter
- Plume
- PostPost
- SocialOomph
- tagdef.com
- The Archivist
- Topsy
- Twazzup
- TweetLevel
- TweetReach
- Tweriod
- Twitalyzer
- Twitter Advanced Search Operators
- Twitter Counter
- twtrland

Bonus! Online Marketing Publications

Remember way back at the beginning of this appendix that we said best practice is to keep your eyes open and a finger on the pulse of the fine online publications that cover social media news and thought-leadership? Yeah. Here are some of them:

- aimClear Blog
- AllFacebook
- BlogWorld
- BlueGlass
- ClickZ
- Copyblogger
- Digital Buzz
- Duct Tape Marketing
- Google Blog
- HubSpot
- KISSmetrics
- Instagram Blog

- Mari Smith
- Marketing Land
- MarketingProfs
- Mashable
- Outspoken Media
- Pinterest Blog
- ProBlogger
- Quick Sprout
- Search Engine Journal
- Search Engine Land
- Search Engine People

- Search Engine Roundtable
- Search Engine Watch
- SEO Book
- SEOmoz
- Social Fresh
- Social Media Examiner
- SocialTimes
- TechCrunch
- Twitter Blog
- TopRank
- YouMoz

72 Must-Follow Online Marketing Geniuses

C *Welcome to a directory of your future super-BFFs! All right, not exactly, but this appendix boasts a selected round-up of folks who know what's up when it comes to social media.*

Not everyone on the list is a community manager—some specialize in PPC, SEO, analytics, or mobile—but, as we hope this book has taught you, it's important for social media CMs to be well informed on all things online marketing. Besides, these are cool people you should know anyway if you're kicking it in this industry.

You can find almost all of them on Twitter, where they often talk shop and trade valuable resources. Reach out and say hi. They don't bite.

- Aaron Wall—@seobook
- Adam Audette—@audette
- Akvile Harlow—@akvileharlow
- Alex Cohen—@digitalalex
- Amy Vernon—@amyvernon
- Andrew Shotland—@localseoguide
- Andy Atkins-Krueger—@andyatkinskruge
- Andy Beal—@AndyBeal
- Annie Cushing—@AnnieCushing
- Avinash Kaushik—@avinash
- Bill Hunt—@billhunt
- Brad Geddes—@bgtheory
- Brent D. Payne—@BrentDPayne
- Brett Tabke—@btabke
- Brian Chappell—@brianchappell
- Brian Ussery—@beussery
- Carri Bugbee—@CarriBugbee
- Casie Gillette—@Casieg
- Chris "Silver" Smith—@silvery
- Chris Sherman—@CJSherman
- Christine Churchill—@keyrelevance
- Cindy Crum—@Suzzicks
- Dana Lookadoo—@lookadoo
- Danny Sullivan—@dannysullivan
- Dennis Goedegebuure—@TheNextCorner
- Derek Edmond—@derekedmond
- Elisabeth Osmeloski—@elisabethos
- Gary Vaynerchuck—@garyvee
- Greg Finn—@gregfinn
- Greg Jarboe—@gregjarboe
- Guy Kawasaki—@guykawasaki
- Heather Lloyd-Martin—@heatherlloyd
- Hollis Thomases—@hollisthomases
- Imelda Khoo—@imeldak
- Jennifer Lopez—@jennita
- Joanna Lord—@JoannaLord
- Joe Kerschbaum—@JoeKerschbaum
- Jonathan Allen—@jc1000000
- Julia Roy—@juliaroy
- Keri Morgret—@KeriMorgret
- Kevin Spidel—@kspidel
- Laura Lippay—@lauralippay
- Lee Odden—@leeodden
- Lisa Barone—@lisabarone
- Lisa Buyer—@lisabuyer
- Lisa Grimm—@lulugrimm
- Liz Strauss—@lizstrauss
- Manny Rivas—@mannyrivas
- Marc Poirer—@marcpoirier
- Mari Smith—@MariSmith
- Matt Siltala—@Matt_Siltala
- Matt Van Wagner—@mvanwagner
- Megan Leap—@meganleap
- Melissa Fach—@SEOAware
- Melissa Mackey—@mel66
- Merry Morud—@MerryMorud
- Michael Dorausch—@chiropractic

- Michael King—@iPullRank
- Michael Streko—@streko
- Mike Grehan—@mikegrehan
- Monica Wright—@monicawright
- Purna Virji—@purnavirji
- Rand Fishkin—@randfish
- Rand Hah—@littleredbook
- Rhea Drysdale—@rhea
- Ric Dragon—@ricdragon
- Ruth Burr—@ruthburr
- Shelly Kramer—@shellykramer
- Ted Rubin—@TedRubin
- Todd Friesen—@oilman
- Todd Mintz—@toddmintz
- Will Scott—@w2scott

Index

Note to the Reader: Throughout this index **boldfaced** page numbers indicate primary discussions of a topic. *Italicized* page numbers indicate illustrations.

INDEX